IN HIS LIGHT

A Path Into Catholic Belief

Rev. William A. Anderson

Religious Education Division
Wm. C. Brown Company Publishers
Dubuque, Iowa

Nihil Obstat
   Rev. John H. McDonnell

Imprimatur
   ✠Joseph H. Hodges, D.D.
   Bishop of Wheeling-Charleston
   October 17, 1984

The Nihil Obstat and the Imprimatur are official declarations
that a book or a pamphlet is free of doctrinal or moral error.
No implication is contained therein that those who have
granted the Nihil Obstat or Imprimatur agree with the
contents, opinions, or statements expressed.

Excerpts from the English translation of *Rite of Baptism for
Children* © 1969, International Committee on English in the
Liturgy, Inc. (ICEL); excerpts from the English translation of
Rite of Penance © 1974, ICEL; excerpts from the English
translation of *Pastoral Care of the Sick: Rites of Anointing
and Viaticum* © 1982, ICEL. All rights reserved.

Excerpts from *The Jerusalem Bible,* copyright © 1966, 1967,
and 1968 by Darton, Longman & Todd Ltd and Doubleday
and Company, Inc.; *The Bible in Today's English Version*
Old Testament: © American Bible Society, 1976; New
Testament: © American Bible Society, 1966, 1971, 1976; *The
New American Bible,* copyright © 1970, by Benziger, Inc.

ISBN 0–697–02111–4

10   9   8   7   6   5   4   3   2

In Memory of
Bishop Joseph H. Hodges, D.D.
(1911–1985)

This book is dedicated to Bishop Joseph H. Hodges, D.D., who succeeded to the See of Wheeling-Charleston (West Virginia) on November 23, 1962 and served the Diocese until his death on January 27, 1985.

Many of us in the Diocese of Wheeling-Charleston remember him as a man of prayer and study, who worked day and night for the Lord and who was open to the direction taken by the Church in the wake of the II Vatican Council.

I am especially indebted to him for his many suggestions made in the original manuscript for this book. Upon receiving the manuscript for the first edition, he read through it page by page and set aside a full day to discuss with me the many pages of notes he had compiled while reading the text. When he received the revision for this edition, he was growing weak from his illness, but he still insisted on reading the text before giving the imprimatur. This was typical of the dedication he brought to every task of his ministry.

As his illness progressed, he tired more quickly and was often too weak to stand for long periods of time, but he continued his ministry in the Diocese until the day before his death. He did not want his illness to become an obstacle to those who sought his advice or needed a decision from him concerning the mission of the Church. He was a dedicated, prayerful man, and we, the people of the Diocese of Wheeling-Charleston, were fortunate to have had him as our Bishop.

Contents

Introduction to Second Edition

Each day, an elderly man would take a three mile walk into town. He would walk past several farm houses surrounded by fields of wheat or corn, and he would arrive in town about an hour before his son finished work. His son owned a hardware store, and the elderly man would sit on a stool behind the counter and talk with his son and the customers about any topic they wished. During the trip home, the man would tell his son about his new discoveries on his three mile trip into town. The son was amazed that his father had walked that road for three years and could still make new discoveries each time he came to town.

A second edition of a book can be like a stroll along a familiar road filled with new discoveries. What was written several years ago can now look a little different, perhaps a little more important or be a little better understood because of the experiences of the past few years. A second edition offers the opportunity to express these new insights which have come from the experiences of a living Church. At the same time, a second edition must not do away with the teachings which have made a first edition so successful. There is always room for growth, but the roots must always remain firm. This edition, although remaining faithful to the first, shares some of the insights and discoveries which have arisen through the past five or more years of ministerial practice in the Church.

In this edition, Scripture quotations are used much more extensively than in the first edition, not as proof texts, but as texts which offer greater insights into the lesson taught. Over the past several years, the use of the Rite of Christian Initiation of Adults (RCIA) has reached a deserved place in sharing the faith with those who wish to become members of our Catholic community. It has swept across the country with a force and power which no one would have imagined several years ago. The continued growth in Scripture studies and developing studies in the understanding of sacraments could not be overlooked in this second edition. Finally, the link between faith and our global concern can not be ignored in any book such as this. A second edition offers an opportunity for sharing all these new and exciting discoveries while, at the same time, remaining faithful to the major portion of the teachings in the first edition.

Over the past years, the first edition of this book has been used in teacher training sessions, parish adult education sessions, high school classes, discussion groups and as a basic text for those entering the Catholic Faith. Several have written that they have used it for spiritual reflection. We are grateful for the many creative uses of this book, and we hope that this edition will find as welcome a place as the first in all these endeavors.

A book such as this plays an important role in the process for the Rite of Christian Initiation of Adults, but it does not attempt to replace the Bible which is the major book for the RCIA process. Nor does this book attempt to replace another important feature of the RCIA process, namely the shared, living stories of those involved in this process. The value of the RCIA process lies in its ability to relate the stories of those sharing in the process with the revealed Word of God in the Scriptures. In the RCIA process, however, there is also a need for a basic text for reflection on the Catholic Faith. This book offers such a text. The intent of this book has not changed since the first edition, namely to present in a clear and concise language a presentation of the Catholic Faith which shares the spirit and teachings of the faith without presenting an overwhelming amount of material. A common error in teaching the faith is the tendency to try to teach everything within the short period of a year or two. This book lays a foundation, realizing that there is much more to learn in the years ahead.

Because the RCIA process places such a great emphasis on the sharing of one's story in relationship to the Word of God, a companion book to *In His Light* has been published for the sake of this process. The book, entitled *Journeying in His Light*, is intended as the first book used in the RCIA process. The opening chapters allow for reflection and sharing during the period of the precatechumenate, and the remaining chapters follow each of the periods of this process. Where the chapters of this companion book follow the chapters from *In His Light*, we have noted this at the end of each chapter in this book.

Whether you are paging through this book for the first time or making a return journey, I pray that you will always find new and exciting insights into God's love and ways of responding to that love.

Using *Journeying in His Light* with *In His Light*

For those using *In His Light* and *Journeying in His Light* for the RCIA process, the following schema might prove helpful. It lists those chapters where these two books parallel each other.

─────────────── Precatechumenate ───────────────

In His Light	Journeying in His Light
	Topic 1 (Invitation)
	Topic 2 (Journey)
	Topic 3 (Insight—Faith)
	Topic 4 (Hope)
	Topic 5 (Love)
Chapter 1 (God)	Topic 6 (God)
Chapter 2 (Knowing God Better—O.T.)	Topic 7 and 8 (Knowing God Better—O.T.)
Chapter 3 (Jesus)	Topic 9 and 10 (Jesus)
Chapter 4 (Holy Spirit)	Topic 11 (Holy Spirit)
Chapter 5 (Sin and Life)	Topic 12 (Sin and Life)

─────────────── Catechumenate ───────────────

Chapter 6 (Church)	Topic 13 (Church)
Chapter 7 (Sacraments)	Topic 14 (Sacraments)
Chapter 8 (Baptism)	Topic 15 (Baptism)
Chapter 9 (Confirmation)	Topic 16 (Confirmation)
Chapter 10 (Eucharist)	Topic 17 (Eucharist)
Chapter 11 (Reconciliation)	Topic 18 (Reconciliation)
Chapter 12 (Marriage)	Topic 19 (Marriage)
Chapter 13 (Holy Orders)	Topic 20 (Holy Orders)
Chapter 14 (Anointing)	Topic 21 (Anointing)
Chapter 15 (Last Things)	Topic 22 (Last Things)

Enlightenment

Mystagogia

Acknowledgments

This book was written at the urging of the Evangelization Commission of the Diocese of Wheeling–Charleston. The Commission was looking for a book that would express in a simple fashion the developing thought in Catholic belief today. These pages are an attempt to present such a book.

I am indebted to the members of the Evangelization Commission for their time and encouragement, most especially to Sister Anne Francis Bartus, S.S.J. for her many insights and corrections, and to Father Thomas Gornick for his helpful suggestions. I would also like to thank Sister Celestine Anderson, S.S.J., for her many hours spent in typing and re-typing this book. I am grateful to Sister Veronica Shellhase, S.S.J., Sister Mary Grace Freeman, S.S.J., and Sister Immaculate Spires, S.S.J., for their time spent in proofreading the manuscript.

The Sisters of St. Joseph of the Diocese of Wheeling–Charleston have contributed a great deal to this book by their prayers. To these, and to so many others who in some way contributed to this book, I express my deepest gratitude.

Prologue

One night, a father decided that his son was now old enough to go out to the barn to feed the horses. The boy, however, told his father that he was afraid of the dark. The father stepped out onto the porch with the boy, lit a lantern, gave it to his son and asked him how far he could see as he held up the lantern.

"I can see halfway down the path," said the boy. The father directed his son to carry the lantern halfway down the path. When the boy reached that point, the father asked the boy how far he could see now. The boy called back to the father that he could see to the gate. The father urged the boy to walk to the gate, and, when the boy was at the gate, the father asked how far he could now see.

"I can see the barn," came the boy's reply. The father encouraged the boy to go to the barn and open the door. When the boy finally shouted back that he was at the barn and could see the horses, the father simply called, "Now feed the horses," and stepped into the house.

The point of this book and the point of the story are the same. The path this book attempts to light up is the path of understanding to God and the Church. As the boy walked with the lantern, he came to see the path, the gate, and the barn. He did not see the whole yard or the fields that surrounded him. Only daylight would provide that gift. Similarly, this book will shed light on only a very small portion of the topics it discusses.

Indeed, whole books have been written on each chapter. As a start, readers must first become familiar with the path of understanding. Having done that, they can look beyond to the wider context which other books illuminate.

In His Light consists primarily of questions in bold print, answers in italic print, and followed by answers explained in ordinary print. These questions and answers are stepping stones toward understanding the larger message. Wherever possible, technical words have been avoided so that readers may easily recognize what is at the heart of Christianity—deep joy and love—and may leave the reader with a desire to know more.

1

If this happens and if it leads to further study of any topic, the book will have served its purpose well. At times, readers may feel that more should have been said on a given topic. When this happens, they are advised to keep in mind that this book was designed merely to light up a small path, not the whole yard.

In Search of God

Introduction

A man and woman strolling along the beach stopped to look at a piece of seaworn driftwood. The woman decided that the driftwood would fit in beautifully beside the fireplace at their bungalow. On another day, when her mood was more sullen, the woman might never have noticed the driftwood. But morning sun, the sound of the waves, and the feel of the cool water and warm sand had lifted her to a greater awareness on this morning.

The man saw only a gnarled piece of wood, caked in mud and seaweed, that had drifted onto the beach with other pieces of sea litter. The sea shells, he decided, were pretty at least, but this old piece of wood had no place in anyone's home. However, he had promised his wife that this would be "her day," so he carried the driftwood back to the bungalow.

Some people view God with the same kind of eyes that the beach-combers turned on the driftwood. Some see God shining throughout the whole of life—in life's joyful, beautiful moments as well as in its sad, tragic moments. No matter what happens, God is there and God is still beautiful. Others see God only in the good moments. When a tragedy strikes, they say, "How can I believe in a good God when God allows this tragedy in my life?" But others live under the strong, fresh breeze of faith.

When we speak of God, we must also speak of how people experience God. This chapter will strive to share an insight into God that will help us to experience God at all moments of life—and perhaps to know God better.

1. Who are we?

a. We are members of the human family and the center of God's creation.

In the opening story of creation found in the book of Genesis, the author describes God's creation of the world, beginning with the separation of light from darkness and ending with the crowning event of creation, the creation of human beings. Only in the creation of human beings does God say that they are created ". . . in our image, after our likeness" (Genesis 1:26). This does not mean that our shape is the shape of God, as though God has hands, legs, or a material body like ours, but it means that we share in some way in God's ability to think, act, judge, love, and choose freely. As members of the human family, we are special and central to God's creation.

The message found in the opening chapters of the Bible points out that every other detail of creation was created for the sake of human creation. The vast and intricate design of the universe not only tells us about the greatness of God, but it also tells of the importance of our human family in the eyes of God. In the Old Testament, we read the prayer of a psalmist who praises God for the goodness shown to human beings when he writes, "You have made him little less than the angels, and crowned him with glory and honor. You have given him rule over the works of your hands, putting all things under his feet" (Psalm 8:6–7).

b. We are people who seek meaning and fulfillment in life.

Although we can live in happiness and contentment for many years, we finally discover that we have a restlessness of spirit which keeps us reaching out for a greater meaning and fulfillment in life. The woman on the beach in the opening story wanted a gnarled piece of wood as a decoration beside her fireplace, but, in time, she and her husband began to take the decoration for granted, and they would eventually be looking for other gifts in their lives. As members of the human family, we eventually discover that we become restless to continue our quest for something more deeply satisfying. Many of us discover the answer to that quest in our response to the love of God in our lives. Augustine, a saint who lived around the late fourth and early fifth centuries, wrote that our lives are restless until they rest in the Lord. A psalmist writing in the Old Testament spoke the same sentiments when he wrote, "My soul yearns and pines for the courts of the Lord. My heart and my flesh cry out for the living God" (Psalm 84:3).

c. Our fulfillment lies in loving and serving God in this life and sharing eternal happiness with God.

As members of the human family, we are called to know, love, and serve God and one another. Our years on this earth are not given to us simply to test us for heaven, but we have a responsibility and call to help develop creation according to God's plan. In the New Testament, we read in the second letter of John about the necessity of loving one another if we wish to claim that we love God. The author writes, "If anyone says, 'My love is fixed on God,' yet hates his brother, he is a liar" (1 John 4:20). Our fulfillment in this life lies in knowing, loving, and serving God and every member of the human family.

Our eternal fulfillment comes through happiness with God which surpasses all attempts to describe it. Paul, the great apostle of the early Church, writes in his letter to a Christian community at Corinth, "Eye has not seen, ear has not heard, nor has it so much as dawned on man what God has prepared for those who love him" (I Corinthians 2:9).

In another letter, Paul faces needs for fulfillment both in this life and life hereafter. As he preaches the message of Jesus, he recognizes his special call on earth and his strong desire to be with God. He writes, "I am strongly attracted by both: I long to be freed from this life and to be with Christ, for that is the far better thing; yet it is more urgent that I remain alive for your sakes" (Phillipians 1:23–24). We have a mission and purpose here on earth, and we have a call to eternal happiness with God. In both of these lies our meaning and fulfillment as members of the human family.

d. We are a people who constantly seek to know more about God, our Creator.

As a group, human beings are curious, wanting to know the deep mysteries of this world as well as the deep mysteries of the spiritual world. We strive to know the meaning of life, and we seek to understand the mind of a Creator who gave us such a creation. Some try to explain away the idea of such a Creator, while most of us accept it with lively faith. Faith consists in believing what we cannot see. Although we cannot see God as God truly exists, we continue to want to learn more about God so that we might love God more deeply. That is the purpose of beginning a study such as the one presented in this book.

2. Who is God?

a. We cannot fully understand the nature of God.

Even before we are born, we begin to experience life around us. Prenatal researchers tell us, for example, that a mother's stress can affect the infant in her womb. After birth, as our capacity for experiencing increases, so does our knowledge.

As a child, we touch a hot stove and learn what the word "burn" means. Some years later, we enter school, and our teachers make use of our past experiences to teach us. "Dry ice can burn us as badly as a hot stove," we are told. We remember how a hot stove burned us and we learn something new about dry ice by comparing it to something in our experience, namely the hot stove.

Because we learn first through our senses, it is not surprising that when we come to speak of God, we have a problem. We find nothing in our experience to compare with God. We learn that God has no limits, but we find nothing in our experience without limits. A house is limited by walls, a sea is limited by shores, and our very person is limited by a body. We learn that God is all powerful, but we know that even the strongest person or machine in the world can only lift so many pounds without breaking. We learn that God is all knowing, yet our experience tells us that even the most intricate computer cannot know everything. Ultimately, we must admit that a person without limits can never be understood by minds that are limited.

We cannot understand the nature of God, because God has no limits. If someone challenged us with the words, "Tell me all about God so that I can know God perfectly," that person would be asking for something absurd. If we could know and describe God perfectly, God would not be God. God is limitless and far beyond our powers of understanding. The psalmist writes of God, "Great is the Lord and highly to be praised; his greatness is unsearchable" (Psalm 145:3).

b. Ancient pagan cultures understood their gods by the way they touched their lives.

When a storm raged among people of ancient times, they would run to their altars to sacrifice animals and at times even human beings to appease the storm gods. Before a voyage, they would worship the sea gods. To these people a god was the power or force who affected the mainstream of their lives. God was the sea who could either become angry or calm, depending upon the way the people treated him. The summer god would hold back the refreshing rains when people ignored him. Many of the unexplained mysteries that brought terror or tragedy into the lives of ancient peoples became gods to these peoples. They understood their gods through the very experiences of their lives. This was the way the gods touched them, and the only way they could speak of their gods.

c. The Old Testament authors often spoke of God as one who related to their lives.

In the story of creation, the authors tell of God preparing the earth for the human family. Even when these people sinned, the love and mercy of God became apparent as God gave them other chances, over and over again. God showed a power greater than that of the Egyptian Pharaoh when Moses was able to lead the chosen people out of slavery. God showed a deep love in preparing a land for the people of Israel, and in forgiving the sins of David, the great Hebrew King. When the writers of the Bible spoke of God, they spoke of God's love, power, mercy, anger, and overwhelming knowledge shown through God's dealings with the chosen people. The ancient Israelites worshipped the one God, not because they understood all about God, but because of the way God touched their lives with power and love. In a prayer from the Old Testament, we read, "Come, let us bow down in worship; let us kneel before the Lord who made us. For He is our God, and we are the people He shepherds, the flock He guides" (Psalm 95:6–7).

d. We can define God by understanding how God relates to us.

When we define God, we must accept our limitations. We have nothing in our experience to compare with God. But like the people of the Scriptures, we too can speak of God who relates to us. When we experience love for our families, we know that a loving God has shared love with us. When we speak of an all-loving God, we reflect on our ability to love and realize that it merely hints at the love that the Creator of the world must possess. The human power of conceiving and constructing a great building points to a greater power that conceived and created our universe. When we stand in amazement at the knowledge that allows us to launch explorers off into space, we recall the creative knowledge that knew that space before it even existed. When we proclaim that God is all-loving, all-powerful and all-knowing, we declare that our experience of love, power, and knowledge reflect only a shadow of God's true person.

3. What do the Scriptures tell us about God?

a. The Scriptures tell us that God is a loving, personal God.

Throughout the Old Testament, we read of God's continual concern and compassion for the chosen people. When they are in slavery, God frees them, and when they sin, God forgives them. When they seek a land and a kingdom, God grants it, and when they seem to lose all, God promises a savior. The psalms sing of the love and protection of God, and they continually proclaim the greatness of the God who has done so much for them. In one of the psalms, we read, "For the Lord loves His people, and He adorns the lowly with victory" (Psalm 149:4). Only a loving, living God could have led the people of the Old Testament to victory against all odds, and gave them hope when all seemed lost.

In the New Testament, Jesus tells us that he reflects the presence of God among the people. In the Gospel of John, we read, "Whoever puts faith in me believes not so much in me as in Him who sent me; and whoever looks on me is seeing Him who sent me" (John 12:44–45). In the person of Jesus, we see the love, compassion, forgiveness, and concern of God for all people. Reflecting on the life and message of Jesus Christ, the author of the first letter of John can write about the love of God, "Love, then, consists in this: not that we have loved God, but that He has loved us and has sent His Son as an offering for our sins" (1 John 4:10).

A central, revealed theme of the Scriptures is that God is a God of love who lives and invites us to respond with love.

b. The Scriptures tell us that God is a spirit who knows all and is present to all.

The Scriptures tell us that God cannot be confined to space and time, since God has no limitations such as a body. God is a spiritual being, present in all places and for all time. No matter where we go or try to hide, we can never escape from the presence of God. Because God is a spiritual being, God is able to know all and see all. The psalmist expresses this belief when he writes, "O Lord, you have probed me and you know me; you know when I sit and when I stand; you understand my thoughts from afar" (Psalm 139:1–2). A few verses later, the same psalmist speaks of the continual presence of God's spirit when he writes, "Where can I go from your spirit? from your presence where can I flee? If I go up to the heavens, you are there; if I sink to the nether world, you are present there" (Psalm 139:7–8).

When Jesus tells the people to fast, pray, and offer alms in secret, he reminds them that God sees their hidden actions and will reward them for these good deeds. Matthew records these words of Jesus when he writes, "Keep your deeds of mercy secret, and your Father who sees in secret will repay you" (Matthew 6:4).

God not only created the world, but God remains present to the world, knowing all and guiding those who respond in faith to this presence. The Spirit of the Lord fills the whole world.

c. The Scriptures tell us that God is without beginning and without end.

Although we live in time, we believe that God had no beginning and will have no end. This is difficult for us to understand since we are familiar with lives that begin and end (at least on this earth). From the Scriptures, we learn that God has neither beginning nor end. The psalmist again puts into words the living faith of the people when he prays, "Before the mountains were begotten and the earth and the world were brought forth, from everlasting to everlasting You are God" (Psalm 90:2). The people of Israel believed that God always existed and would continue to exist into eternity.

In the New Testament, we read about the creation of the world in the opening verses of the Gospel of John. When the author uses the expression, "In the beginning . . . ," he is actually speaking of God's existence before the beginning. The author of this Gospel writes, "In the beginning was the Word; the Word was in God's presence, and the Word was God. He was present to God in the beginning" (John 1:1–2). The New Testament speaks not only of the presence of God before the beginning of time, but it speaks of the continued presence of God at the end of time. This presence is one we too will share—the eternal presence of God. The author of the first letter of John writes, "God gave us eternal life, and this life is in His Son" (1 John 5:11).

God is eternal, and we too have a hope of sharing in this eternal glory.

d. The Scriptures reveal these and many other insights into God.

Throughout the Scriptures, we are continually learning more about God through the people of the Old Testament and through Jesus Christ. To say that God is a living, loving, personal God who exists eternally, and who, as a spiritual being, is able to know all and be present to all is only the tip of the iceberg. We must reflect upon these truths, apply them to our lives, and understand how they touch us in our desire to know and love God more deeply. Our journey consists not only in knowing about God, but of a desire to serve and love God and every member of the human family.

4. Can we know about God from our human experience alone?

a. We cannot know God through human experience alone.

Nature provides us with many signs of God's presence and powers. Without the gift of faith in God we do not fully accept these signs of God in the universe. We do have natural proofs of God's existence, but without faith, we can simply keep saying, "Maybe we have not discovered the answer yet. We know a lot more now than we did a century ago, and perhaps in the next century we shall learn the answer to these mysteries in nature." With faith the natural proofs of God's existence help to reinforce our faith by showing that belief in God's existence is not contrary to our human experience.

Paul, in writing to the Romans, reminds them that the pagans among them had faith in God through the "things he has made," but they refused to accept this as an incentive to worship the one true God. The basic faith was there, but they ignored the evidence of the world around them. Paul writes, "God punishes them because what can be known about God is plain to them, for God Himself made it plain. Ever since God created the world, these invisible qualities . . . have been clearly seen; they are perceived in the things God has made. So those people have no excuse at all! They know God, but they do not give Him the honor that belongs to Him, nor do they thank Him" (Romans 1:19–21). In Paul's eyes, the sin of the pagans was their unwillingness to develop their faith, despite the evidence given by God in the world around them.

b. Our human experience supports our faith by showing that God must always have existed, without beginning.

When a baby is born, we congratulate the parents. The baby did not just suddenly appear in the world; every infant came from parents. When we see a painted picture, we ask the name of the artist. The painting did not suddenly fall together on the canvas. Everything in our experience had something or someone preceding it. Even the first parents had to come from someone, along with the earth they stood on and the food they ate. We keep going back in our experience until we stand alone with God who has no beginning but who put all this in motion. At some point, our experience tells us that someone must have existed with no one before that person. And if this is so, that person, God, always existed, with no beginning. The psalmist writes, "Before the mountains were begotten, and the earth and the world were brought forth, from everlasting to everlasting you are God" (Psalm 90:2).

c. Our human experience supports our faith by showing that God is an intelligent God.

As we look at the universe that surrounds us, we smile in wonder that anyone could ever suggest that it happened by chance. The perfect nervous system that a child shows at the moment of birth astounds the greatest minds. The many stars and planets of the universe that hold each other in place by varying forces of gravity could never be fully understood or repeated, even on a minor scale. Only a perfect, powerful, intelligent God could have planned so intricate a universe and a creation that works so well. The psalmist writes, "You made the moon to mark the seasons; the sun knows the hour of its setting. You bring darkness, and it is night" (Psalm 104:19–20).

d. Our human experience supports our faith by showing that God is a loving God.

Parents who know nothing about cars do not lead their children out to the garage to rebuild an engine. Since they know nothing about cars, they have nothing to share with their children regarding this particular field. They do, however, love their children. Through the actions of their parents, the children, in turn, learn to love. Love is central to our creation. When we experience love, we experience lightheartedness, tenderness, simple contentment, and happiness. When we lack the experience of love, we grow sad, lonely, and deeply unhappy. Since love affects the whole of human experience so deeply, we look to the Creator, namely God, and conclude from our experience that only a loving person can share love. For this reason, we believe in a loving God, not only because of the message of God's love learned from the Scriptures, but also because of our own human experience of loving.

5. How does God show concern for the world God created?

a. God keeps the world in existence.

Not only did the world need God for its creation, but it needs God to continue in existence. God created a world that is continually developing and growing. For this to happen, God must keep the world and all its creatures in mind, or the world ceases to exist. The mere fact of our existence tells us that God is showing concern for the world God created.

In the Gospel of Matthew, we read about God's concern for creation. The author of the Gospel gives us a message of Jesus who says, "For only a penny you can buy two sparrows, yet not one sparrow falls to the ground without your Father's consent. As for you, even the hairs of your head have all been counted. So do not be afraid; you are worth much more than many sparrows (Matthew 10:29–31).

b. God shared with us the dignity of being co-creators.

God shared with us all the gifts of creation. We are called to understand these gifts more fully and use them more effectively in building up the world. By understanding the process of healing in the human body, doctors are able to heal more quickly and painlessly. By understanding the laws of gravity and stress, great minds achieve spectacular results that allow large bridges to span rivers and tall buildings to stretch skyward. As co-creators, we reach out in the universe to explore God's gifts and discover greater uses for these gifts. Because of the hope God had for human creation, God placed in our hands the ability to struggle with an incomplete world and to help God bring it to the completion God has planned. By doing so, human beings share in the dignity of being co-creators with God.

From the very beginning, human beings were destined to share in God's creative work. The message found in the first book of the Bible speaks of God's creation of human beings with a special co-creative task. The author writes, ". . . male and female he created them. God blessed them, saying: 'Be fertile and multiply; fill the earth and subdue it' " (Genesis 1:27–28). The mission to work does not come to us as a result of sin, but, as the opening book of the Bible tells us, it comes to us from God's creative plan. From the beginning, we have been called to the dignity of being co-creators with God.

c. God gives help and guidance as we seek it.

God helps and guides us in our quest to understand and develop the world. God is an inviting God. God does not force this help and guidance upon us, but allows us to respond to an invitation to call upon God. With our belief in God's help in our lives, we dare to attempt more than we would attempt alone. We do not depend solely upon our talents or knowledge, but we learn to depend upon God for help. The prayer of the psalmist reminds us of our need to call upon God as we read, "When I called, You answered me; You built up strength within me" (Psalm 138:3).

d. God loves the world.

Some portray God as a condemning God, just waiting for people to step out of line in order to punish them. This unfortunate image of God has caused many to deny or to fear God. The Scriptures do not portray this image of God. The Scriptures speak of a God who continually seeks to forgive and to show love. Throughout the Scriptures, we learn that God will never abandon God's people, even if they should abandon God. A psalmist again captures the true image of God when he writes, "We feast on the abundant food you provide; you let us drink from the river of Your goodness. You are the source of all life, and because of Your light we see the light. Continue to love those who know you and to do good to those who are righteous" (Psalm 36:8–10).

6. What name do we give people who deny or doubt God's existence?

a. An agnostic is a person who claims ignorance of God's existence.

An agnostic neither denies nor accepts the existence of God. The agnostic simply says, "I do not know if God exists."

b. An atheist is a person who claims that God does not exist.

For the atheist, there is no doubt. Belief in God is absurd. Many atheists feel so strongly about their denial of God, that they spend a great deal of time and money spreading their message. Atheism is not something new in our modern world. In Old Testament times, we read the words of a psalmist who proclaims the foolishness of the atheist. The psalmist writes, "The fool says in his heart, 'There is no God' " (Psalm 14:1).

c. Some people who proclaim a belief in God live as though God does not exist.

Some people who glibly say that God exists often betray a disbelief in God by their daily lives. By their actions and their lack of adverting to God's presence in life, these people lead lives that some refer to as the life of a "practical atheist." Life moves along with all its decisions, tragedies, joys, and pleasures with no thought of God. The fact of God's existence has no effect on their lives—to the point that in the real day by day living of their lives, God does not exist. Because their lives lack the awareness of God's presence, we could say that such people are atheists in practice.

d. A person who believes in God may pass through periods of doubt or nonbelief.

As we grow and mature throughout life, we relate to people around us in different ways. As children, we fully depend upon our parents. To approach God with child-like dependence comes easily in our early years. During the teenage years and early twenties, breaking away from the authority of the Church comes as easily as breaking away from the authority of the home. Just as parents no longer have wise answers to all the problems in life, so God no longer has wise answers. Instead of learning how to relate to God in a new way during these years, many pass through stages of doubt or nonbelief. During the years when we struggle to break away from the nest and all images of authority, we change our way of relating to God. Some never learn how to relate as a mature adult to God. Others will gradually move from rejection to a greater understanding of God in their lives. We should not panic during these years of doubt, but rather pray for those struggling with this stage in their growth pattern. Hopefully, they will return to the faith of their roots, with a deeper, more mature relationship with God.

Jesus told a parable about weeds and wheat which reminds us that we cannot always identify those who are good and bad at every period of life. A farmer had planted some wheat, and an enemy came during the night to plant weeds among the wheat. The farmer decided to allow the weeds and the wheat to grow together, lest in an attempt to root out the weeds, the wheat would also be lost. At harvest time, the wheat would be separated from the weeds. Through this parable, Jesus is telling us that some people, who seem to be the "weeds" of creation, may, at a later time in their lives, prove to be the true wheat and harvest of God's creation. History abounds with the stories of sinners who eventually became saints. The wisdom of Jesus recognized the fact of God's grace and human conversion in creation (cf Matthew 13:24–30).

7. Why does God allow suffering?

a. Suffering in life is one of the great mysteries of God's creation.

Why is there disease or sickness in the world? Why do innocent babies die and good, loving people suffer so agonizingly as they near death? Sometimes, the wicked of this world seem to die well or live in luxury. It is a fact of life that the good as well as the bad suffer. Some suffering comes from human selfishness and carelessness. This we can accept as a partial answer for suffering in the world. But why does the innocent baby die at birth when the mother has followed all the rules? Why does the loving, concerned father suddenly die from a heart attack? No matter how many answers we seek for these questions, we must finally admit that they are part of the mysteries of God's creation. If we were to believe that our lives ended here, the answer would be even more difficult. Somewhere, in God's loving plan, lies the answer to suffering in the world.

b. God does not cause suffering in the world.

Suffering reminds us of the incompleteness of our creation. God set up the world to move in a certain direction, and God gave the human person free will to share in bringing the world to completion. The striving for this completeness will go on as long as the world exists and we must never stop working in this direction. When we do stop reaching for perfection and completion of this creation, we will only increase suffering.

When a person suffers, we can never say that God directly caused or planned that particular suffering. In the plan of creation, God allowed suffering, but God did not cause suffering. Suffering and death happen as a normal process of life. God does not decide that on a particular day at a particular time we shall suffer or die. God set up the process of life and we become part of that process. How we live; the cautions we take; the health received from our parents; the carefulness of others, and our continual use of free will will often affect the amount and type of suffering and, at times, the moment of our death. God set up a process of life that shares with us health and happiness, sickness and sadness. We continually strive to bring this process to completion by alleviating causes of sickness and sadness and other forms of suffering, but we recognize the fact that suffering and death are part of our incomplete creation.

Paul, the apostle, recognizes the struggle of the world as it reaches toward its fulfillment. He writes, "For creation was condemned to lose its purpose, not of its own will, but because God willed it to be so. Yet there was the hope that creation itself would one day be set free from its slavery to decay and would share the glorious freedom of the children

15

of God. For we know that up to the present time all of creation groans with pain, like the pain of childbirth" (Romans 8:20–22). Despite the suffering found in creation, Paul has a living hope that the end will bring freedom from suffering.

c. God's love calls us to heal suffering.

When we suffer, our faith in God is tested. Without suffering as part of the normal process of life, we might never have a chance to prove just how deeply we love God. In reality, it is not what happens to us that speaks of our love and faithfulness, but rather how we respond to what happens to us. A small pain can cause continual complaining on the part of some, while deep, continuous pain can cause others to reflect on their dependence upon God's strength. A suffering person can often renew the faith of others who see the love of God reflected even in the midst of suffering.

Even though we do not know fully the answer to the mystery of pain, we should still strive to alleviate pain and suffering wherever possible in God's creation. As co-creators with God, we share in the call to bring healing to a broken world. This includes physical as well as spiritual healing. The story of the Good Samaritan, told by Jesus, describes a virtuous Samaritan who helps a battered stranger by dressing his wounds and providing housing for him. Jesus praises the Samaritan for his concern for the physical well-being of the stranger (cf Luke 10:25–37).

8. How do we touch God in our daily lives?

a. We can touch God through a continual awareness of God's presence in our lives.

Because God is all-knowing and all-loving, we believe God constantly keeps us in mind. God is always with us, knowing us and loving us. We should strive to return this love of God by reminding ourselves of God's presence. At times, we become so involved in our day to day joys and struggles that we often forget that God is sharing these joys and struggles with us. At any moment of the day, we can say to ourselves, "God is with me and loves me right now." By doing so, we are touching God and growing in consciousness of God's presence with us. The more we grow aware of this presence, the more perfectly we will live our lives.

b. We can touch God by setting aside a quiet time each day for prayer.

We tend to love the people with whom we communicate often throughout our lives. Husbands and wives learn the importance of communication in marriage. As long as they communicate, they continually meet each other and love each other. When communication ceases, loss of love often follows. Prayer is simply communicating with God. What we say to God is not as important as the fact that we spend time in communication. Because we are made for God, our lives will never reach fulfillment unless we spend some time communicating with God. We actually need this communication. When we neglect to pray, we try to make others fill the gap in our lives that only God can fill. This leads to frustration and unhappiness. We should set aside a quiet time each day to speak with God or simply to sit in silence and let God speak to us. This quiet time can exist when all is quiet around us or even when all is noisy around us. The quiet time is within. On a bus going to work, while preparing lunch, or while jogging, we can withdraw alone into ourselves to speak with God. Through this quiet time for prayer, we reach out to God's presence in our lives.

c. We can touch God through "formal" or "informal" prayer.

In the Bible, the disciples asked Jesus to teach them to pray. Jesus responded with the words and ideas that have shaped the "Lord's Prayer" recited by Catholics today. We pray:

Our Father, Who art in heaven,
Hallowed be thy name;
Thy Kingdom come;
Thy will be done
On earth as it is in heaven.
Give us this day our daily bread;
And forgive us our trespasses
As we forgive those who trespass against us;
And lead us not into temptation,
But deliver us from evil. Amen.

Prayers that have preformulated words such as the "Lord's Prayer" are called "formal prayer." "Informal prayer" refers to those prayers spoken in our own words, expressing our love for God either silently or in sharing with others. Both forms of praying have their place in loving and praising God.

Conclusion

The piece of driftwood has found a home beside the fireplace in the bungalow. The man and woman have long since forgotten the day they brought it home from the beach. Other gifts from the sea have found their way into the bungalow since that piece of driftwood arrived. Although the man and woman are no longer aware of the driftwood, they would notice something missing if it were stolen.

Their bungalow is a creation of their "vacation mind," rustic and reflective of the sea. The piece of driftwood sits clearly in the back of their minds, not drawing attention to itself, but one part of the whole picture.

Like that piece of driftwood, God becomes part of the fabric of our lives. God underlies the whole picture. Every now and then, we must take a steady look at God in our lives so the presence of God does not fade into the shadows. The world around us, with its children, its gardens, its furnishings, and its painted walls, reflect our part in creation. In the midst of them all, the touch of God, the Creator and lover of creation, must always be felt.

_____

For Scripture reflection and discussion concerning this chapter, see Journeying in His Light, *"In Search of God."*

Knowing God Better

Introduction

The man pushed a junk cart through the streets of Brooklyn, and called up to the open windows for old newspapers. One young boy of the neighborhood often joined the other boys in taunting the "junk man" until he would suddenly turn and take a few threatening steps in their direction. At that, the boys would scramble off down the street.

One day, the young boy was picnicking with his family at a neighborhood park. To his amazement, he saw the "junk man," cheaply dressed but clean, playing with some children who were apparently his own. The boy felt ashamed and sad when he saw that the "junk man" was actually someone's father. He realized that his own father could have been a "junk man." Life had treated his father a little more kindly.

The young boy never met the "junk man," but he felt he knew him a little better because he saw him playing with children in a park.

In this chapter, we get to know God a little better. We look not only through our own eyes to understand God, but also through the eyes of the Old Testament people. We try to understand these people, why they wrote, how they wrote, and what they tried to tell us about God. Through their histories, messages, prayers, and poetry, we come to know God better.

1. Where do we learn about God?

a. We first learn about God from people who touch our lives.

Most of us have first learned about God from our families. As we grew, we heard more about God from our teachers, our friends, and our minister or priest in church. The very exceptional person first learns about

God through books. Unknowingly, we were developing ideas about God from the world around us and the people who shared in that world. Only later would we turn to books.

b. We deepened our understanding of God by listening to God's message as shared in the Bible.

Although many people are familiar with Bible stories, very few people have read the Bible from beginning to end. Most have heard certain stories drawn from the Bible that teach messages about living life in union with God. When a Bible story or lesson teaches something special, it very often reinforces what we have already learned through our growing process. By reading the Bible we can begin to understand more about God and how God related to the chosen people. Through these readings, we learn how we, too, can relate to God in our world today. The Bible challenges us to clarify any false impressions we may have formed about God. We must not only read the Bible, but we must understand how to read it so we can understand the message of the author.

c. We also learn about God from prayers and reflections found in other writings besides the Bible.

Some people have responded to God's presence in their lives by writing down their experiences of God or their innermost prayers and reflections on God's message. Through these writings, we learn how others have responded to God's presence in their lives. We should never view their way of approaching God as the only way, but we can learn from these people. In their writings, we can learn a great deal about God's dealings with others who, in turn, share their gifts with us. We must realize, however, that God deals with each of us in a slightly different manner according to our own personalities.

2. Why is the Bible considered an important source of knowing God?

a. Revelation about God comes to us through the Bible.

Through reading about the community of the chosen people, we gradually learn intimate details about God and God's concern for the people. These people looked back to God's presence in their midst and reflected on that presence. Under God's special guidance, they drew conclusions about God that would give insight to power, love, mercy, and many other of God's unique attributes. Gradually, the community shaped an image of God that God had shared with that community. The writers rarely came to new conclusions themselves. They simply reflected the knowledge of God as known through the community. We call this sharing of intimate knowledge of God with God's people "revelation."

b. God inspired certain people who compiled these revelations.

Throughout their history, the community shared among themselves stories and messages about God's presence in their midst. At certain points in history, these ideas were committed to writing under the guidance of God. Not all the preaching and teaching of the people found its way to the written page, but only those parts of the message that the writer, under the guidance of God, chose from the oral traditions of God's people. We call this guidance "inspiration." God did not dictate the message to these writers. The writers wrote according to their own world view and their own style. The writers did not know they were committing the inspired word to writing. They simply reflected the revelation shared by the community in the language and style of the age in which they wrote. Occasionally, the writer might become the receiver and sharer of a new revelation to the community.

c. The Bible, taken as a whole, reflects the true message of God's revelation.

In order to decide the truth of any individual passage of the Bible, we must test that passage against the overall, constant teaching of the Bible. This constant teaching of the Bible is the inspired, revealed truth that the Bible teaches free from error.

For example, in some Old Testament writings the authors expressed ignorance or doubt about life after death. For many of them, their life and spirit continued in their children and their children's children. In the Book of Job, we read how death ends all: "But a man dies, and that is the end of him; he dies and where is he then? Like rivers that stop running, and lakes that go dry, people die, never to rise. They will never wake up while the sky endures; they will never stir from their sleep" (Job 14:10–12). In the New Testament, we read statements of Jesus that point to life after death. Jesus promised the thief crucified alongside him that he would enter paradise that day because he sought forgiveness. As we look to the Bible as a whole, we read clear statements of life after death. To quote the book of Job as a proof that we have no life after death is to miss the gradual unfolding message of the Bible.

The individual message of Bible passages must stand the test of the constant teaching of the Bible. It is this constant teaching of the Bible which is the inspired, revealed truth that the Bible teaches free from error.

3. Is the Bible a single book?

a. The Bible consists in a collection of many writings composed or compiled at different stages of history.

Long before the messages of the Bible were committed to writing, they were shared through the spoken word. Eventually, the stories and preaching that the people shared concerning the action of God in their midst were written down for further generations. Certain writings took a central position in the lives of the people of God. In time, these writings were gathered together into the one book of the Bible.

b. Some books of the Bible had several different authors.

Throughout the Bible, we find that some books are collections from several different sources. On close inspection, for example, biblical scholars found different styles and emphasis in the Book of Genesis. They even found different words used for "God." They concluded that the Book of Genesis was a collection of four different writings (called Traditions) brought together by an editor at a later date. The editor was able to fit these stories into their proper place, thus giving later generations the impression that the Book of Genesis was the work of a single author.

c. The Bible consists of the Old Testament and the New Testament.

The word "Testament" means a covenant or agreement made between God and God's chosen people. The Old Testament records the events from the creation of the world to the coming of Jesus. It describes the formation, development, and hopes of God's chosen people. The New Testament treats the events of Jesus' life, his message, and the effect of that message on the early Church.

4. What is literary form?

a. The Bible consists of many different types of writings.

The Bible consists of hymns, prayers, poems, stories, historical narratives, prophecies, exhortations, and letters. To understand its message more fully, we should attempt to understand the type of writing chosen to convey the message. We should not read a story as though it were history, nor should we read a hymn as though it were a prophetic message. Besides trying to understand the type of writing, we should strive to understand the people who wrote the Bible. For example, our conception of historical writing differs vastly from that of the people who wrote history more than two thousand years ago, in a culture that had its birth almost halfway around the world from our own.

b. These different types of writing or forms of literature are called "literary forms."

As we read a newspaper, we encounter several different forms of writing, or "literary forms." On the first page, we may read about a bombing somewhere in the world, and we are saddened that a killing has taken place. The front page gives us factual news of the world. On the second page, we might read a small section that tells us of a certain pill that will cure arthritis. We recognize that this is an advertisement for the pill, so we pay little attention. Somewhere in the middle of the paper, certain writers express their opinion of world events. We listen to what they have to say, but we know what they say is only opinion. On the sports page, we read that one baseball team has bombed another. If our team has taken the "bombing," we feel sad because our team lost the game. The word "bombing" has a different meaning on the sports page than it does on the first page of a newspaper. As we turn from page to page and read a different "literary form," we do not have to be reminded to change our mind-set. We have lived with these different literary forms and we automatically accept them.

Unfortunately, when we pick up the Bible we often expect that the people of ancient Israel are writing in the same literary forms used within our own history books. This is rarely the case. The people of ancient Israel were a more poetic people, interested in expressing the experience of the event and message rather than the event itself. If they had a message to share, they would package that message neatly in a story that the people could listen to and repeat. In our century and past centuries, we often misunderstood the literary form of many biblical writings and read these stories as though they expressed historical events exactly as they happened. This led to many problems in trying to unnecessarily defend the scientific accuracy and historical truth of the Bible.

5. What is an example of literary form in the Bible

a. In its early chapters the Book of Genesis, the first book of the Bible, shows a good example of literary form.

Several centuries before Christ, while the Israelites were in exile from the Promised Land, they needed to keep alive the message of God's relationship to the world. Stories of the creation of the world originated during this period which were later joined with other creation stories to form the first chapters of Genesis. Many of the ideas for these stories could be found in even more ancient stories of other countries—for example, in the Egyptian stories about the tree of life. By reading the creation stories closely, we can conclude that God used the genius of the people to share God's message of creation.

b. The story of creation is a literary form in which the message, not the history nor the science, is inspired by God.

In the first story of creation, the author makes use of the people's knowledge of a seven day week with the special day of rest, namely the Sabbath. He draws a poetic balance between the first three days of creation and the next three days. He uses a common poetic device that portrays the first three days of separation and the next three days as days of decoration. What God separates on the first day, God decorates on the fourth; what God separates on the second day, God decorates on the fifth, and what God separates on the third day, God decorates on the sixth. In diagram, the days line up as follows:

Separation	Decoration
1—Light from Darkness	4—Sun, Moon, Stars
2—Sky from Water	5—Birds and Fish
3—Land from Water	6—Animal and Human Life

7—God Rests (Sabbath Rest)

On the second day of creation, the author reveals an ignorance of the shape of the earth and the universe. The author has God creating a world that fits in perfectly with the world view of ancient times, but does not correspond to our current knowledge of the world and universe.

We read in the Bible, "Then God commanded, 'Let there be a dome to divide the water and to keep it in two separate places'—and it was done. . . . Then God commanded 'Let the water below the sky come together in one place, so that the land will appear'—and it was done" (Genesis 1:6,9). The ancient view described here and accepted by people of biblical times could be drawn as follows:

From these observations, we conclude that the "biblical days of creation" were not intended to be scientific explanations of the order of creation. Instead, through a poetic literary device the sacred writer conveys God's message: that God created the world out of chaos, and that God put order into the world. God is greater than the "elements" and "the gods" that ride upon the dome of heaven. Indeed, these are not gods, but simply creations of the one true God. As God rested on the Sabbath, so every good Israelite should rest on the Sabbath. The story moves from the lesser creations to the greater, from light to the peak of creation, the human person.

c. In the second chapter of the Book of Genesis (2:4ff), the author contradicts chapter one by telling us that human life was created first, then animal life.

Chapter 2 tells its own story of creation as though chapter one does not exist. Apparently, the editor found another creation story and simply placed it where he felt it belonged in the Book of Genesis. It differs in style from chapter one and contradicts chapter one by having God create human life before animal life. Chapter two tells the story of Adam and Eve, who were placed in a Garden of Paradise, failing a great test given by God. Because they failed, they must work the land by the sweat of their brow and bear the pain of childbirth. This chapter suggests that human life is higher than animal life by moving from the greater form of life to the lower. It also conveys the message that marriage is God's idea, ". . . the two of them become one body," and that human beings, not God, are responsible for sin in the world. Again, the message, not the history nor the science, is the essential point conveyed by this story told about our first parents. The Garden of Paradise, the first man and woman placed in that garden, and the events that led to the fall are simply literary devices in story form used to convey a message to God's people.

d. The use of this literary form continues to chapter eleven (Genesis 11:9) to show how sin is gripping the world.

Genesis 1 to 11:9 conveys in story form the creation of the world and its subsequent fall into the grip of sinfulness. These chapters are termed prehistory. The Bible does not intend to give a history of the world from creation to Abraham, but rather a religious explanation or inter- pretation of the origin of sin and suffering in creation. In these chapters, we read about Cain killing his brother Abel, and the continued growth of sin in the world. When the world becomes filled with sin, God de- stroys it with a flood, saving only Noah and his family. Ham, a son of Noah and the father of the nation of Caanan, commits a sin shortly after the flood ends, and he is cursed by Noah. The final sin of these chapters oc- curs when the people of the world decide to share their knowledge and build their own tower to heaven. The author pictures God as one who is concerned about the ability of these people to do whatever they want, even if it is contrary to God's will. God "confuses their tongues" so that they begin to speak different languages and can no longer work together. Abraham is the first truly historical person of the Bible.

6. What does the rest of the Book of Genesis tell us?

a. The Book of Genesis continues with the era of the patriarchs.

God chose Abraham as the father of the Israelite nation. While reading the portion of the Bible which speaks of him, we should keep in mind that the story of Abraham was passed on from generation to generation before being written down. Within that time legend grew. Although Abraham is apparently the first historical person in the Bible, we cannot say the narration about him is history in the modern sense. We are reading the epic of Abraham and his sons, bits of history embellished as the story passed from generation to generation. Again, we look to the message and find that Abraham's gift is his great faith and trust in God. In this narrative, God promises Abraham that he will be the father of a great nation and grants Abraham and his wife, Sarah, a child in their old age. The faith of Abraham is challenged when an angel of the Lord directs him to sacrifice his son Isaac, and Abraham's trust in God is shown as he prepares to kill Isaac. God, pleased with Abraham's faith, stops him from sacrificing Isaac. The faith of Abraham will become an example of perfect faith in the writings of the New Testament.

b. Genesis continues with the story of Isaac, Jacob, and the twelve sons of Jacob.

Short sections of the book of Genesis tell of Isaac and Jacob and their special duty in carrying on the tradition of Abraham. Isaac, the son of Abraham, has two sons, Esau and Jacob. Although Esau is the first born, God chooses Jacob to carry on the traditions of Abraham. Jacob has twelve sons, whose names will play an important role in establishing the families of Israel centuries later.

c. A large portion of Genesis deals with one of Jacob's sons named Joseph who becomes responsible for the family of Jacob settling in Egypt.

Of Jacob's sons, Joseph becomes a favorite, and the other sons of Jacob become jealous of Joseph. Joseph is a dreamer who sees his brothers symbolically bowing down to him in his dreams. When he relates his dreams to his brothers, they become angry with him and eventually sell him into slavery to some merchants. They tell Jacob that Joseph was killed by a wild animal.

In Egypt, the Pharaoh's wife, rejected by Joseph, accuses him of trying to seduce her, and the Pharaoh has him cast into prison. Years later, the Pharaoh has a dream and has Joseph, the interpreter of dreams, brought to him. Joseph interprets the dream, telling the Pharaoh that there will be seven years of plenty and seven years of famine over the land. The Pharaoh places Joseph second to him in charge of the land. For the first seven years, Joseph leads the people in storing up enough food to feed the people for the seven years of famine. During these last seven years, the family of Joseph come to Egypt for food. Joseph recognizes them, and, after causing them some difficulty, has them all brought to Egypt to settle.

The story of Joseph takes up a large portion of the book of Genesis, and its purpose is to relate how the Hebrew people came to settle in Egypt. This sets the scene for the next book of the Bible, the Book of Exodus.

7. How did the Israelites come to settle in Palestine?

a. The Book of Exodus records the journey of the Israelites out of slavery in Egypt, through the wandering in the desert, to the borders of the Promised Land, Palestine.

Four hundred years elapse between the end of the book of Genesis and the beginning of the Book of Exodus. During that time, Egyptian rulers, called Pharaohs, came into power. Before this, Egypt was ruled by Semitic Pharaohs of the same background as the Hebrews (who were later called Israelites). The new Egyptian Pharaohs, fearing that the rapid growth of the Hebrew tribes would threaten their hold on the kingdom, forced the Hebrews into slavery. When the Book of Exodus begins, they had struggled and suffered under slavery for some time.

When Moses was a child, the Pharaoh ordered that all male children be killed. But Moses escaped death when the Pharaoh's daughter found him in a basket among the reeds and eventually adopted him. When Moses grew up, he killed an Egyptian who was striking one of his Hebrew kin, and he fled into the desert lest the Egyptians discover his crime and kill him. In the desert, he married, had a son and lived as a shepherd.

After some years, an angel of the Lord appeared to him in a burning bush, and God spoke from the bush, directing Moses to free the Hebrew people from the slavery of Egypt. Since the people were not allowed to use the name of "God," Moses was told to say to the people that "I Am" sent him. In this title, the people would recognize that the source of all creation sent him to lead them from slavery.

On the night they fled Egypt, the Hebrews first celebrated the most significant event of their history. Each household killed a lamb, painted its blood on the doorposts, and ate the lamb as people ready for a journey. The author of the Book of Exodus tells how the angel of death passed over the doors painted with the blood and killed the first-born children and animals of the Egyptians. Each year, the Hebrew nation would celebrate this feast of the Passover, and it would play a central role in the passion of Jesus. Because of the slaughter of this evening, the Pharaoh called Moses and ordered him to take his people and leave.

b. In the desert of Mount Sinai, God delivers to Moses the Ten Commandments.

The most famous and best known moral teachings of many western religions center in some way around the Ten Commandments. As Moses received these in the story of Sinai, the number was not so clearly given.

28

However, down through the years, the Church has numbered these Commandments as ten and lined them up as follows:

1. *"I, the Lord, am your God, who brought you out of the land of Egypt, that place of slavery. You shall not have other gods besides me."*
2. *"You shall not take the name of the Lord, your God, in vain."*
3. *"Remember to keep holy the sabbath day."*
4. *"Honor your father and your mother. . . ."*
5. *"You shall not kill."*
6. *"You shall not commit adultery."*
7. *"You shall not steal."*
8. *"You shall not bear false witness against your neighbor."*
9. *"You shall not covet your neighbor's house."*
10. *"You shall not covet your neighbor's wife. . . ." (Exodus 20:2–3, 7–8, 12–17)*

The Book of Exodus goes on to explain these laws and others more at length.

The Ten Commandments became the central law of the people of Israel, and Jesus emphasized their importance by quoting some of them to the people of his own day. In the Gospel of Matthew, when a rich man asked Jesus what he must do to possess eternal life, Jesus tells him, "Keep the commandments if you want to enter life." "What commandments?" he asked. Jesus answered. "Do not commit murder; do not commit adultery; do not steal; do not accuse anyone falsely; respect your father and your mother; and (Jesus adds) love your neighbor as you love yourself" (Matthew 19:17–19). Jesus, however, invites the man to live beyond the commandments and to come to perfection. He tells him, "If you want to be perfect, go and sell all you have, and give the money to the poor, and you will have riches in heaven; then come and follow me" (Matthew 19:21). Although Jesus honored the commandments, he asked his followers to do even more than was demanded by the commandments.

c. *After the death of Moses, Joshua led the people into the Promised Land.*

The next three books following upon the Book of Exodus (Leviticus, Numbers and Deuteronomy) tell of the extensive laws governing the people of God in their daily lives and in worship. They also describe how the Promised Land is parcelled out among the twelve tribes of Israel. The Book of Joshua tells of the Israelites' entry into the Promised Land and their battles with the inhabitants of that land. The years of struggle continue during which certain great military leaders, called judges, played a major role in the conquest of the Promised Land. Many legends surround the stories of these judges.

29

8. What happened to the people of God in the promised land?

a. After the days of the judges, Israel was ruled by kings.

God allows the Israelites to have a king and set up a kingdom similar to those of their surrounding neighbors. Saul, the first king, gradually goes insane, turns his back upon God, and is killed in battle. Samuel, the prophet of the Lord, anoints David the new king of the Israelites. The Scripture stories tell of God's great love for David, but because David is a warrior and a man of blood, God will not allow David to build the temple. David establishes the great city of God, Jerusalem. Solomon, David's son, follows David as king of Israel. He builds a magnificent temple, but eventually succumbs to the pleasures and soft life of the pagan religions. Solomon is the most powerful of the first three kings of Israel and he is the last king to rule the whole nation as one.

b. At the death of Solomon, his kingdom was broken into the northern kingdom (Israel) and the southern kingdom (Juda).

Under the heavy hand of Solomon's son, the northern kingdom rebelled and chose one of Solomon's generals as its king. Solomon's son was left with only two tribes to rule in the southern kingdom. A line of kings followed in both the northern and southern kingdoms until the Assyrians invaded the northern kingdom in the eighth century before Christ and led most of the inhabitants into exile. At the beginning of the sixth century before Christ, the Babylonians invaded the southern kingdom and led its inhabitants into exile. Eventually, some of the tribes of Juda returned from exile to rebuild the temple. From this point onward, the Israelite nation is referred to as the Jewish nation, an allusion to the only known people to return to the Promised Land from exile.

c. The Book of Maccabees tells of the Jewish nation's heroic attempt to overthrow foreign domination.

About the second century before Christ, an attempt was made to suppress Judaism in Palestine. The title of Book of Maccabees refers to the heroic leader, Judas Maccabee, who led the revolt of the Jewish people. This book stands as an important link between the Old Testament and the New Testament since it gives some insights into conditions only a few centuries before Christ. The Book of Maccabees ends the line of historical books of the Old Testament.

9. What is a covenant?

a. A covenant consists of an agreement between people by which they bind or commit themselves to each other at their deepest level.

A contract and a covenant are both agreements made between people by which they bind themselves in some way. In a contract, a builder promises to build a house within a certain period of time for a certain amount of money. When the building is finished, the builder receives his pay and the terms of the contract have ended. In a covenant, people bind or commit their whole person to each other, not just for a short period of time, but permanently. When a man and woman enter marriage, they enter a covenant that binds them to each other for life. If they place a period of time on their agreement or a condition that must be fulfilled, then they are simply sharing in a contract, not a covenant, and they would not truly be sharing in marriage.

b. God made a covenant with the people of Israel through Abraham, the father of the nation.

Abraham and God committed themselves to each other through a covenant. God would be the special God of the Israelites and they would be God's special people. We read in the Scriptures, "When Abram prostrated himself, God continued to speak to him: 'My covenant with you is this: you are to become the father of a host of nations' " (Genesis 17:3-4). God then reminded Abraham of his duty toward the covenant. "God said to Abraham, 'On your part, you and your descendants after you must keep my covenant throughout the ages' " (Genesis 17:9). God renewed this covenant with Abraham's son, Isaac, and Isaac's son, Jacob. Abraham and his descendants promised to serve the Lord, God, and to live with faith in God's promises. In return, God promised Abraham that he would be the father of a great nation, and that God would guide this nation to a fruitful land. As a sign of this covenant between God and the Israelite nation, all male children would be circumcised.

c. A familiar word used also for covenant is the word testament.

When we speak of the Old Testament and the New Testament, we are speaking of the specific covenants God made with the people. The first Covenant consists of the Covenant made between God and the people before the coming of Jesus Christ. The second Covenant consists in a covenant made between God and God's people in the person of Jesus Christ.

31

10. How does the Bible refer to prophets?

a. A prophet was a person who spoke or acted in the name of God.

Under God's guidance, certain men and women of the Old Testament would remind the people of the covenant that bound their nation to God. They reminded the family of God that God would always keep God's part of the covenant, but they cautioned the people that God would punish them if they broke their part of the covenant. These prophets would share insights into God's work among the people, and on rare occasions, would share a message about some future event. The prophets were not always popular, since they were telling the people (including kings) when God was not pleased with them and that they would soon experience God's wrath. They often predicted such catastrophies as the destruction of the northern kingdom of Israel, and the tragic exile in Babylon of the people of Judea.

b. We meet some of the prophets of the Old Testament through their writings while we meet others through the historical books of the Old Testament.

In the Old Testament, we find seventeen books of prophecy. Among the names of these "writing prophets," are prophets such as Ezekiel, Jeremiah, Amos, and Isaiah. Others come to life in the historical narratives of the Old Testament through stories steeped in messages and legend. Elijah confronts King Ahab of the northern kingdom in an effort to save Israel from the grip of the treacherous Jezebel. Elisha, a follower of Elijah, is called by God from his poverty to eventually destroy Jezebel. The call of these prophets stands upon the need to draw the people back to God's love and message in their lives and to save the nation from the threat that seeks to seize Israel from God's hands.

c. A book of prophecy may also portray a prophet who may never have existed.

The Book of Jonah tells of a man seeking to hide from God to avoid his call to spread the Word of God to the nation of Nineveh. A whale brings Jonah to the land of Nineveh where Jonah preaches and converts the lives of the people of that land. The Book of Jonah is a prophetic book, even though the events most likely never occurred. The message of the book concerns God's care for a sinning nation. God sends whom God wills to send, even against that person's wishes. Several books of prophecy use stories to share their great prophetic message.

11. What is wisdom literature?

a. Wisdom literature deals with the question of living successfully in God's world.

Wisdom literature, for the most part, has its roots in the wisdom writings of other ancient countries, especially Egypt. The Wisdom Books have a good deal of natural secular wisdom. What makes the Wisdom literature of Israel different from that of other cultures lies in its view of the world as God's world and the theme of fear of the Lord. Through poetry, wise sayings, prayers or love songs, the different wisdom writers portray a successful response to life in God's world.

b. Wisdom literature faces some of the difficult questions of life.

Wisdom literature includes the Books of Job, Proverbs, Ecclesiastes, Sirach and the Wisdom of Solomon. Some include Psalms and the Song of Songs under this heading, but others would deny that these properly belong to Wisdom Literature. Whether we speak of suffering or joy, love or hatred, we find these moments touched upon by the Books of Wisdom. The Book of Job faces the question of evil and suffering in life. Through short, pointed proverbs, the Books of Wisdom speak to living daily life with a knowledge of the sacredness of God in ordinary life. The Song of Songs touches the intimate love that exists in the very nature of creation. The Book of Psalms stands out as prayerful responses to every condition of life in relation to God.

12. Do angels exist?

a. The Scriptures presume but never prove angels.

To the people of biblical times, God had a visible hand in everything that happened. One means used to show God's concern and guidance of the people of God was through special messengers, commonly referred to as "angels." The word "angel" really means "messenger." Problems arise concerning angels when we look more closely at the use of angels in the Scriptures. For instance, the angel who tells Abraham to sacrifice his son Isaac suddenly speaks as God in praising Abraham for his faith. Jacob wrestles with an angel all night long and speaks of the event by proclaiming that he has seen God face to face and has lived.

Nowhere in the Scriptures do we read of proofs concerning angels, nor do we read of angels as spiritual beings. Later philosophers, in trying to explain angels in the Scriptures, identified them as spiritual beings.

The writers of the Scriptures spoke in picturesque language. They would always use visible signs of God's presence, even if these visible signs had to call an inspiration of God a visitation by an angel. From this evidence, we do not necessarily deny the existence of angels, but rather recognize the fact that we cannot use Scripture as a proof of angels. The Scriptures presume, but never prove, angels.

b. In the same way, the Scriptures presume but never prove devils.

In light of the New Testament words of Christ, it seems difficult to deny the existence of the devil. When the disciples returned from their mission full of enthusiasm with their new spiritual powers, Jesus told them, "I watched Satan fall from the sky like lightning" (Luke 10:18). We must remember, however, that Jesus was speaking to his followers in a language they would understand. In referring to evil, Jesus would speak the language of his own culture and tradition. In the Old Testament story of Job, Satan is actually visiting with the Lord, and appears more as a tester rather than an evil spirit. If we contend that devils are fallen angels, then the same presumption that led to scriptural acceptance of angels must also apply to the acceptance of devils. For the reasons given above, we cannot use the Scripture as a proof of devils.

c. The Church has traditionally taught the existence of angels.

The Church has taught the existence of angels throughout its history. Along with the Scriptures, the Church presumes but never proves angels. This presumption of the existence of angels has been a constant teaching of the Church. In its prayer life, the Church joins its voice with that of the angels in praising God, and the Church sets aside certain feast days to honor the angels. Although the Scriptures and the Church have presumed but never proven angels, we cannot definitively deny the existence of angels for that reason alone.

As we look off into the universe, we face the real possibility that God has created life on other planets, perhaps in other galaxies. Within this same possibility lies the creation of angelic creatures. God's power and love is certainly open to the possibility of many types of creation.

d. We must accept a presence of good and evil in the world.

Whether God's messenger be an angel or an act of direct inspiration through the Spirit of God, we know that we are guided to good actions. We also recognize that evil exists in the world and takes root within the human person. Some claim that the sinner is a person who accepts evil suggestions in the world, allows them to grow and develop, and tries to draw others into this evil. Evil becomes personal, not because of the devil, but because we make it part of our person and part of our world. Others would claim that evil is the work of the devil. Whatever the cause of evil in the world, we must still act against evil in the same way, namely through avoiding sinful situations and through prayer. Belief or nonbelief in the devil does not change our need to guard against sin and seek God's help in avoiding evil.

Conclusion

The young boy in the introduction to this chapter never again joined the other boys on the street in taunting the "junk man." He tried to explain to the others how he felt, but no one seemed to understand. Perhaps they had to see the man playing with his children to really understand the boy's feelings.

In this chapter, we studied how people of Old Testament days experienced God. Through their writers and prophets, they tried to explain to us their understanding of God as God related to their lives. Throughout their history, they strove to reveal to future generations an image of their loving God. Some would share that feeling and respond to the goodness and love of God and others would know their history and ignore God. Still others would never take time out of their daily routine to listen to their experience of God.

What happened to the young boy in trying to share his experience of the "junk man" could happen to the writers and prophets trying to share their experience of God. People very often do not listen. But some people do listen, and many people have listened to the message of God's dealing with the people. Our world has grown closer to an understanding of God because of these people who have listened and understood.

For Scripture reflection and discussion concerning this chapter, see Journeying In His Light, *"Knowing God Better: Parts 1 and 2."*

Jesus Is Lord

Introduction

The newspapers told of a man who had fallen through ice while fishing. While he struggled and screamed from the water, he saw a man rushing across the ice with a rope over his shoulder. In a few moments, that man had the fisherman out of the water and on his way to the nearest hospital. The man left the half-frozen and frightened fisherman in the emergency room of the hospital, shook his hand and said, "Someday you may find someone in need, and help that person because of this." Only after the man left did the fisherman realize that he did not even know his rescuer's name.

The fisherman told the newspaper reporter that encountering this man had changed his life. As he lay in the hospital nervously realizing that he could have been a frozen corpse at the bottom of a lake, he wondered what he would have done if someone else needed his help. "Never get involved if you don't have to," was his life's slogan. He thanked God that his rescuer did not have the same slogan to guide his life. This fisherman now determined to erase that attitude from his life and to reach out and share with people. He marvelled at how the kindness and courage of one man, who passed through his life for a little more than an hour, had changed his life.

In this chapter, we meet Jesus Christ. Within the course of a few short years, he drastically changed the direction of history. We shall study this person, Jesus, and see how his "stopping to help" has affected the lives of billions of people from his time to ours.

1. Where do we learn about Jesus?

a. A major source of information about Jesus comes from the New Testament.

The New Testament consists of a collection of twenty-seven books or writings compiled by early Christian believers. These Christians listened to the preaching concerning the life and message of Jesus and eventually committed this preaching to four books called the Gospels. The preaching surrounding the early days of the Christian community after Christ's physical departure from this earth was eventually gathered into a book called the Acts of the Apostles. During these early days, missionaries would send letters to the people they had brought into belief in Christ to correct, guide, and encourage them to hold to their new beliefs. There are twenty-one such letters, and the majority are attributed to Paul the Apostle. Other letters are attributed to Peter, James, and John. Finally, a highly symbolic book concerning Christianity's final conquest during the last days became known under the name of the Book of Revelation or the Apocalypse. The twenty-seven books make up the New Testament.

b. We understand these writings more clearly by understanding the "literary form" used, as we did in the Old Testament.

At the beginning of the last chapter on the Bible, we spoke of the "literary form" used in the early part of the Old Testament. In reading the New Testament, we should become aware of the culture in which the books were written and the types of writing used. Almost two thousand years have passed since the writing of the New Testament. Cultures and styles of writing have changed in that time. Recent studies and discoveries have provided a new and deeper insight into the writings of the New Testament. We should respect these insights. They should help us understand the message of the New Testament more fully.

c. We understand these writings by understanding the world in which Jesus lived.

Jesus was a true Jew, filled with a love for the law and the traditions of the Israelite nation. Although we often see Jesus challenging the leaders of the people in their interpretation of the law, he himself remains faithful to the spirit of the law. He often went to the synagogue for worship, and he challenged his listeners to live up to the law of Moses. In time, he built his new law upon the law of Moses, explaining that it was the spirit of the person and not just the living of external precepts which led to the fulfillment of the law.

During the time of Jesus, the land of Israel and its inhabitants belonged to the Roman Empire. The land was ruled by men such as Herod and Pilate who acted on behalf of Rome. Despite the Roman rule, the leaders who seemed to have the greatest influence upon the daily lives of the Jewish people were the religious leaders, consisting of several groups.

The Sadducees were the rich, priestly cast, liberal in politics and conservative in religion. They accepted only the first five books of the Bible as the inspired Scriptures.

The Pharisees were more liberal in religious developments, but conservative politically. They accepted the writings of the prophets and other writings as part of the inspired Scriptures. Being an educated class, they were accepted as the interpreters of the Scriptures. The Pharisees are portrayed as the leading opponents of Christ in the Gospels.

The Scribes consisted of the judges, writers, and interpreters of the law. All the Scribes belonged to the Pharisee party, but not all Pharisees were Scribes.

The Sanhedrin was the official ruling body of religious leaders within Judaism, and it had in its ranks members from both the Pharisees and the Sadducees. It also had the high priest at its head. The Sanhedrin play a significant role in the passion of Jesus.

The Zealots were a war-like faction within Judaism who believed that they had a divine call to free the nation from its foreign oppression.

A group considered by the Jewish people of the day to be sinful were the tax collectors and others who worked for the foreign rulers. Jesus often mixed with these tax collectors and sinners, much to the unhappiness of the religious leaders.

2. How were the Gospels written?

a. The Gospels came from the Good News as preached by the early Christians.

In the early Church, the events and message of Jesus' life, death, and resurrection were preserved through the preaching of the early disciples of Jesus. People listened to their preaching, reflected on its message, and passed the reflections of the community on to other members of the early Christian community. Only after many years of reflecting and preaching the message did writers gather the result of this preaching into written form.

The Gospel of Mark, the first Gospel, appeared sometime between A.D. 65 and 70. The Gospels of Matthew and Luke appeared sometime after the year A.D. 70, but before the year A.D. 90. Scholars believe that Matthew and Luke used Mark as part of the outline of their Gospels, and that they both used another common source (called "Q") which was unknown to Mark. They also had their own private source, known to none of the others. For Matthew, this is called the "M" source, and for Luke it is called the "L" source. If we were to put this into a formula, we would have the following:

$$\text{Mark} + Q + M = \text{Matthew}$$
$$\text{Mark} + Q + L = \text{Luke}$$

Writers have given the name, "Synoptic Gospels" to the Gospels of Mark, Matthew, and Luke. The word "synoptic" comes from a Greek word which means "seeing together." These three Gospels share so much in common that we find ourselves seeing many of the same events and messages (with slight changes) in each of the Gospels.

At least thirty years elapsed between the resurrection of Jesus and the first Gospel. The Gospel of John, the last of the Gospels, appeared between A.D. 90 and 100. This Gospel expresses many of the developments in understanding the divinity of Jesus which took place over the sixty or seventy years between the resurrection of Jesus and the writing of the Gospel.

b. The Gospels are not biographies of Jesus, but reflections of the early Christian community about the person of Jesus as they understood him after his resurrection.

The Gospels were written by followers of Jesus who knew the end of the story. After the resurrection of Jesus, his followers looked back on the events of Jesus' life and saw them in a different light. In preaching about the life of Jesus, the early Christians wanted to share the message that "Jesus is Lord." With a style proper to their own culture, they could portray events of Jesus' life in ways that proclaimed that Jesus was God. The Gospels are more than a simple biography of the life of Jesus. They are a reflection of the faith of the early community who knew Jesus and who knew that he was the Lord who was raised from the dead.

c. The events of Jesus' life highly influenced the writing of the Gospels.

Although we cannot call the Gospels biographies of Jesus, we must also be careful not to give the impression that the events of Jesus' life had no influence on the writing of the Gospels. The writers did not simply

fashion a false image of Christ to emphasize their message. The Jesus they spoke about had a definite history, and this history is portrayed in the Gospels. The early community reflected upon this history and saw it in a new light after the resurrection of Jesus. They understood a great deal more about the person of Jesus and the life of Jesus as they saw his life through the resurrection. In the Gospel of Mark, we read of a centurion at the cross of Jesus. When Jesus expired, the centurion exclaimed, "Clearly this man was the Son of God" (Mark 15:39). As the early community looked back over the life of Jesus and reflected in faith on the events of this life, they too wanted to share this message with us. . . . . "*Clearly* this man was the son of God!" The events of Jesus' life highly influenced this reflection in faith.

d. The condition of the Church at the time of the writing and the audience for whom the Gospels were written also influenced the authors of the Gospels.

The authors at times arranged the events of Jesus' life and his message for a particular audience or to emphasize a particular point needed at the time of the writing. Matthew, for example, wrote for Jewish converts to Christianity. He wanted to show Jesus as the new Moses and the new Israel. As Moses went up the mountain to receive God's law for his chosen people, Christ went up the mountain to give the new law to his followers. To show that Jesus is the fulfillment of the Old Testament prophecies, Matthew often makes reference to the words of the prophets fulfilled in Christ. Concerning the return of Jesus to Egypt, for instance, Matthew writes, " . . . to fulfill what the Lord had said through the prophet: 'Out of Egypt I have called my son' " (Matthew 2:15). These Old Testament references are found throughout the Gospel of Matthew. Luke, who had no need to portray Jesus as the new Moses, describes Jesus as coming down from the mountain in that same scene. Both authors describe a similar message from Jesus, but the backdrop for that message changes according to the audience and the more subtle message intended by the inspired author.

3. What do the Gospels tell us about the birth of Jesus?

a. The Gospels tell us little about the historical birth of Jesus.

The infancy narratives, which tell of the birth of Jesus and the events surrounding that birth, are found only in the Gospels of Matthew and Luke. When the narratives were written, the authors already knew that

41

Jesus had been raised from the dead. They were written long after the resurrection of Jesus. The writers wanted to explain the person of Jesus and the message of his life. Unlike the present forms of writing today, the literary forms used during the early years of Christianity enabled the writers to present historical facts through events that may not have been historical. They knew that Jesus was the son of Mary, that he was the confirmation of Old Testament hopes, that he was rejected by his own people, and that he would be accepted by many others throughout the world. With these ideas in mind, the writers set out to share the message through a style of writing acceptable in their own day.

b. Matthew and Luke both give a family line for Jesus.

When we look at the family trees presented by both Matthew and Luke, we discover how their purpose in writing affected what they wrote. In recording the family tree of Jesus, Matthew, who wrote for converts from the Jewish belief, wanted to portray Jesus as the hope of the Israelite nation. For this reason, Matthew begins with Abraham, the father of the Israelite nation, and traces the family tree from Abraham to Jesus. Luke, wishing to show that Jesus came for all people, begins with Adam and traces the family tree of Jesus from Adam to Jesus. As we compare the two Gospels, we discover that Matthew and Luke do not always agree on the names contained in the family tree. The fact that the family lines do not match each other would scarcely have disturbed the writers. They were not writing an exact history, but rather sharing a message about the mission of Jesus.

c. Both Gospels show Jesus as the fulfillment of the Old Testament expectation.

Matthew shows that Jesus is the new Israel and the new Moses. He draws events from the life of Moses and applies them to Jesus. At the birth of Moses, all male children two years old and under were put to death. Only Moses was spared. At the birth of Jesus, all male children two years old and under were also put to death. Only Jesus was spared. In the Gospel of Matthew, Jesus is taken to Egypt by Mary and Joseph. He later comes out of Egypt, as the Israelite nation came from the land of Egypt centuries before under the leadership of Moses.

Luke shows that Jesus is "the prophet." In the Old Testament, Hannah begged God for a child, and God heard her prayer. Hannah gave birth to a son named Samuel, who became the great prophet chosen to anoint the first kings of Israel. When Hannah came to worship the Lord in thanksgiving for Samuel, she proclaimed a song of praise to God that closely

resembles the same type of prayer that Mary recited at the home of Elizabeth: "and as she worshiped the Lord, she (Hannah) said 'My heart exults in the Lord my horn is exalted in my God . . .' " (I Samuel 2:1). By the events chosen in structuring the infancy narratives, both Matthew and Luke portray the message they wish to emphasize in developing these narratives. Their purpose, as stated earlier, is not primarily history, but rather the sharing of a message about Jesus.

d. Both Gospels use stories to portray historical facts.

At the time the Gospel of Matthew was committed to writing, others besides Judeans had joined the early Christians in their belief that Christ was the Messiah. Matthew realized this historical fact as he recounted the story of the astrologers who came from a pagan land. These wise astrologers followed a star that led to Jesus while his own people did not recognize him. Pagans, out of a pagan land (the east), came to pay homage to Christ. The story may not be true, but the historical fact, namely the pagan recognition and acceptance of Christ, was true.

When Luke wrote his Gospel, a surprising number of sinners were flocking to Christianity. In the Judean mind, the shepherds who tended their flocks on the Sabbath day of rest and who took their sheep to graze on foreign soil clearly defied the Judean laws. Luke, through the story of the Shepherds called to worship the Christ Child, portrays the historical fact that sinners recognized Christ. Luke also recognizes that Jesus was rejected by his own people, so he narrates the story of the rejection of Jesus' parents as they sought lodging at the inn at Bethlehem. Just as there was no room at the inn, so Jesus would find no room among his own people. The fact that Mary and Joseph found no room at the inn is used by Luke to portray the historical facts of the rejection of Jesus by his own people throughout his life.

Both Matthew and Luke use the literary forms of their own day to share a deep insight into the life and message of Jesus. Through their stories, they are able to summarize historical facts that surrounded Jesus and his message.

e. Both infancy narratives speak of the birth of Jesus as a special event.

The birth of Jesus was no ordinary birth. Jesus, the Messiah and Christ, came into the world. In the Gospel of Matthew, an angel tells Joseph in a dream that Mary has conceived a child by the power of the Holy Spirit. In the Gospel of Luke, an angel appears to Mary to announce that she will conceive a child who will be called "Son of the Most High." (Luke 1:32) Without doubt, a virgin birth is no ordinary birth, and it does point to the fact that a great event has taken place in history.

Some writers feel that the virgin birth of Jesus contains more message than fact. The wide use of symbol and story in the infancy narratives points to the fact that these narratives are more concerned with message than with history. The message simply tells us that a great event has taken place, namely a miraculous birth of the child Jesus. God has joined our human condition.

Other writers agree that we cannot use the infancy narratives to prove the virgin birth of Jesus, but we also cannot lightly discard the common teaching of the Church that Mary remained a virgin in the conception of Jesus. For them, the fact of the virgin birth cannot easily be denied, even if not able to be proven from the Scriptures.

One of the merits of this difference of opinion is the fact that the central message becomes more dominant. The message is not merely the virgin birth, but rather the special call of Mary to become the mother of Jesus, who is the Christ. Mary was the highly favored person chosen to give birth to the Saviour of the world. What more could be said?

At Christmastime, we should continue to use the nativity scene as a portrait of the birth of Christ. Just as the infancy narratives tell a message surrounding the birth of Christ, so the nativity scene reminds us of that message. As in the infancy narratives, if the historical events are not accurate the historical fact is still there. The *message* of Christmas is far more important than the *events* of Christmas.

4. What do the Gospels tell us about the public life of Jesus?

a. The public life of Jesus began with his baptism at the Jordan by John the Baptist.

John the Baptist, a cousin of Jesus, lived in the desert and preached repentance along the shores of the Jordan River. He invited those who wished to commit themselves to God by a change of life to enter the waters of the Jordan and seal their commitment with baptism. The baptism of John consisted in a public commitment, much as we might witness at a revival when some come forward to commit themselves to God. Jesus entered the waters to commit himself to his mission of preaching and sharing the reign of God. At this point, when Jesus was about thirty years of age, he left the obscurity of his private life to begin his public life which would last two or three years.

The custom of being bathed in water as a sign of some spiritual change in a person's life was a practice used by many religions of Jesus' day, including Judaism. Although this custom offers some insight into the meaning of the Sacrament of Baptism used in Christianity today, we should not confuse the two. The baptism by John was not the same as our Sacrament of Baptism. The people who accepted the baptism of John recognized their own sinfulness and responded to John's call to change their way of life. Their going down into the water was an external sign of an internal change which had already taken place.

Some of the people of the early Church thought that John the Baptist was the awaited Messiah. The Gospels remind us that Jesus is greater than John as we read the words of the Baptist himself who tells us in the Gospel of Luke, "I am baptizing you in water, but there is one to come who is mightier than I. I am not fit to loosen his sandle strap. He will baptize you in the Holy Spirit and in fire" (Luke 3:16).

b. Jesus chose special followers.

When a great Rabbi appeared in Palestine, people sought to become his followers to learn from him. Jesus changed this tradition as he changed so many. Jesus chose his own followers. In the Gospel of Mark, we read that Jesus approached some fishermen and said, "Follow me. . . . I will make you into fishers of men" (Mark 1:17). Jesus gathered around himself fishermen, tax collectors, and known sinners as his followers. Of these, Jesus chose twelve to serve as special companions whom he would instruct throughout the years of his public life. These twelve, called apostles, would pass on the message of Jesus to the early Christian community.

Besides choosing his own followers, Jesus invited them to spend some time with him, learning about him and his message. In the Gospel of John, two disciples of the Baptist decide to become followers of Jesus, and they ask him where he is staying. He tells them, "Come and see" (John 1:39). Instead of a short instruction, the disciples must travel with Jesus, listen to him, and "see" as witnesses to his mission and message. Unlike other rabbis of the day who merely teach their disciples, Jesus calls his followers to learn his life and message and to share it with others. This understanding of discipleship is important since we today, as followers of Jesus, are called to the same mission. During this time of study and reflection, we are called "to come and see" so that we might share with others the true message of Christ.

c. Jesus performed miracles.

In the Gospels, we read of miraculous powers of Jesus extending from calming the seas to healing a paralytic. Nature miracles, such as calming the storms, were certainly acts of God, and only God could control the elements at will. Some writers proposed that these nature miracles were postresurrection stories intended to teach that Jesus is God. Perhaps we will never definitely know the extent of Jesus' miraculous powers, but we do know that Jesus had a clear reputation as a miracle worker. Miracles are central to the Gospels, and miracles are also part of the message. They point to something more than themselves. When the followers of John asked Jesus if he were the one whom they were awaiting, Jesus responded on the authority of his message and miracles. "Go back and tell John what you hear and see; the blind see again, and the lame walk, lepers are cleansed, and the deaf hear, and the dead are raised to life and the Good News is proclaimed to the poor" (Matthew 11:4–5). Matthew chooses these words of Jesus to answer, "Yes," he is the one who is to come. In reading the miracles of Jesus, we should strive to understand the truth they point to in the message of the Gospels.

Many writers see the miracles of Jesus as a living sign of the presence of God and a sign pointing to the presence of the reign of God on earth. Jesus came preaching that the reign of God is here among us, and the miracles are signs of this presence. Not only do we see the healing and caring gifts of God in the miracles, but we also see the dawn of a new era ushered into God's creation with the coming of Jesus.

d. Jesus proclaimed a new message for the people.

The central message taught by Jesus concerned the reign of God which entered the world in a dramatic way with the coming of Jesus. This reign of God, preached by Jesus, is not a reign or kingdom which has a specific boundary in this world, but an invisible reign whereby God is properly recognized as the One reigning over all. But, Jesus' message had some surprising elements. The reign of God is now present with Jesus and the world in a new way. As people united with Jesus, we can call out to God in an intimate manner, using the title "Abba" which comes from the Hebrew and means "Daddy" or some intimate equivalent. The call of the reign of God is a call of love—love for God, our neighbor and ourselves. The reign of God, although existing in the world in a special way now, is yet to reach its fulfillment in our eternal call to glory and happiness in Christ. The reign of God becomes visible not just in our individual response to God, but primarily in our community response to God in Christ. Because the message of the reign of God is so important, we are called not only to hear, but also to spread the message.

In preaching his message, Jesus used an approach not easily accepted by the people of his own day. Rabbis based their conclusions upon rabbis of the past. Jesus drew his conclusions on his authority, and this disturbed the chief priests and elders of the Israelite nation. "As he was walking in the temple precincts, the chief priests and the scribes and the elders approached him and said to him, 'On what authority are you doing these things? Who has given you the power to do them?' " (Mark 11:27–29). His message condemned the hypocrisy of the leaders of the people, called sinners to repentance, and promised eternal happiness to those who suffer and die for justice's sake. Jesus came with the intention of fulfilling the law, not doing away with the law.

After a public life lasting about two or three years, Jesus entered the period of his passion. Within the context of this narrative, we find a description of Jesus celebrating the Last Supper with his disciples. The authors of the synoptic Gospels place this supper within the framework of the passover meal, although some commentators on the Scriptures wonder whether or not the meal actually took place at the time of passover. By placing it in the framework of the passover meal, the writers are telling us that Jesus is the new Lamb of God and the event is the New Covenant between God and all people.

e. Jesus suffered and died on the cross.

After the meal, Jesus went to the ordinary place of rest used whenever he and the disciples came to Jerusalem. Judas led the temple guards to the spot and betrayed Jesus with some sign of affection. The pain of the passion not only includes the physical pain Jesus endured, but the pain of being betrayed by one he loved and trusted.

Jesus was brought to trial before the Sanhedrin, and they accepted the testimony of false witnesses in condemning Jesus to death. Because they did not have the authority to put Jesus to death, he was brought before Pilate, the Roman procurator, and they demanded that Jesus be crucified. Although Pilate showed little reluctance in the past when it came to condemning someone to death, the Gospels present him as a sympathetic ruler, trying to free Jesus. The leaders of the people accused Jesus of plotting against Rome, and Pilate, afraid that the people would riot, condemned Jesus to death by crucifixion. Before Jesus was led out to his death, he was flogged according to custom and some of the soldiers mocked him by putting a crown of thorns on his head.

When they came to the place of crucifixion outside the city of Jerusalem, the Gospels tell us simply that "they crucified him." The common place for crucifixion was near a main road where people passing by would witness the punishment, and, where necessary, would hesitate to commit any crimes against the laws of the land. After the death of Jesus, a centurion pierced his side and blood and water flowed forth.

f. Jesus was raised from the dead.

The Gospels tell the story of some women coming to the tomb on the morning of the third day and finding it empty. Through the resurrection stories of the Gospels, we learn that Jesus has been raised from the dead, and that he has appeared to many. The fear and confusion of the followers of Jesus turned to amazement as the word spread, "He is raised." With the resurrection of Jesus, the real beginnings of Christianity began to take root. Because Jesus was truly raised, the Church could now preach of Jesus, the living messiah. Now they could say with the apostle Paul, "JESUS CHRIST IS LORD" (Philippians 2:11).

5. Was Jesus human like us?

a. The son of God is one with the Father, and existed with the Father from all eternity.

Although God is neither male nor female, the people of the ancient Jewish culture ordinarily used the male image in referring to God. For this reason, many of our words used for God in the Scriptures present God as our Father, and Jesus as the eternal Son of God. This Son of God is one with the Father, i.e., equal to the Father. The Son became human in the person of Jesus, the son of Mary.

John's Gospel refers to the Son as the "Word" of God, and he tells us that the Word existed with God the creator from all eternity. John writes, "In the beginning was the Word; the Word was in God's presence, and the Word was God. He was present to God in the beginning. Through Him all things came into being, and apart from Him nothing came to be" (John 1:1–3). Later, in the same Gospel, Jesus gives himself the same eternal title given by God to Moses from the burning bush. Jesus said to the Jewish leaders, "I solemnly declare it: before Abraham came to be, I AM" (John 8:58). Christians believe that "The Word became flesh and made his dwelling among us" (John 1:14). Our faith tells us that the Word is eternal, one and equal with the Father.

b. An ancient hymn proclaims that Jesus was human like us.

In a letter to the Christians at Philippi, Paul includes a hymn that predates the letter and apparently was used shortly after Christ's resurrection. This hymn spoke of Jesus during his life as emptying himself and becoming like us. He became fully human.

"Though he was in the form of God,
*   he did not deem equality with God*
*   something to be grasped at.*
Rather, he emptied himself
*   and took the form of a slave,*
*   being born in the likeness of men.*

He was known to be of human estate,
and it was thus that he humbled himself,
obediently accepting even death,
death on a cross!" (Phillipians 2:6–8)

How Jesus emptied himself is hard to understand. Somehow, he became like us in all ways, with the exception of sin. We must admit that we are facing a mystery when we declare that Jesus became fully human and that he emptied himself of the powers and gifts of his Godhood while still being God. This hymn does not tell us how it happened, but simply tells us that it did happen. The passage would imply that Jesus had to go to school to learn as we do; that he grew tired, hungry, and weak as we do; that he had to live with the insecurity of searching for the correct words to share a message as perfectly as possible or the insecurity of wondering what tomorrow would bring, as we do, and that he lived by faith and feared suffering and death, as we do. In simplest terms, Jesus was human like us, yet still God.

c. Some parts of the Gospels show the humanness of Jesus.

In a Gospel story taken from Luke, we read of Jesus around the age of twelve. Although he was God, Jesus still had to grow in wisdom. Jesus had been lost for three days when Mary and Joseph found him and took him home. Luke tells us, "And Jesus increased in wisdom, in stature, and in favor with God and men" (Luke 2:52). The Gospels tell about Jesus sleeping, eating, weeping and experiencing fear—all human qualities. At one point, Jesus professed a lack of knowledge about the end of the world: "But as for that day or hour, nobody knows it, neither the angels of heaven, nor the Son; no one but the Father" (Mark 13:32). In the past, we often spoke of Jesus as having the full and continual experience of God's presence. With this experience, suffering becomes impossible due to the extreme joy of this experience. As humans, we can experience this presence only in a partial way. We must wait for our resurrection to experience the fullness of this presence. The fact that Jesus feared and suffered implies that Jesus "emptied himself" of this full experience of God's presence. Otherwise Jesus would have been acting as he cried out in pain from the cross. This, of course, would contradict the complete openness and honesty of Jesus.

d. Knowledge of the human condition of Jesus helps us to understand why the followers of Jesus continually misunderstood him.

Jesus' own townspeople, who grew up with him and saw him in a very human light, wanted to put him to death because of his message. Despite his miracles and his debates with some of the Pharisees, the apostles still saw Jesus as a human person. They thought Jesus foolish to head for certain death in Jerusalem and they tried to persuade him to avoid the trip to that city. Through many of the reactions of the followers of Jesus in the Gospels, we see them as viewing Jesus in a fully human way.

e. In becoming human, Jesus showed his great love for all people.

That the Son of God would take upon himself a human nature and join us in the struggles of life could never have been imagined by anyone except God. The act of love shown through this entry into our human existence tells us more about the loving God. The fact that Jesus "emptied himself," and became like us in all ways but sin shows the degree of his love. If he had kept the powers of his Godhood, we would still marvel at his love. The fact that he emptied himself of these powers makes his sign of love more astounding.

Another message we receive from the "new Adam" (as Jesus is called in the writings of Paul) reminds us of the wonders of our human calling. Although sin has a deep effect upon our human condition, we remember that God created human beings and saw that the act was good. God's creation is a good creation. In the story of the first sin, we read that Adam and Eve sinned because they wanted to be like God. In the story, the serpent tells Eve that she will be like God if she grasps the forbidden fruit and eats it. The Son of God, on the other hand, who is totally one with God, "does not deem equality with God something to be grasped at . . ." (Phillipians 2:6). Instead, he empties himself and becomes one with our human condition. In this way, the new Adam overwhelms us with a great act of love and, at the same time, lifts our humanness to a new dignity.

6. Did Jesus come to die?

a. Jesus came to give life.

Past theologies drew an image of God the Father as experiencing a deep hurt at the sin of Adam and Eve. In order to appease this God, the people of the Old Testament offered animal sacrifices, fasts, and long hours of worship. But these were never enough. Finally, this God's innocent Son became man, suffered, and died. Now God the Father was appeased and God showed His pleasure by raising His Son from the dead and bringing redemption to all people. This was an unfortunate image of God not drawn in the Scriptures but pieced together by a misunderstanding of certain Scripture texts. We can say that Jesus did not come to die to appease a hurt God the Father, but rather that Jesus came to give life.

In the Gospel of John, we read that Jesus is the Good Shepherd who is willing to lay down his life for his sheep. A shepherd protects the sheep and shares his life with them. Jesus himself says, "I came that they might have life and have it to the full" (John 10:10). In protecting the sheep, Jesus, the Good Shepherd, would remain faithful to protecting them to the end, even with his life.

b. Jesus came to give life by confronting the power of evil and sin in the world.

Jesus came into a world controlled by evil and sin. Throughout the Old Testament, people tried to overcome evil but often found themselves caught up in its power. Even if someone was able to live a good life, the final weapon of evil, namely death, would have its day. Jesus came to confront evil head-on. Evil attempted to have Jesus join with it. The temptations in the desert portray in story form the weapons evil used. If Jesus would kneel to evil and worship its existence, Jesus would control the whole world. Jesus rejected in his life this temptation to join with evil. Evil then tried to embarrass Jesus or frustrate him in striving to share his message. Still Jesus did not give in to evil. Finally, evil moved the hearts of the people to bring Jesus to suffering and ultimately to death. When Jesus was raised from the dead by God the Father, evil had no weapons left and for the first time in history had to admit defeat. Jesus did not come to die, but to give life. The fact that he confronted evil head-on inevitably led to his death.

c. By confronting death in obedience to God the Father, Jesus' actions brought redemption to the world.

Jesus' mission of bringing redemption to the world came not simply because he confronted evil, but because he committed himself, in his human condition, to confronting evil on behalf of God. He showed a great love of God the Father by obediently living out his commitment in confronting evil, even when he saw that this confrontation would lead to a horrible death. Jesus did not seek suffering, but suffering came to Jesus. In the same way, Jesus did not seek death on the cross, but his obedience led him to accept this death in carrying out his mission. St. Paul writes in the letter to the Philippians, ". . . he was humbler yet, even to accepting death, death on a cross!" (Philippians 2:8). Through this obedience to God the Father, Jesus was raised up and brought redemption to the world.

In the garden on the Mount of Olives, Jesus prays to the Father to take the cup of suffering away from him, but, if it be the Father's will, Jesus willingly accepts the cup. Jesus prays, "Father, if it is your will, take this cup from me; yet not my will but yours be done" (Luke 22:42). The mission of Jesus asks that he be obedient to his commitment to the end, even if that commitment demands suffering and death. When Jesus began his passion, the power of evil had reached its peak. Jesus tells those who come out to take him, "When I was with you day after day in the temple you never raised a hand against me. But this is your hour— the triumph of darkness" (Luke 22:53). In the death of Jesus, evil would triumph, but, in his resurrection, evil would be overcome.

d. To understand our part as Christians in the world, we must imitate the love and commitment of Jesus.

Like Jesus, we too are called to confront evil head-on. We have the special gifts of Jesus' resurrection to help in this mission. Because suffering shows the grip of evil in the world, we should strive to alleviate suffering wherever possible. If Jesus came to die and if suffering alone had a redemptive power, then we should seek to keep suffering in the world. If love and commitment are the acts that make suffering redemptive, then we should strive for love and commitment in all we do rather than strive for suffering. Love leads us to overcome the grip of suffering and evil in the world.

When Mark wrote his gospel, Christians were facing persecution in Rome, and they wondered why they were called to suffer. If Jesus had overcome the power of evil and suffering in the world, why did suffering still exist? Mark wrote his Gospel to tell the disciples of Jesus that they must not expect anything to be easier for the follower than it was for the master. In Mark's Gospel, Jesus tells us, "If a man wishes to come after me, he must deny his very self, take up his cross, and follow in my steps. Whoever will preserve his life will lose it, but whoever loses his life for my sake and the Gospel's will preserve it" (Mark 8:34–35). Although we should not seek suffering, we must realize that the message of the life of Jesus will often demand sacrifice and suffering on our part. Like Jesus, we, the disciples, must be willing to travel the same road.

7. What were the effects of the resurrection?

a. Through his resurrection, Jesus Christ could properly be called "Lord."

The word "Lord" was used in many different ways in the Scriptures. Here, however, we use the term as referring to the divine nature of God. At the resurrection of Jesus, his human nature entered fully into union with his divine nature. He now received into his human nature the fullness of his Godhood with all its powers. Now the name of Jesus became sacred and the power and knowledge of Jesus was fully that of the Son of God. Again we tread on mystery. In the same early hymn we quoted under the humanness of Jesus, we find the reward of Jesus' human obedience:

For this reason God raised him to the highest place above and gave him the name that is greater than any other name. And so in honor of the name of Jesus all beings in heaven, on earth, and in the world below will fall on their knees, and all will openly proclaim that Jesus Christ is Lord, to the glory of God the Father (Philippians 2:9–11).

Because of the exaltation of Jesus, we can now say for the first time "Jesus Christ Is Lord!" How it happened, we do not know. That it did happen in the resurrection, we learn from the Scriptures.

b. Through the resurrection, Jesus could properly be called the Christ, or the Messiah.

The Jewish tradition expected a kingly ruler to rise up and bring the Jewish nation to victory over its enemies. By the time Jesus came upon earth, this tradition was not as strong as it had been in the past. Throughout the Gospels, we often find Jesus rejecting the title given to this ruler, namely, the Messiah. Jesus thought as the rest of the people of his own age, and he knew he would not lead an uprising against the

Roman authorities. Only after the resurrection did the early Christians see the title of Messiah as referring to a saviour in the spiritual sense rather than the earthly ruler mistakenly sought after by the Israelites. Once the idea of Messiah was properly understood as referring to this spiritual saviour, the title could be applied to Jesus. Although Jesus, at times, denied that he was the Messiah, (especially in the Gospel of Mark), at other times he accepted the title where it was fully understood. When Jesus asks his disciples who people said he was, Peter answers, "You are the Messiah . . . the Son of the living God" (Matthew 16:16). Immediately after Peter's profession of faith found in Matthew's Gospel, the author of the Gospel offers us the true meaning of Messiah through the words of Jesus who states that he must suffer, die, and then rise. When Peter tries to deny that Jesus, the Messiah, must pass through his death to his resurrection, Jesus answers him sharply, saying, "Get out of my sight, you satan" (Matthew 16:23). Despite his profession of faith, Peter would not understand the meaning of the title "Messiah" until after the resurrection of Jesus. Through his death and resurrection, Jesus properly became the Messiah or the Christ. The word, Christ, is the Greek equivalent of the term, Messiah.

c. Through his resurrection, Jesus could properly be seen as one with God the Father, that is as God.

After the resurrection, the early Christians recognized Jesus as the "Lord." In calling him "Lord," they were professing a faith in his Godhood, using the same term for Jesus that was used for God the Father in other Scripture writings. By the time the Gospel of John was written (c 90–100 A.D.), the early Church clearly accepted Jesus as one with God the Father. When Philip approached Jesus and asked to see the Father, Jesus replied, "Have I been with you all this time, Philip, and you still do not know me? To have seen me is to have seen the Father, so how can you say, 'Let us see the Father'?" (John 14:9–10). Jesus declares flatly in another section of the Gospel of John, "The Father and I are one" (John 10:30). The Gospel of John shows a belief in Christ that has developed to a point of fully accepting his Godhood.

d. Through the resurrection, a new hope and new life were brought to all of God's people.

If Jesus had not been raised from the dead by God the Father, we would still be in our sins. Death was the last weapon of evil, and by the resurrection of Jesus, death and evil were overcome. A new life came into the world through the resurrection. As Jesus' humanness was raised up on the day of his resurrection, so our humanness was lifted up. We are now capable of entering into a special union with Christ. Our belief that sin has been overcome likewise flows from Jesus' resurrection. "If Christ has not been raised," writes St. Paul, "You are still in your sin" (1Corinthians 15:17).

8. What is the meaning of the ascension of Jesus?

a. The death, resurrection and ascension of Jesus are all the same one act of redemption.

In our world, we live in time. Eternity is timeless, with no past and no future. We are faced with a mystery outside our experience and we have no way to explain timelessness. In speaking of the Ascension of Jesus, the Scriptures follow a time sequence. In reality, at the moment of Jesus' death, he was raised and exalted at the right hand of the Father. Christ ascended at the same time he died and was raised. In St. Paul's letter to the Philippians, Paul actually skips the resurrection of Jesus and reports that the exaltation, or ascension, took place immediately upon the death of Jesus. Paul writes,

He was humble and walked the path of obedience all the way to death—his death on the cross. For this reason God raised him to the highest place above and gave him the name that is greater than any other name (Philippians 2:8-9).

In the resurrection of Jesus, we see his glory. This glory belongs to his heavenly glory which actually comes through his place at the right hand of the Father. This presupposes that an ascension had already taken place.

b. Forty days after the resurrection of Jesus, the Scriptures portray a visible ascension of Jesus into heaven.

We read in the Acts of the Apostles, "After saying this, he was taken up to heaven as they watched him, and a cloud hid him from their sight. They still had their eyes fixed on the sky as he went away, when two men dressed in white suddenly stood beside them and said, 'Galileans, why are you standing there looking up at the sky? This Jesus who was taken from you into heaven, will come back in the same way that you saw him go to heaven'" (Acts 1:9–11). In this reading, the Gospel speaks of the ancient view of the world. Jesus ascends to heaven upon a cloud and will pass through the dome into the heavenly realm. In this picturesque narrative, The Acts of the Apostles is telling us that the apostles had the mission of continuing the mission of Jesus. In the early preaching, a definite point in time was chosen to portray the end of Jesus' sojourn on earth and the beginning of the new era of the early Church.

9. Was Jesus really raised from the dead?

a. The effect of this belief in the resurrection of Jesus was too dramatic to deny that he was raised from the dead.

The early followers of Jesus changed so drastically from fear to courage and from doubt to belief that it would be impossible to presume that Jesus' resurrection was a hoax. We must remember, however, that when we speak of the resurrection of Jesus, we are speaking of a new form of life. Unlike Lazarus, who was raised from the dead and who would die again, Jesus would no longer face death. He now lived in his new, eternal, and glorious life. In one of the resurrection stories, two men are walking along a road to a town called Emmaus. Jesus joins them in this walk, but they do not recognize him. In speaking of resurrection in general, St. Paul writes, "It is the same with the resurrection of the dead: the thing that is sown is perishable, but what is raised is imperishable; the thing that is sown is contemptible, but what is raised is glorious; the thing that is sown is weak, but what is raised is powerful; when it is sown it embodies the soul, when it is raised it embodies the spirit" (1 Corinthians 15:42–44). Because Christ was sharing in his resurrected, glorious body, the friends of Jesus on the road to Emmaus did not recognize him. However, they recognized him as he broke bread with them and disappeared from their midst. When they ran to tell the other apostles, they were greeted with "The Lord has risen and has appeared to Simon" (Luke 24:34).

b. We do not know exactly what took place since each Gospel tells a slightly different story.

Although each of the Gospels speaks of the empty tomb, no one actually saw Jesus raised from the dead. They only report the evidence after the resurrection. Even this evidence varies from Gospel to Gospel. In Matthew's Gospel, Mary Magdalene and the other Mary are at the tomb as the stone is rolled back by an angel in dazzling garments. Jesus is not in the tomb when the stone is rolled back. In Mark, Mary Magdalene, Mary the mother of James and Salome come to the tomb to find the stone already rolled back and find a young man inside dressed in a white robe. Jesus is not there. In Luke, Mary Magdalene, Joanna and Mary the mother of James come to the tomb and find the stone rolled back and the tomb empty. Suddenly, two men in dazzling garments are beside them. In John's Gospel, Mary Magdalene comes to the tomb and finds the stone rolled back. Instead of entering, she runs to tell Peter and John that the body has been taken from the tomb, apparently stolen. John and Peter rush to the tomb and find it empty. In John's Gospel, there are no angels, no young man or young men present. Some today claim that this resurrection story of the empty tomb was the early Christian faith simply saying that Jesus was raised. Some feel that the body of Jesus was placed in an unmarked potter's grave, but this is simply a conclusion drawn from the differences in the stories of the resurrection. All we can say is that Jesus actually was raised from the dead but we do not know how this happened.

c. The Christian Church centers its belief on the resurrection of Jesus.

What type of experience of the resurrection the apostles had cannot be definitely stated, due mainly to the different literary forms used in the Gospels. The writers could simply be trying to tell us that the apostles knew with certainty that Jesus was raised and they expressed this belief by showing that Jesus was alive and living with them through the resurrection narratives. From the reading of the Scriptures, we know that the apostles had more than an inner experience of Christ's resurrection. They had a real experience of a special presence of Christ among them. Whether we accept the stories as written or whether there was another experience of Christ that led the apostles to preach the message in this way is not the center of our faith. Our faith centers on the fact that Jesus Christ was raised, that he is Lord and that he lives in his resurrection. The resurrection narratives, under the inspiration of God, share this message and today we celebrate the fact that "Jesus is alive; He has been raised."

10. What is the second coming of Jesus?

a. In the Scriptures, we read of a presence of Christ in creation that is yet to happen.

We know very little about the second coming of Jesus. Christ told us to be on our guard for the end of the world, but he claimed that only the Father knew when this would come. Many of the writings of St. Paul tell us that the early Christians expected this coming shortly after the ascension of Jesus. After some time, when the second coming did not take place, the tone of the letters of Paul changed and he no longer spoke of the second coming as being near. St. Luke expressed the imagery that told of the second coming of Jesus when he writes, "And then, they will see the Son of Man coming in a cloud with power and great glory. When these things begin to take place, stand erect, hold your heads high, because your liberation is near at hand" (Luke 21:27–29). We still await the second coming of Jesus Christ, whatever that second coming may entail.

b. The second coming of Jesus should fill us with hope rather than fear.

A majority of people tend to fear the second coming. They read in the Scriptures that great earthquakes and catastrophies will occur upon the earth just before the end. But even here, the Scriptures do not clearly state exactly what we are to look for. The earth has had earthquakes, war, and catastrophies almost every decade since the beginning of recorded history. We simply must be ready for the great day of the coming of the Lord, when we "stand erect, hold . . . heads high" (Luke 21:28). On that day, the Son of God will invite the just into the everlasting joy of Heaven, and this is a cause for rejoicing.

Conclusion

As the fisherman in the introduction to this chapter grew to a wise old age, he often told his grandchildren about the stranger who saved his life. The story had grown over the years, but the kindness of the stranger was always there. The more the fisherman thought of the stranger, the more he realized his goodness. This realization found its way into his story. When he told the children about this adventure, he embellished by adding that the stranger had a great appointment he missed because of this encounter. The parents of the children who heard the story and actually knew what had happened just shook their heads and smiled that the fisherman could add these details with such enthusiasm. But the parents had to admit that perhaps the fisherman had captured the real personality of the stranger. After all, he was a definite part of the experience and he had to have the deeper insight.

For scripture reflection and discussion concerning this chapter, see Journeying in His Light, *"Jesus Is Lord: Parts 1 and 2."*

The Holy Spirit in Our Lives

Introduction

The newspaper told of a skydiver whose parachute did not open and who fell two thousand feet to the ground. Miraculously, the man did not die, although he broke almost every bone in his body. After twelve months in the hospital, he was able to limp back into the world. The doctors predicted that he would always have that limp. The man began to walk everyday and finally to jog. Gradually, the limp disappeared and the man was able to run in a marathon race in a major city. He did not win the marathon, but he celebrated the fact that he could jog respectfully along with hundreds of others in that marathon.

In the last chapter, we looked at Jesus' resurrection and ascension. We are specially chosen to share the message of Christ through our lives, but in many ways we are a broken, weak people. We need strength to carry out this task, and God gives this strength through the presence of the Holy Spirit in our lives. We take faltering steps in the faith, but with the help of the Holy Spirit, we can begin to move more firmly, trusting in his guidance and continual presence.

1. Where do we hear of the Holy Spirit?

a. The Gospels speak of the Holy Spirit as possessing or being in Jesus.

The Holy Spirit is mentioned often in relationship to Jesus during his earthly life. In the Gospel of Luke, the author uses a dramatic story to show the Holy Spirit entering Jesus' life. "Now when all the people had been baptized and while Jesus after his own baptism was at prayer, heaven opened and the Holy Spirit descended on him in bodily shape

59

like a dove. And a voice came from heaven, "You are My Son, the beloved; my favor rests on you" (Luke 3:21–22). In the following chapter, the author of Luke has the Spirit guiding Jesus and being with Jesus. "Filled with the Holy Spirit, Jesus left the Jordan and was led by the Spirit through the wilderness, being tempted there by the devil for forty days" (Luke 4:1–2). The Gospels proclaim the presence of the Holy Spirit in Jesus from the lips of Jesus himself: "And they handed him the scroll of the prophet Isaiah. Unrolling the scroll he found the place where it is written: 'The Spirit of the Lord has been given to me . . . this text is being fulfilled today even as you listen" (Luke 4:17–18, 21). As we read these and other similar declarations throughout the Gospels, we conclude that the Holy Spirit worked in, with, and through Jesus throughout his life. The Holy Spirit filled him, guided him, inspired him, and worked through him.

b. The New Testament proclaims that Jesus would send the Holy Spirit upon the world.

In the Gospel of John, we read that the work of the Holy Spirit will take place in the followers of Jesus after his resurrection. Jesus tells his apostles, "it is for your own good that I am going, because unless I go, the Advocate will not come to you; but if I do go, I will send him to you" (John 16:7). Only through his death and resurrection will the early followers of Jesus receive this Holy Spirit. He must go before he can send the Spirit. On a special festival day, Jesus talks about the living waters that would flow forth from him. John makes a commentary here when he writes, "He was speaking of the Spirit, which those who believed in him were to receive; for there was no Spirit as yet because Jesus had not yet been glorified" (John 7:39). Through the glorification of Jesus will the waters of the Spirit flow forth. As we read through the writings of John, we realize that the later community understood the Spirit as being in Jesus while he lived on this earth, and as being sent by Jesus into the world after his glorification.

c. Jesus speaks of the Holy Spirit as an independent person.

In the Gospels, Jesus speaks of the Holy Spirit as a person separate from himself: "I shall ask the Father and he will give you another Advocate, to be with you forever: that Spirit of truth whom the world can never receive, since it neither sees nor knows him; but you know him because he is with you, and he is in you" (John 14:16–17). In another section of the same discourse, Jesus speaks of the Paraclete as a separate person, ". . . Advocate, the Holy Spirit, whom the Father will send in

my name, will teach you everything and remind you of all I have said to you" (John 14:26). Although the Holy Spirit guided Jesus while on earth, he is still independent of Jesus, a separate person.

d. The Old Testament speaks of the Spirit of God as an action of God rather than as a separate person.

In the story of creation, the Spirit of God sweeps across the waters and brings order into creation. This action of God refers more to a wind or a breath that moves across the waters. When Isaiah the prophet first used the expression of the Spirit's presence, he was probably speaking of the guidance of God rather than the action of another person: "The Spirit of the Lord Yahweh has been given to me, for Yahweh has anointed me: He has sent me to bring good news to the poor, to bind up hearts that are broken" (Isaiah 61:1). This action of God fully possesses a person and enables the person to live out the Word of God. In this case as in other cases in the Old Testament, God's Spirit affects people for a short time, to preach the Word or to perform some action. At certain prophetic moments in their lives, the prophets feel the Spirit of the Lord upon them. In these and other uses of the Spirit in the Old Testament, we can hardly refer to the Holy Spirit as we understand the Spirit through the New Testament. But the Old Testament can easily pave the way for a deeper New Testament understanding of the action of the Spirit. As we look back today from our understanding of the Holy Spirit as a person separate from the Father, we can see a far more significant message than even the prophets saw.

2. Is the Holy Spirit God?

a. The Gospel of John tells of the Holy Spirit as coming from both the Father and the Son.

The Holy Spirit is described as coming directly from the Father and being sent by the Son. Implied here is an equality of mission in sharing the truth: "When the Advocate comes, whom I shall send to you from the Father, the Spirit of truth who issues from the Father . . . will be my witness" (John 15:26). When Jesus speaks of the Holy Spirit, he says that the Spirit will not speak on his own, but only what he receives from the Son, who in turn will always be reflecting the Father. This shows the independence of each person, yet the unity of the three persons.

b. In giving the apostles the power and mission to baptize, Jesus also proclaims the oneness of the Father, the Son, and the Holy Spirit.

In the Gospel of Matthew, Jesus speaks of the three separate persons, the Father, the Son and the Holy Spirit, yet he places these three under a single "name." "All authority in heaven and on earth has been given to me; Go, therefore, make disciples of all the nations; baptize them in the name of the Father and of the Son and of the Holy Spirit" (Matthew 28:18–19). Just as Jesus proclaimed that he and the Father were one, he here proclaims that the Father, Son, and Holy Spirit are one. We are again treading on the mystery of trying to understand God.

c. In the early centuries, the Church struggled with this mystery of three persons in one God calling this mystery the Blessed Trinity.

The Scriptures clearly speak of only one God, yet they also speak of the Father as God, the Son as God, and the Holy Spirit as God. All are equal, all are one yet all are independent of each other. If God had not revealed this mystery to us through the Scriptures, we would never have known it. We are at a loss fully to understand this mystery because we have nothing in our experience to compare with this idea of three persons having only one nature. Each of us is an individual person having an individual human nature. God is three persons having a common divine nature. A common picture of the Trinity (which means "three-in-one") is the three-leaf clover. But three leaves on one stem still do not portray the Trinity. Each leaf does not act independently, nor can we look upon God as having one stem. A legend is told of St. Augustine in the fifth century walking along a beach trying to understand the Trinity. He met a little boy on the beach who had dug a hole in the sand and was running back and forth from the water to the hole with a pail, continuously putting water into the hole. Augustine asked the boy what he was doing, and the boy told Augustine that he was going to put the ocean into this hole. Augustine laughed and told the boy that this was impossible. The boy answered, "It is more possible for me to put all the water from the ocean into this hole than it is for you to understand the Trinity." Although this story most likely never happened, the message it teaches is a good one. We can never understand how there can be three persons in the one God, since this is one of the mysteries of God. We simply accept this revelation on Faith.

3. Why did God reveal the Trinity?

a We could never say with full certainty why God revealed the Trinity.

The ways of God will always remain a mystery, and perhaps we can never really know why God does anything. We can guess, but only God truly knows God's own inner thinking. In the case of the Trinity, God did not have to tell us about the three persons in one God. God could have left us with the revelation that the one true God became man and the one true God is sharing personal guidance with us in life. But God revealed that each of these works was the work of an individual person who is also the one true God. God revealed this mystery, and instead of asking "why" we should ask ourselves what the revelation teaches us.

b. The three persons in one God tells us of the value of unity.

In the Book of Genesis, we read under the sixth day of creation, "Let us make man in our own image, in the likeness of ourselves" (Genesis 1:26). Besides the ability to think, judge, will, and act as sharing in the image of God, we should see as our goal another image in God through revelation, namely the unity of three distinct persons. Our aim as God's human family and as an image of God is not to destroy our individuality, but rather to make our own personhood work toward unity. By remaining different, yet working with a unity of concern and love, we are more truly reflecting the image of God.

4. Do the Scriptures reveal when the disciples received the Holy Spirit?

a. The Scriptures reveal that Christ gave the Holy Spirit to his disciples shortly after his resurrection.

In the Gospel of John, the apostles gathered together in fear in the upper room, apparently the room of the Last Supper. Jesus suddenly stood in their midst and said, "As the Father sent me, so am I sending you. After saying this he breathed on them and said: 'Receive the Holy Spirit. For those whose sins you forgive they are forgiven; for those whose sins you retain, they are retained' " (John 20:21–23). In the Gospel of John, Jesus promised to send the Holy Spirit upon the disciples after his resurrection, and he fulfilled this promise as one of his first acts after the resurrection.

b. In the Acts of the Apostles, we read that the Holy Spirit came upon the apostles on Pentecost.

On the feast of Pentecost, the apostles were gathered together in one place. The Acts describe a strong, driving wind and "tongues as of fire" that rested upon each of them. The Acts go on to say simply, "All were filled with the Holy Spirit" (Acts 2:4). Courage comes with this gift of the Spirit, and Peter goes out to preach to crowds of people from many distant lands, who heard his words in their own languages. Again, the Scriptures present us with a problem. When did the apostles first receive the Holy Spirit, immediately after the resurrection of Jesus or on Pentecost Sunday? We must look to the message and realize that although we too have received the Holy Spirit, the awareness and guidance of the Holy Spirit is not always strongly felt in our lives. At times, however, we can fully experience the guidance of the Holy Spirit that fires us up to share Christ's message in some special way. Exactly what happened on Pentecost must remain a mystery, but the fact that the Holy Spirit shares special gifts with us is the revealed message.

5. What is the mission of the Holy Spirit?

a. The Holy Spirit enables us to understand the message of Jesus.

In the Gospel of John, we read the words of Jesus, "This much have I told you while I was still with you; the Paraclete, the Holy Spirit, whom the Father will send in my name, will instruct you in everything, and remind you of all I have said to you (John 14:25–26). Just as the Holy Spirit instructed the early disciples, so the work of the Holy Spirit guides us that we too may be better able to understand the message and life of Jesus. The Holy Spirit comes as the Spirit of Truth; "But when the Spirit of Truth comes, he will lead you to the complete truth" (John 16:13). The continuing mission of the Holy Spirit is to guide the followers of Jesus in understanding the truth about Jesus.

b. The Holy Spirit guides us in witnessing to Christ.

We again read in the Gospel of John, "When the Advocate comes, whom I shall send to you from the Father, the Spirit of Truth who issues from the Father . . . will be my witness. And you too will be witnesses because you have been with me from the outset" (John 15:26–27). The Gospel tells us that just as the Holy Spirit will bear witness on behalf of

Jesus, so the disciples, filled with the Holy Spirit, must also, in their turn, bear witness to Jesus. We too, under the guidance of the Holy Spirit, receive our call to witness to Jesus by our words and the way we live.

In the Acts of the Apostles, Jesus reminds them that this witness must reach to the very ends of the earth: "You will receive power when the Holy Spirit comes on you; and then you will be my witnesses not only in Jerusalem, but throughout Judea and Samaria, and indeed to the ends of the earth" (Acts 1:8). The ministry of the Holy Spirit is to witness to Jesus to the whole world.

c. The Holy Spirit shares different gifts for the sake of the ministry.

The Holy Spirit provides different gifts for the sharing of Jesus' message throughout the world. Although there are many gifts shared, they all come from the one and the same Holy Spirit. The Holy Spirit decides on the distribution of these gifts, and freely distributes them as the Spirit wills. St. Paul writes:

There are different kinds of spiritual gifts, but the same Spirit gives them. There are different ways of serving, but the same Lord is served. There are different abilities to perform service, but the same God gives ability to everyone for their particular service. The Spirit's presence is shown in some way in each person for the good of all. The Spirit gives one person a message full of wisdom, while to another person the same Spirit gives a message full of knowledge. One and the same Spirit gives faith to one person, while to another person He gives the power to heal. The Spirit gives one person the power to work miracles; to another, the gift of speaking God's message; and to yet another, the ability to tell the difference between gifts that come from the Spirit and those that do not. To one person He gives the ability to speak in strange tongues, and to another He gives the ability to explain what is said. But it is one and the same Spirit who does all this; as He wishes, He gives a different gift to each person (1 Corinthians 12:4–11).

All of us share in some gifts of the Holy Spirit. In sharing in these gifts, we should never become proud of our accomplishments, but remember the words of Paul in this same letter, "The particular way in which the Spirit is given to each person is for a good purpose" (1 Corinthians 12:7). God shares the gifts of the Spirit that the Christian community might grow.

d. The Holy Spirit calls us to holiness.

We cannot achieve holiness on our own, since holiness comes from faith, and faith comes through a gift of the Holy Spirit. In his letter to the Corinthians, Paul tells us, ". . . no one can say: 'Jesus is Lord,' except in the Holy Spirit" (1 Corinthians 12:3). In his letter to the Galatians, Paul reminds them that those who follow the ways of the world experience every kind of evil, while those who follow the Spirit experience the fruit of the Spirit which leads to holiness. Paul writes, ". . . the fruit of the Spirit is love, joy, peace, patient endurance, kindness, generosity, faith, mildness, and chastity" (Galatians 5:22–23). He urges his readers, "Since we live by the Spirit, let us follow the Spirit's lead" (Galatians 5:25).

6. How does the Church honor the Holy Spirit and the Trinity?

a. The Church encourages all Christians to seek continually the guidance of the Holy Spirit.

Before any great work or decision in life, the Church encourages prayer to seek the guidance of the Holy Spirit. Even for the simple decisions of life, the Church encourages this devotion, realizing that nothing is too tedious for God. A prayer often used in invoking the Holy Spirit is the following:

Come, Holy Spirit,
fill the hearts of your faithful
and kindle in them the fire
of your divine love. Send forth
your Spirit and they shall
be created, and you shall
renew the face of the earth.

b. The Church honors the Blessed Trinity by the sign of the cross accompanied by the words of faith in the Trinity.

At the beginning of prayer, a Catholic will often make the sign of the cross. The ordinary way of making the sign of the cross is to touch the forehead, the chest, the left shoulder, then the right with the right hand, praying as we do so:

In the name of the Father,
and of the Son,
and of the Holy Spirit, Amen.

c. The Church also proclaims a prayer for glory to the three persons in one God.

The Church has a special prayer which praises God in God's glory and proclaims that the Godhood of the three persons is eternal. We pray:

Glory to the Father,
and to the Son,
and to the Holy Spirit.
As it was in the beginning,
is now, and will be,
forever. Amen.

Conclusion

As Christians, we believe in sharing in God's presence on earth. We live our days with the conviction that we are filled with the power of the Holy Spirit. Like the marathon runner at the beginning of this chapter, we do not run the race to outrun everyone else, but we celebrate the fact that God has chosen to give us the power to move along with the rest. We have our particular task within the human family, whether the task be rearing a family, studying at school, working in an office or a factory, or simply accepting the inactivity of sickness or aging. Whatever our call at this moment, we are racing along with the rest of the human family, doing our special tasks under the guidance of the Holy Spirit. And like that marathon runner, we must struggle to realize fully the great power and hope of the gifts within us.

For Scripture reflection and discussion concerning this chapter, see Journeying in His Light *"The Holy Spirit in our Life."*

Sin and Life

Introduction

The counselor listened to the story he had heard so many times before. The mother and father told him how their teenage son had gone on picnics with them in his early years, how he had gone to church each Sunday and even stopped into church for special visits, how he had brought his friends home and played in the yard and how he had hated to see his father smoke. Now he no longer wanted to join the family in outings; he never went to church; they never met his friends; he left home early and came back late; he skipped school, and not only did he smoke, but he also drank. The reason they had come to the counselor was an event that happened just a week ago. The boy had cursed at his mother when she asked where he had been and the father, when he had heard the boy swear at the mother, had slapped the boy so hard he had stumbled across the room and tripped over a chair. In a tirade of angry words and in tears, the boy had slammed out the door and had not returned till early the next morning. The parents were seeking help in relating to their son.

The counselor tried to explain to the parents how children often rebel as they grow. In some cases, the rebellion takes form in simple laziness, irritability, and a desire to get their own way, while others make a complete rejection of their younger years. The child had to break away from the nest, and for some this becomes more violent than for others. The counselor advised the parents never to break with the boy no matter what he did while at the same time they must continue to keep before the boy's eyes the fact that he must learn to live in a mature society which demands that he give as well as receive. Hopefully, the boy would return in some way to the lessons of his youth.

1. What is sin?

a. Sin is a weakening or breaking of a love relationship between a person and God.

Love is filled with relationships. We relate in one way to the person who works at the grocery store; we relate in another way to our friends; and we relate in an even different way to our families. These relationships are based upon some degree of love. We know that God loves us deeply, and so we can claim a deep love relationship between ourselves and God. The parents in the introduction love their teenage son, and they see him weakening or breaking that love relationship. Their son is moving away from them, and they feel his alienation. Because the relationship is growing weaker, they seek the help of a counselor before the relationship breaks completely. When we sin, we act in a fashion similar to that of the son in the introduction. We either forget about God's love for us and ignore it; or, at times, we might completely reject God's love just to have our own way in life. Whenever we ignore God's love for us or reject that love, we commit sin because we are weakening or breaking that love relationship between ourselves and God. As the parents in the introduction will never stop loving their son, so God will never stop loving us. We are the ones who choose to break that love relationship or to weaken it, and so we are the ones who commit sin.

In the Gospel of Luke, Jesus speaks of his helplessness as the people of Jersualem refuse to respond to his love. In face of this rejection, Jesus tells them, "O Jerusalem, Jerusalem, you slay the prophets and stone those who are sent to you! How often have I wanted to gather your children together as a mother bird collects her young under her wings, and you refused me" (Luke 13:34). Despite their rejection of him, Jesus will continue to reach out to the Judean leaders until his death.

b. This sin which consists in weakening or breaking a love relationship with God occurs when we hurt our neighbor.

The author of the first letter of John reminds us that we cannot love God unless we first love our neighbor: "Anyone who says, 'I love God,' and hates his brother, is a liar, since a man who does not love the brother that he can see cannot love God, whom he has never seen. So this is the commandment that he has given us, that anyone who loves God must also love his brother' " (1 John 4:20–21). When someone asked Jesus who his neighbor was, Jesus told the story of the Good Samaritan. "A man was beaten by robbers and thrown into a ditch. A priest and a Levite passed the man by, but a Samaritan stopped to help the man. He bound his wounds, took him to an inn for lodging and told the inn-keeper that he would pay whatever he owed on his return." Jesus then let the questioner answer his own question: "Which of these three, do you think proved himself a neighbor to the man who fell into the brigand's hands?" The answer came, "The one who took pity on him." Jesus said to him, "Go, and do the same yourself" (Luke 10:36–37). Our neighbor is all around us. As we relate to him or her, we relate to God. As we hurt our neighbor, we hurt God, and as we love our neighbor, we love God. Whenever we weaken or break a love relationship with our neighbor, even an unknown neighbor in need, we weaken or break a love relationship with God. In this way, we commit sin.

c. We sin by weakening or breaking a love relationship with God even when we hurt ourselves.

God has made us a most precious part of creation and has even commanded us to love ourselves: "You must love the Lord your God with all your heart, with all your soul, with all your strength and with all your mind, and your neighbor as yourself" (Luke 10:27). Love of self differs from selfishness which is often destructive of self. When we accept our dignity as special creations of God and strive to develop our gifts in a proper fashion, we show love of self. When we abuse the gifts God gives us or allow them to be destroyed by our own laziness or negligence, then we hurt ourselves and weaken our relationship with God who is deeply and lovingly concerned for us. The parents of the boy in the introduction agonize over their son as they see him drinking into the early hours of the morning. So it is with God. As the parents seek the good of their son, so God seeks our good.

To truly love oneself consists in living with appreciation of the gifts God has given us with the realization that God truly loves us.

We are closest to God when we love, and we are farthest from God when we lack love. In the first letter of John, we have a summary of the need for love in our lives if we wish to remain aware of God's presence within us. The author writes, "God is love, and he who abides in love abides in God, and God in him" (1 John 4:16). Since God is love, we cannot truly know God unless we love.

2. How do we explain sin in the world?

a. We do not know how sin began in the world.

In the story of Adam and Eve, we read that human beings are responsible for sin in the world. God granted them many gifts and only one small precept: "You may eat indeed of all the trees of the Garden.

71

Nevertheless of the tree of knowledge of good and evil you are not to eat, for on the day you eat of it, you shall most surely die" (Genesis 2:16–17). A serpent tempted Eve to eat the fruit and Eve enjoyed the taste so much she ran to share the fruit with Adam who also ate it and sinned. By this action, they broke the love relationship between God and themselves. They covered themselves with leaves in order to hide from each other. They also tried to hide from God. The love that once bound them together in an open, free way was destroyed by the sin of eating the fruit. The message behind the story tells us that human beings, not God, had broken this love relationship and brought sin into the world.

b. The early stories of the Book of Genesis following upon this sin share the message that sin gradually gained a grip on the world.

After Adam and Eve were cast out of the garden of paradise, the story of Cain and Abel, the sons of Adam and Eve, told of another sin being committed. God was pleased with Abel's gift, and Cain, in his anger, killed Abel. In this destruction of his brother, Cain, broke his love relationship with God. Shortly after this, the story teller drew a story from mythology. Just as the gods of mythology married human beings, so the story teller wrote, "When men had begun to be plentiful on the earth and daughters had been born to them, the sons of God, looking at the daughters of men, saw they were pleasing, so they married as many as they chose" (Genesis 6:1–2). Finally, in a world filled with sin, only Noah and his family were sinless and worthy of salvation. Noah built the ark and saved his family and all the animals from the terrible flood that covered the earth. No sooner had the ark landed than Noah's son, Ham, committed sin by looking upon his father's nakedness and ridiculing his father. These early stories end with the building of the tower of Babel by which these people attempted to reach God in their own way. The tower would soar to the dome of heaven and give vain glory to its builders. Because of the pride of these people, God mixed up their languages that they might not work together. Instead of using their common gift for good, they sinned through this gift. By the time we come to the end of chapter 11 in Genesis, we have read through the stories that tell of sin gaining a grip on the world. When Abraham comes on the scene, sin already controls the world.

c. The grip of sin in the world is called original sin because it now stands at the very base of our creation.

This build-up of sin in the world has never ceased, even down to our present day. Whenever we accept sinful attitudes that become part of the thinking of society, we contribute to original sin. The acceptance of racism, excessive profits, abortion, and "taking care of number one first" are all attitudes of sin existing at the very base of our creation. By the "base of our creation," we simply mean those sins that have rooted themselves in a people, society, or a culture. Nowhere in the Scriptures do we have the expression "original sin." The term seems to have its birth somewhere in the early centuries after Christ.

When we speak of being born in original sin, we not only refer to the sinful attitude of the world that surrounds us, but we also refer to our own inability to confront and overcome this sinful attitude that grips the world. Through the resurrection of Jesus, we are able to share in a new strength and new life that enables us to do our share in overcoming the sin of the world. Christ came to confront this grip of sin in the world, and he successfully overcame sin. Now, through the gifts of Christ's resurrection, we too are called to do our part in overcoming these sinful attitudes that surround us. In his letter to the Romans, Paul reminds us of the power of Christ over sin. He writes, ". . . just as a single offense brought condemnation to all men, a single righteous act brought all men acquittal and life" (Romans 5:18).

3. What are some examples of actions that are considered sinful?

a. The Scriptures enable us to understand sinful actions by listing activities considered sinful by their very nature.

In the Old Testament, we read of the commandments given to the Israelite community (cf. page 29). These commandments still have importance and value, and are taught by the Church today. In the New Testament, we also find listings of sinful actions to be avoided.

In the letter of Paul to the Colossians, we read:

You must put to death, then, the earthly desires at work in you, such as sexual immorality, indecency, lust, evil passions, and greed (for greed is a form of idolatry). Because of such things God's anger will come upon those who do not obey Him. At one time, you yourselves used to live according to such desires when your life was dominated by them. But now you must get rid of all these things: anger, passion, and hateful feelings. No insults or obscene talk must ever come from your lips. Do not lie to one another. For you have put off the old self with its habits and have put on the new self. This is the new being which God, its Creator is constantly renewing in His own image, in order to bring you to a full knowledge of Himself (Colossians 3:5–10).

Although these listings cover many sinful actions, they do not cover all sinful actions. They can, however, enable us to understand the types of actions considered sinful.

b. For people to sin, they must freely and consciously choose actions they know to be sinful.

The actions mentioned above are sinful by their very nature. They are sinful because they are contrary to the good order of God's creation. But if the person performing the action does not know it is wrong, then that person is not guilty of sin before God. If a cannibal believes that the killing and eating of a young warrior is a form of worshipping his gods, the cannibal is not responsible for any personal sin in the eyes of God. In the same way, a person cannot commit a sin if a person does not know right from wrong. There is, however, an obligation to search out what is right. The Church serves as a guide in this search to understand right and wrong in God's creation.

A person cannot commit a sin if that person does not have the ability to know right from wrong. A person who suddenly loses his or her mind is not responsible for his or her actions. Some of the things he or she does may be wrong, but because he or she does not do these actions freely and consciously, they are not sinful actions. The person must also be physically capable of avoiding sin. A person sitting at a beach house with a broken leg cannot go running down the beach into the water to save a drowning child. There is a big difference between "I don't care," and "I am not physically able."

4. Are some sins more serious than others?

a. The seriousness of a sin depends upon a person's basic attitude or "fundamental option" in life.

By basic attitude or fundamental option, we refer to the basic stance a person continually takes toward life, in other words, a person's common way of thinking. When a person marries and dedicates his or her life to loving and respecting a spouse, the basic attitude is one of love and respect. If a person marries and still feels free to date other people whenever he or she wishes, this basic attitude of mind is one that lacks love and respect for his or her spouse. A person who seriously strives to show love and respect for God's presence in life has a continual way of thinking that seeks to live this love and respect. On the other hand, if a person decides on one's own will over the will of God, that person's basic option is toward oneself and against God. For the seriousness of a sin, we do not look to the individual actions, but rather to the "fundamental option" that guides a person through life. We must remember, however, that our actions flow from our basic attitude of mind. They are signs of our fundamental option. In speaking of good and bad actions, Jesus said, "A good man draws what is good from the store of goodness in his heart; a bad man draws what is bad from the store of badness" (Luke 6:45).

A Vatican document on sexual ethics recognizes the idea of "fundamental option," but it rightly warns that we should not go to the extreme of saying that an individual action, especially if it results from a series of lesser sinful actions, cannot change one's basic stance. The document states, "In reality, it is precisely the fundamental option which in the last resort defines a person's moral disposition. But it can be completely changed by particular acts, especially when . . . these have been prepared for by previous more superficial acts. Whatever the case, it is wrong to say that particular acts are not enough to constitute mortal sin" (*Vatican Declaration on Sexual Ethics No. 10*). In the same way, we can say that an individual act of love can totally change a person's fundamental way of thinking from one of rejection of God to one of total love of God.

b. A serious sin is a fundamental option to seek one's own will and to reject a love relationship with God.

When a person consciously decides to follow one's own will in life, this person rejects God and commits a serious sin. This is a continual way of thinking, a "fundamental option" to choose oneself over God. Just as we cannot say that one act of love makes a person a loving person (although there are cases where this does happen), we cannot say that one nonloving act can make a person an unloving person. In this way, the seriousness of a sin can be determined by the fundamental way of thinking of an individual. If one unloving act can change a person's whole direction of thought, then that person commits a serious sin. Ordinarily this does not happen.

c. A less serious sin occurs when a person retains an attitude of loving God yet at the same time commits an individual action that weakens or eventually could lead to a breakup of a love relationship with God.

A person could love and respect a marriage partner, yet, at times, have some very hurtful arguments with that partner. If a person continues to prolong these arguments, he or she could be weakening the fundamental attitude of love and respect toward the partner. By seeking an early reconciliation, the partners can admit they have hurt each other while at the same time admitting that their love and respect still remain. By delaying the reconciliation, the couple could be seriously hurting their relationship. When we speak of less serious sins, we realize that some of them happen quickly and are reconciled quickly. They do little harm to our fundamental option of loving God. Other less serious sins may actually hurt this fundamental option as in the case of a person who continuously pulls more and more from a neighbor till he or she has completely broken the love relationship and concern for his or her neighbor. The fundamental option that says, "I don't care," gradually takes over and the person is then living with a fundamental option that could be seriously sinful.

All of us must struggle with weaknesses in our lives, and we easily find ourselves performing those very actions which we do not wish to do. Even Paul, the great apostle to the Gentiles, complained about this weakness in himself when he writes, " What happens is that I do, not the good I will to do, but the evil I do not intend. . . . My inner self agrees with the law of God, but I see in my body's members another law at war with the law of my mind" (Romans 7:19, 22). Although he recognized these small faults within himself, Paul eventually proclaims that it is Christ who will save him and us from this power of sin.

5. What do the Scriptures tell us about God's love and sin?

a. Christ tells us about the love of God for sinners

In the Gospel of Luke, we read a story about a son who asks his father for his inheritance so he could leave home and spend his time with friends. The father sadly granted the request, and the boy left. Eventually, he squandered the inheritance and went to work tending. He would eat the husks fed to the pigs had eaten. Finally, he to return to his father's house, not to regain his right to son father to work as a hired hand. The story tells of the merciful father:

He (the son) was still a long way from home when his
him; his heart was filled with pity, and he ran, threw his
his son, and kissed him. The father called to his servants
get the prize calf and kill it, and let us celebrate with a
son of mine was dead, but now he is alive, he was lost
been found. And so the feasting began (Luke 15:20,

76

decides on one's own will over the will of God, that person's basic option is toward oneself and against God. For the seriousness of a sin, we do not look to the individual actions, but rather to the "fundamental option" that guides a person through life. We must remember, however, that our actions flow from our basic attitude of mind. They are signs of our fundamental option. In speaking of good and bad actions, Jesus said, "A good man draws what is good from the store of goodness in his heart; a bad man draws what is bad from the store of badness" (Luke 6:45).

A Vatican document on sexual ethics recognizes the idea of "fundamental option," but it rightly warns that we should not go to the extreme of saying that an individual action, especially if it results from a series of lesser sinful actions, cannot change one's basic stance. The document states, "In reality, it is precisely the fundamental option which in the last resort defines a person's moral disposition. But it can be completely changed by particular acts, especially when . . . these have been prepared for by previous more superficial acts. Whatever the case, it is wrong to say that particular acts are not enough to constitute mortal sin" (*Vatican Declaration on Sexual Ethics No. 10*). In the same way, we can say that an individual act of love can totally change a person's fundamental way of thinking from one of rejection of God to one of total love of God.

b. A serious sin is a fundamental option to seek one's own will and to reject a love relationship with God.

When a person consciously decides to follow one's own will in life, this person rejects God and commits a serious sin. This is a continual way of thinking, a "fundamental option" to choose oneself over God. Just as we cannot say that one act of love makes a person a loving person (although there are cases where this does happen), we cannot say that one nonloving act can make a person an unloving person. In this way, the seriousness of a sin can be determined by the fundamental way of thinking of an individual. If one unloving act can change a person's whole direction of thought, then that person commits a serious sin. Ordinarily this does not happen.

c. A less serious sin occurs when a person retains an attitude of loving God yet at the same time commits an individual action that weakens or eventually could lead to a breakup of a love relationship with God.

A person could love and respect a marriage partner, yet, at times, have some very hurtful arguments with that partner. If a person continues to prolong these arguments, he or she could be weakening the fundamental attitude of love and respect toward the partner. By seeking an early reconciliation, the partners can admit they have hurt each other while at the same time admitting that their love and respect still remain. By delaying the reconciliation, the couple could be seriously hurting their relationship. When we speak of less serious sins, we realize that some of them happen quickly and are reconciled quickly. They do little harm to our fundamental option of loving God. Other less serious sins may seriously hurt this fundamental option as in the case of a person who continuously steals more and more from a neighbor till he or she has completely broken the love relationship and concern for his or her neighbor. The fundamental option that says, "I don't care," gradually takes over and the person is then living with a fundamental option that could be seriously sinful.

All of us must struggle with weaknesses in our lives, and we easily find ourselves performing those very actions which we do not wish to do. Even Paul, the great apostle to the Gentiles, complained about this weakness in himself when he writes, "What happens is that I do, not the good I will to do, but the evil I do not intend. . . . My inner self agrees with the law of God, but I see in my body's members another law at war with the law of my mind" (Romans 7:19, 22). Although he recognizes these small faults within himself, Paul eventually proclaims that it is Christ who will save him and us from this power of sin.

5. What do the Scriptures tell us about God's love and sin?

a. Christ tells us about the love of God for sinners.

In the Gospel of Luke, we read a story about a son who asked his father for his inheritance so he could leave home and spend his time with his friends. The father sadly granted the request, and the boy left home. Eventually, he squandered the inheritance and went to work tending pigs. He would eat the left overs after the pigs had eaten. Finally, he decided to return to his father's house, not to regain his right to sonship, but rather to work as a hired hand. The story tells of the merciful, forgiving father:

> *He (the son) was still a long way from home when his father saw him; his heart was filled with pity, and he ran, threw his arms around his son, and kissed him. The father called to his servants . . . go and get the prize calf and kill it, and let us celebrate with a feast! For this son of mine was dead, but now he is alive; he was lost, but now he has been found. And so the feasting began (Luke 15:20, 22–24).*

76

Although these listings cover many sinful actions, they do not cover all sinful actions. They can, however, enable us to understand the types of actions considered sinful.

b. For people to sin, they must freely and consciously choose actions they know to be sinful.

The actions mentioned above are sinful by their very nature. They are sinful because they are contrary to the good order of God's creation. But if the person performing the action does not know it is wrong, then that person is not guilty of sin before God. If a cannibal believes that the killing and eating of a young warrior is a form of worshipping his gods, the cannibal is not responsible for any personal sin in the eyes of God. In the same way, a person cannot commit a sin if a person does not know right from wrong. There is, however, an obligation to search out what is right. The Church serves as a guide in this search to understand right and wrong in God's creation.

A person cannot commit a sin if that person does not have the ability to know right from wrong. A person who suddenly loses his or her mind is not responsible for his or her actions. Some of the things he or she does may be wrong, but because he or she does not do these actions freely and consciously, they are not sinful actions. The person must also be physically capable of avoiding sin. A person sitting at a beach house with a broken leg cannot go running down the beach into the water to save a drowning child. There is a big difference between "I don't care," and "I am not physically able."

4. Are some sins more serious than others?

a. The seriousness of a sin depends upon a person's basic attitude or "fundamental option" in life.

By basic attitude or fundamental option, we refer to the basic stance a person continually takes toward life, in other words, a person's common way of thinking. When a person marries and dedicates his or her life to loving and respecting a spouse, the basic attitude is one of love and respect. If a person marries and still feels free to date other people whenever he or she wishes, this basic attitude of mind is one that lacks love and respect for his or her spouse. A person who seriously strives to show love and respect for God's presence in life has a continual way of thinking that seeks to live this love and respect. On the other hand, if a person racism, excessive profits, abortion, and "taking care of number one first" are all attitudes of sin existing at the very base of our creation. By the "base of our creation," we simply mean those sins that have rooted themselves in a people, society, or a culture. Nowhere in the Scriptures do we have the expression "original sin." The term seems to have its birth somewhere in the early centuries after Christ.

When we speak of being born in original sin, we not only refer to the sinful attitude of the world that surrounds us, but we also refer to our own inability to confront and overcome this sinful attitude that grips the world. Through the resurrection of Jesus, we are able to share in a new strength and new life that enables us to do our share in overcoming the sin of the world. Christ came to confront this grip of sin in the world, and he successfully overcame sin. Now, through the gifts of Christ's resurrection, we too are called to do our part in overcoming these sinful attitudes that surround us. In his letter to the Romans, Paul reminds us of the power of Christ over sin. He writes, ". . . just as a single offense brought condemnation to all men, a single righteous act brought all men acquittal and life" (Romans 5:18).

3. What are some examples of actions that are considered sinful?

a. The Scriptures enable us to understand sinful actions by listing activities considered sinful by their very nature.

In the Old Testament, we read of the commandments given to the Israelite community (cf. page 29). These commandments still have importance and value, and are taught by the Church today. In the New Testament, we also find listings of sinful actions to be avoided.

In the letter of Paul to the Colossians, we read:

You must put to death, then, the earthly desires at work in you, such as sexual immorality, indecency, lust, evil passions, and greed (for greed is a form of idolatry). Because of such things God's anger will come upon those who do not obey Him. At one time, you yourselves used to live according to such desires when your life was dominated by them. But now you must get rid of all these things: anger, passion, and hateful feelings. No insults or obscene talk must ever come from your lips. Do not lie to one another. For you have put off the old self with its habits and have put on the new self. This is the new being which God, its Creator is constantly renewing in His own image, in order to bring you to a full knowledge of Himself (Colossians 3:5–10).

The forgiving, merciful father is an image of God the Father who rushes out to greet the sinner who returns. Through this parable, Jesus tells of the great love of the Father for sinners. Jesus tells of the joy of God over the sinner who returns to God. He tells of having a hundred sheep and losing one. The sheep herder will leave the ninety-nine to look for that one and will celebrate when that one is found. Jesus goes on to say, "I tell you, there will be more rejoicing in heaven over one repentant sinner than over ninety-nine virtuous men who have no need of repentance" (Luke 15:7). Sinners who recognize a need for God's forgiveness have a special place in God's heart.

b. In the infancy narrative, Joseph receives the message, "you are to name him Jesus because he will save his people from their sins" (Matthew 1:21).

The mission of Jesus is to save the people from their sins. The same idea stated in the infancy narrative of Matthew, is repeated in the words spoken at the Last Supper: "For this is my blood, the blood of the covenant, which is to be poured out for many for the forgiveness of sins" (Matthew 26:28). These texts at the beginning and end of Jesus' life remind us of the mission of Jesus toward sinners.

c. Jesus associated with sinners.

While Jesus dined at the house of a Pharisee, a woman known to be a sinner came to the Pharisee's house to wash Jesus' feet. Jesus knew what his host was thinking concerning the woman, and Jesus responded to his host, "You did not anoint my head with oil but she has anointed my feet with ointment. For this reason, I tell you that her sins, her many sins, must have been forgiven her, or she would not have shown such great love" (Luke 7:46–47). In the Gospel of Luke, we read, "The tax collectors and the sinners, meanwhile, were all seeking his company to hear what he had to say, and the Pharisees and scribes complained, 'This man', they said, 'welcomes sinners and eats with them' " (Luke 15:1–2). Throughout his life, Jesus never hesitated to mix with sinners.

d. Jesus overcame sin by his death and resurrection and shared this gift with us.

In the letter to the Romans, Paul tells how Christ overcame sin and shared that gift with us: "When he died, he died, once and for all, to sin, so now his life is life with God, and in that way, you too must consider yourselves to be dead to sin but alive for God in Christ Jesus" (Roman 6:10–11). Through the death and resurrection of Jesus, we have a new life. We now live for God in the name of Christ Jesus, and we now dare to approach God more closely in the name of Jesus who overcame sin and shared the gifts of his conquest with all of us.

In the first letter of John, we read, ". . . if anyone should sin, we have, in the presence of the Father, Jesus Christ, an intercessor who is just. He is an offering for our sins, and not for our sins only, but for those of the whole world" (I John 2:1–2).

6. What do the Scriptures tell us about the new life brought by Jesus?

a. With the coming of Jesus, the reign of God entered the world.

Through the parable of the mustard seed, Jesus tells us that this reign of God will flourish and offer spiritual protection for many. In the Gospel of Matthew, Jesus tells us, "The reign of God is like a mustard seed which someone took and sowed in his field. It is the smallest seed of all, yet, when full-grown it is the largest of plants. It becomes so big a shrub that the birds of the sky come and build their nests in its branches" (Matthew 13:31–32).

In a question in chapter 3, we spoke about the reign of God coming into the world through Jesus. In speaking of the reign of God, Jesus presented the manner of life demanded of those who accept this reign of God in their lives. These guidelines, found in the Gospels, enable us to understand the high call of living the Christian life.

b. Jesus gave a new law to his disciples.

In the Gospel of Matthew from chapter five to seven, we learn of a new law of the reign of God based upon love. When he writes his Gospel, the author of the Gospel of Matthew links the new law of Christ with that of the Commandments of the Old Testament. Just as Moses went up the mountain and received the Ten Commandments from God, so the disciples went up the mountain and received the precepts of the reign of God from Christ. Where the Commandments gave specific laws (mostly in a negative way by telling people what to avoid), the message of Jesus centered more on an attitude of mind or way of thinking. Some writers today use the Ten Commandments as a framework for the moral law, and they apply Christian principles to the law which were never intended in the original Commandments. In this way, they are able to make the Ten Commandments applicable to a Christian audience. The law given by Christ goes far beyond the original precepts of the Ten Commandments.

c. Many of the basic ideas of the new law given by Jesus are found in the Sermon on the Mount as presented in the Gospel of Matthew.

In his famous Sermon on the Mount, Jesus called his disciples to have an attitude of mind which reflected the presence of Christ in the world. He called them and (through them) all his followers, the salt of the earth and the light of the world. The basis of the Christian life are the following words of Jesus:

How blest are the poor in spirit; . . .
Blest too are the sorrowing; . . .
Blest are the lowly; . . .
Blest are they who hunger and thirst for holiness; . . .
Blest are they who show mercy; . . .
Blest are the single-hearted; . . .
Blest too the peacemakers; . . .
Blest are those persecuted for holiness sake; . . .
Blest are you when they insult you and persecute you and utter every kind of slander against you because of me . . . (Matthew 5:3–11).

Jesus calls his followers to recognize that this new law builds upon the old and fulfills the old. Where the old law forbade killing, the new law forbids any kind of destruction of the dignity of another, whether by abusive language or words. Reconciliation is central to the message of the reign of God.

Where the old law forbade adultery, the new law forbids any form of sinful or lustful glances or thoughts which destroy the dignity of others and makes them objects. The new law calls for personal sacrifice of some kind to overcome any sinful tendencies.

Where the old law allowed divorce with a written notice of divorce, the new law states that a divorced person commits adultery in a case of divorce and remarriage. This will be explained more at length under the chapter on the Sacrament of Marriage.

Where the old law stated that people should avoid false oaths, the new law states that no one should take an oath lightly. Honesty should be so much a part of a person's life that there should be no need of an oath to convince another of one's truthfulness.

Where the old law allowed equal retribution for an offense, the new law calls for total forgiveness of those who offend us.

Where the old law called for love of the people of one's nation and allowed for hatred of one's enemies, the new law calls for love of all, enemies, persecutors, and those who love us. The central law of Christianity is to love God and our neighbors as we love ourselves.

Jesus warned his followers against seeking earthly rewards or praise for their actions. Almsgiving from one's need is seen as an act of virtue and a great source of blessings from God. But the person who gives for the sake of praise has already received his or her reward. As Christians, we are called to share our goods with those in need.

Christians are also called to pray with simplicity, perseverance, trust, and patience. Prayer should not be done for personal praise, but for the sake of honoring and praising God. Those who constantly ask and seek will be heard.

Christians are called to fast and perform works of penance. For Catholics, Friday becomes a special day of penance in union with the suffering of Jesus who suffered and died on a Friday. The Lenten Season, which recalls the suffering and death of Jesus, is a special season for penance in union with the suffering Christ. In fasting, people should not seek the praise of others, but should fast in such a way that no one knows of the fasting. In this way, God will reward them.

Jesus calls Christians to a total attitude of trust. They should seek the things of God rather than the things of the world, and they should serve God and not the needs of the flesh as their true master. Jesus, although he encourages people to use their talents, cautions them against being overly concerned about material needs. They should trust God.

The true Christian has no right to judge others. Because we cannot know the motives behind actions, we have no ability to judge. We look only to the surface, and our judgement is often wrong and unfair.

Jesus warns that others will come with new laws and ways of acting, but we should avoid these. They will have an appeal about them, but their call must always be measured against the guidelines of the New Testament message. A person's basic way of thinking (fundamental option) will be betrayed by his or her way of acting. Jesus tells us, "Any sound tree bears good fruit, while a decayed tree bears bad fruit. You can tell a tree by its fruit" (Matthew 7:17,20).

To be a true and firm Christian in the world, we must take these words of Christ and put them into practice in our lives. Our call as a Christian is to be a light to the world, reflecting the presence of Christ through our words and actions.

7. What is Grace?

a. Grace is a special gift from God consisting of a deeper relationship or union with God.

The word grace means gift or favor. Some have falsely pictured grace as a type of spiritual liquid pouring into us and filling us. In simple terms, grace deepens our relationship with God. Just as two people who love each other experience a deepening of their love-relationship each time they share in love through their everyday life, so grace is simply a deeper experience of loving as we share with God through our daily lives. Through our prayers, our good works, our loving concern for our neighbor, we are deepening our relationship with God. We say that people grow in grace as they share more deeply in a loving union with God.

In speaking to his disciples, Jesus tells them that they now have a special relationship with him. They are no longer slaves to sins, but they are friends who have the special gift (grace) of knowing him and the Father. In the Gospel of John, Jesus says to his disciples, "You are my friends if you do what I command you. I do not call you servants any longer, because a servant does not know what his master is doing. Instead, I call you friends, because I have told you everything I heard from my Father" (John 15:14–15).

b. This gift of a deeper relationship with God is a gift freely given to us by God.

God freely chooses to share this gift with us. Even when we act in a way pleasing to God, we still do not have a right to this grace. God does not have to share this love with us, but out of God's goodness God has freely chosen to do this. The writer of the first letter of John shows an admiration of God's love when he writes, "This is the love I mean: not our love for God, but God's love for us when He sent his son to be the sacrifice that takes our sins away" (1 John 4:10). True love is recognizing the grace of God, namely that God first loves us. This is freely given. In writing his letter to the Ephesians, Paul tells us, "For it is by God's grace that you have been saved through faith. It is not the result of your own efforts, but God's gift, so that no one can boast about it" (Ephesians 2:8–9).

Paul, goes on to write, "You yourselves used to be in the darkness, but since you have become the Lord's people, you are in the light. So you must live like people who belong to the light, for it is the light that brings a rich harvest of every kind of goodness, righteousness, and truth" (Ephesians 5:8–9).

81

c. A person sharing in God's grace is often prompted to perform more good works.

A person who deeply loves his or her spouse will often strive for ways to show this love. Since grace is a love relationship with God, a person who shares in this love will also strive to find some way to express this love for God. Each time a person acts out of love, this love relationship deepens and the person grows in grace.

Conclusion

To the surprise of the parents, the boy in the introduction graduated, went to work on road construction during the summer, and planned on entering a school of engineering in the early fall. Christ once told a story about the weeds and wheat growing up together. The owner of the wheat field did not allow his hired hands to pull up the weeds because they looked too much like the wheat in their young growth. In pulling up the weeds, some valuable wheat would be destroyed. On the day of graduation, the parents of the boy could easily understand the meaning of this parable of Jesus. Just when they thought the relationship with their son had been shattered, he grew closer. Their love had gradually won his love. Their relationship with their son had moved from a broken one to a loving one. In reviewing this chapter, we could say the boy's relationship to his parents had moved from one of sin to one of grace.

For Scripture reflection and discussion concerning this chapter, see Journeying in His Light, *"Sin and Life."*

82

6
Our Christian Family—Church

Introduction

A Catholic priest was speaking at an interfaith convention when he turned to two Methodist ministers who happened to be very close friends and who were sharing the stage with him. As he looked at them, he told a very surprised audience, "It would be the happiest day of my life if these two Methodist ministers would become Catholic. They mean so much to me. They are so special that I would love to share my faith with them.

An embarrassed silence followed as he looked back to the audience. "And I would hope," he continued, "that their concern for me is so deep that they would wish with all their hearts that I would become Methodist."

He went on to say that all people should see their belief as so precious that they would wish with all their hearts to share that faith with people close to them.

In this chapter, we take a look at the mission and structure of the Catholic Church. In choosing or receiving any gift from God, we should strive to know that gift as well as possible. If we love someone, and wish to share a gift with the one we love, we should know the gift we are sharing. In this chapter, we touch upon the gift of the Catholic Church.

1. How did the Church develop?

a. Jesus chose twelve men from among his disciples who shared and spread his message.

During his earthly life, Jesus gathered a community of twelve apostles. These men would share in a special way in Jesus' everyday actions. He would share with them insights into his messages and parables. Finally, he would send them out to bear witness to his message. "He called the twelve together and gave them power and authority over all devils and to cure diseases, and he sent them out to proclaim the kingdom of God and to heal'' (Luke 9:1–2). In Matthew's Gospel, we read that Jesus commissioned them in a special way after his resurrection:

The eleven disciples went to the hill in Galilee where Jesus had told them to go. When they saw him, they worshiped him, even though some of them doubted. Jesus drew near and said to them, "I have been given all authority in heaven and on earth. Go then, to all peoples everywhere and make them my disciples: baptize them in the name of the Father, the Son, and the Holy Spirit, and teach them to obey everything I have commanded you. And I will be with you always, to the end of the age (Matthew 28:16–20).

In looking back, we see how Jesus through his public life and under the guidance of the Holy Spirit, shaped this early community. This community, along with other followers of Jesus, began to lay the foundations for a new Church after the ascension of Jesus.

b. The Acts of the Apostles describe the development of the early Church after the ascension of Jesus.

On Pentecost Sunday, the Holy Spirit filled the apostles with a new understanding and a new courage. On that day, they converted masses of people to Jesus. The message of Jesus spread first to the Jewish communities, then outside these communities to the Gentile communities. The apostles and followers of Jesus went about preaching the message of the reign of God. Small groups of people joined them and spread the faith along with them. The early Christian Jews had no idea of breaking away from their Jewish traditions or their Jewish faith. They went to the temple daily to pray and to offer sacrifices with the Jewish community. Their habits, customs, language, and religious practices were those of normal Jewish life. Only in the way that they spoke of the man Jesus did they differ from the ordinary people in Jerusalem. Eventually, these Jewish converts to Christianity were rejected by their own people and not permitted to share in temple worship. A man named Saul, later known to us as Paul, was an early convert to Christianity. From a great persecutor of the Faith, he became a great defender of the Faith. Paul would be one of the first to see the Christian community as a continuation of Christ's presence here on earth. In the Acts of the Apostles we read of his conversion: "He fell to the ground, and then he heard a voice saying, 'Saul, Saul, why are you persecuting me?' 'Who are you, Lord?' he asked. 'I am Jesus, and you are persecuting me' " (Acts 9:4–5). In this reading is a vision in which Christ identifies himself with the suffering members of

84

the Church, as though he were these members. After this experience, Paul began to speak and to witness about Christ's presence in his life. He traveled throughout Asia Minor setting up small communities and continually speaking the praises and the message of Jesus. Because many new converts came into the Church from the non-Jewish sector of the world, Paul strongly requested that the Jewish traditions not be imposed upon these new converts. At the Council of Jerusalem (A.D. 54), the leaders of the early Church agreed with Paul. This decision would eventually move Christianity even further away from Judaism.

c. The Church struggled from persecution to acceptance.

Around the year A.D. 64, a fire raged through Rome. Rumors spread as quickly as the fire that the Christians were responsible for this burning of Rome. From that year until the year A.D. 311, frequent persecutions were inflicted upon the Christian community. Finally after three centuries, a Roman Emperor, Constantine the Great, converted to Christianity. The Church now became associated with the world-wide Empire. This changed the Church in many ways and influenced the very structure of the Church. From 311 to our present day, the Church has passed through many kingdoms and many cultures. But through the changing times the Church has often turned back to its roots, to assure itself that it still carries out the message and commission of Jesus Christ.

2. What do we mean when we say that the Church is a community?

a. A community consists of a group of people working together with a common goal.

We use the word community in many different ways. A group of people living and working together in a certain town is called a community. A community could refer to families on one street, or members of a club, or to a family group. Whenever a group of people join together with a common goal, we call this group a community.

b. The Israelites of the Old Testament formed a community, "The People of God."

In the Old Testament, the Israelites were often referred to as the "chosen people" or the "people of God." The Israelite community responded to their convenant by accepting the true God as the God of the

85

community. In the Old Testament, we saw how God related to a community. God chose the family of Abraham and guided that family as it grew into a nation. That nation was the chosen people of God, the people of Israel. The Old Testament tells the story of God as God related to the special community of the people of God.

c. St. Paul used the image the "Body of Christ" to speak about the community of the New Testament.

In speaking of the Church in the New Testament or the community with which Christ has shared his gifts, St. Paul speaks of the image of the "Body of Christ." We read in St. Paul:

Christ is like a single body, which has many parts; it is still one body, even though it is made up of different parts. In the same way, all of us, whether Jews or Gentiles, whether slaves or free, have been baptized into the one body by the same Spirit, and we have all been given the one Spirit to drink. For the body itself is not made up of only one part, but of many parts (1 Corinthians 12:12–14).

In speaking of the image of the Body of Christ, St. Paul points out that we, the Church, need one another to truly make Christ present here on earth. Just as the whole body is in pain if one part of the body feels pain so the whole community feels the loss of any single member. St. Paul writes, "If one part is hurt, all parts are hurt with it; if one part is given special honor, all parts enjoy it" (1 Corinthians 12:26). The community of the Church is more than a street or a club or a family. It is a community joined to Christ in such a way that Christ and the community become one with each other. Christ brings redemption to the community and we, by entering community, share in this redemption.

d. The Church is a group of baptized people joined together for the common purpose of sharing Christ's redemption.

The Church is not a building nor an organization, but rather a community of people who are joined together in a special way. The people forming this community believe that Jesus Christ is both God and Man; that he came upon this earth, suffered, died, and was raised from the dead to glory. People of this community also believe that Jesus shared a message and a life with his people which in turn must be shared with all people. This community comes together in the one Christ, shares each other's joys, and experiences each other's sorrows. This community, which knows that Christ is God and responds fully to the knowledge, is called the Christian community or the Church.

e. The community called Church is a mystery which can never be fully understood.

We often confuse the words, problem and mystery. A problem can be solved. If I owe a friend five dollars, I solve that problem when I pay my friend. A mystery, however, is a continual search to reach into the depths which seem bottomless. Human beings can never be solved. They are mysteries to be continually discovered, continually learned anew but never fully understood. The Church is a mystery. St. Paul uses the image of the Body of Christ to explain the mystery of Church. The Scriptures, however, use several other images to try to help us discover the mystery of Church. The Church is a sheepfold. It is the flock led by Christ who is the Good Shepherd. It is the vineyard; it is a seed placed in the ground; it is God's temple; the holy city, the new Jerusalem. The Church is God's house, with Christ as the cornerstone. In these images and others, the New Testament continually strives to help us to reach more deeply into the mystery of Church. We can never fully solve the idea of Church. However, we can continually search more deeply to understand many of the surprises contained in the mystery of Church and the mystery of Christ among us in his Church.

3. What sources are used as a basis for Catholic Teaching?

a. A written source for the teachings of the Catholic Church is the Bible.

Catholics, along with all Christians, believe that the Bible is the inspired Word of God, through which God speaks to all people. As mentioned earlier in this book (page 20), the inspired message of God is called revelation. Through this revelation, we not only learn about God; we learn about our manner of relating in love with God. Christians look to the Old and New Testaments as the source of their faith, with special emphasis on the message of the New Testament. The New Testament not only offers us guidelines by which we should conduct our lives as Christians, but it also tells us about the love of God for us, shown through Jesus Christ, and it offers us a motive for responding in love to God.

b. A written and lived source for the teachings of the Catholic Church is tradition.

Before any of the New Testament was written, it was lived and preached by the early Church community. After a period of reflection and preaching, writers committed some of the message to written form, while other aspects of the message continued to be lived and practiced in Christian teaching. Tradition refers to the manner in which the Church understood and lived the faith. The New Testament writings actually have their roots in the tradition of the Church, but tradition covers a far wider area than the New Testament alone.

The earliest records (called the "apostolic tradition") consist of writings from other authors besides those who wrote New Testament books, and any other form of creed or prayers found in the early Church writings. The value of tradition is that much of it has its origin before the writing of the New Testament, and it reflects the manner in which the early Church lived the message of Christ in their daily lives. In later centuries, the teachings of Church councils, the creeds, and the widely accepted teachings of the Church continued to reflect these traditions in a manner and language familiar to the people of a specific age in history. In this way, although tradition may be expressed in various ways throughout history, its expression always remains faithful to the roots from which it springs.

c. For the sake of common practice and order within the Church, the Church has compiled a summary of laws and guidelines which is called the "Code of Canon Law."

In 1917, the first Code of Canon Law was compiled by the Church. Until that time, most of the laws and guidelines for the daily practice and order of the Church could be found in many different documents. To help those who were not able to know or understand all these previous documents, the Church gathered together the laws and guidelines and placed them in one book which was called the "Code of Canon Law."

Since 1917, many new insights into tradition have been expressed through documents from the Church, and the 1917 Code became outdated. In 1984, a new Code of Canon Law took the place of the old, gathering together many of the guidelines which have their source in the II Vatican Council and other recent Church teachings. As important as it is to the Church, the Code of Canon Law cannot propose any laws which contradict the constant tradition of the Church.

4. What is the mission of the Church?

a. The mission of the Church is to proclaim Jesus Christ and his message.

When we speak of the life of Jesus and his message we should bear in mind that the life of Jesus is his message. The message of Jesus and his life, death, resurrection, and ascension flow together as the one proclamation of the whole person, Jesus who became Christ. The mission of the Church is to share this message to the very ends of the earth so that all might be able to proclaim together with the Church. "Jesus Christ is Lord" (Philippians 2:11). "Jesus came forward and addressed them in these words: 'Full authority has been given to me both in heaven and on earth; go, therefore, and make disciples of all the nations' " (Matthew 28:18–19). The word catholic actually means universal and it shows the call of the Church to reach out to all people.

b. The mission of the Church is to carry out the mission of Jesus in sharing the gifts of God's reign with all people.

By his life and message, Jesus continually proclaimed that the reign of God had already come into the world. He also proclaimed that the future of this reign is yet to be fulfilled. The Church proclaims the presence of this reign in the world today by pointing to the gifts that God is sharing through Christ's resurrection and ascension. At the same time, the Church shares these gifts with all people so that the fullness of the reign may more easily be attained. Christ shares gifts with all people through his Church and these gifts enable people to reach the eternal fullness of the reign of God's presence for all eternity. Through these gifts the Church announces the present reign and through these gifts, we will be able to attain the fullness of that reign in the future.

c. All people are called to share in the mission of the Church.

From the moment of their baptism, all people share in the mission of living and sharing the message and gifts of Jesus Christ. In fulfilling this mission of the Church in an orderly fashion, there exists in the Church a structure of service which includes the laity, the ordained, the bishops and the pope. Instead of viewing this image as a type of pyramid with the pope at the top, the bishops next, the ordained under the bishops and the laity at the bottom of the pyramid, we should see it more as a circle, with all working together for the mission of the Church, yet with each one having a particular function of service to the world and to each other. In diagram form, it would look like this:

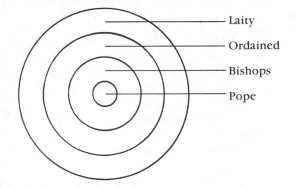

5. What is a Bishop?

a. In carrying out its mission, the early Church established a set order in its ministry.

The apostles held a special position of honor and respect among the Christians of the early Church. Even before Pentecost we saw them establishing a set order in the ministry of Christ's message. Peter announced that Judas had betrayed his right to apostleship and now they elected a new member to replace Judas. This member had to be a person who had witnessed Christ from the time of his baptism by John the Baptist to his resurrection. Two men were chosen, Joseph and Matthias, and they drew lots to see who would become the new apostle. "As the lot fell to Matthias, he was listed as one of the twelve apostles" (Acts 1:26). The apostles exercised leadership within the Church and within their own particular communities. Eventually, we see others joining them in this leadership. From the earliest centuries, we read of chosen men to succeed the apostles and to act as bishops in the Church. The ceremony for passing on this power becomes the symbol of "laying on of hands."

b. A bishop often serves as pastor of a large area called a diocese in which there are many parishes.

Bishops may serve the Church in various ways. Today, we are familiar with bishops who serve over a large area called a diocese. Within this diocese, there are usually many parishes which are served by parish priests. The bishop who serves in the leadership role in this way in a diocese is referred to as the "Ordinary" of the Diocese. Other bishops may assist him within that diocese. Those who assist in this way are called "auxiliary bishops" or "coadjutor bishops" which mean co-helpers.

c. Every bishop is ordained for the whole Church.

From among many candidates, the visible head of the Church, the pope, appoints a bishop. Although a bishop receives his appointment from the pope, he does not receive his power from the pope but rather from God. He is ordained a bishop in the Catholic or Universal Church. He might serve one area of the world and one diocese of that area, but a bishop still has a great responsibility in sharing the message of Christ throughout the whole world. He must be concerned not only for his own diocese but for every person on God's earth.

d. We refer to the entire community of bishops as the "college of bishops."

The group or college of apostles received a call from Christ himself. The "college of bishops" is the successor of this group of college of apostles, and as a member of this "college of bishops," a bishop shares in its apostolic power. When the bishops meet together in Rome, as a council, the college of bishops becomes much more visible to the world.

e. Some bishops are given the honorary title of "Cardinal."

During the middle ages, the Church established the title of cardinal as an honorary title for bishops who served the Church in a significant way. It is a title of honor that adds no new spiritual powers to the one who receives this title. Cardinals are usually bishops of a large diocese or bishops who serve in some central position in the Church. By Church law, cardinals are responsible for electing the pope. If a pope decides for the good of the Church to open future elections to others besides cardinals, he may change the law. Throughout the centuries, the cardinals have elected one of their number to the papacy, although they may choose for pope someone who is not a cardinal.

6. How did the office of pope develop?

a. Tradition in the Catholic Church honors Peter as the first pope and believes that Peter died in Rome under Nero between A.D. 64 and A.D. 67.

An early tradition in the Church claims that Peter went to Rome and served there as bishop for several years. He was put to death under Nero around A.D. 64. The early Church saw this as referring to the words of Christ which said of Peter.

I am telling you the truth: when you were young, you used to get ready and go anywhere you wanted to; but when you are old, you will stretch out your hands and someone else will tie you up and take you where you don't want to go (John 21:18).

What he said indicated the sort of death by which Peter was to glorify God.

b. Throughout the Gospels the authors portray Peter as having a special role among the apostles.

The Gospel of Matthew reflects this special role as seen by the early Church in an episode between Jesus and Peter. Jesus had just asked his followers who people say that the Son of Man is.

Simon Peter answered, "You are the Messiah, the Son of the living God." "Good for you, Simon son of John!" answered Jesus. "For this truth did not come to you from any human being, but it was to you directly by my Father in heaven. And so I tell you, Peter: you are a rock, and on this rock foundation I will build my church, and not even death will ever be able to overcome it. I will give you the keys of the kingdom of heaven; what you prohibit on earth will be prohibited in heaven, and what you permit on earth will be permitted in heaven (Matthew 16:16–19).

In the Gospel of John written much later, we see a special honor and commission given to Simon Peter by Jesus after his resurrection.

After they had eaten, Jesus said to Simon Peter, "Simon son of John, do you love me more than these others do?" "Yes, Lord," he answered, "you know that I love you." Jesus said to him, "Take care of my lambs." A second time Jesus said to him, "Simon son of John, do you love me?" "Yes, Lord," he answered, "you know that I love you." Jesus said to him, "Take care of my sheep." A third time Jesus said, "Simon son of John, do you love me?" Peter became sad because Jesus asked him the third time, "Do you love me?" and so he said to him, "Lord, you know everything; you know that I love you!" Jesus said to him, "Take care of my sheep" (John 21:15–17).

To say something three times in Scripture writing is to say it in a most emphatic way. The Gospel of John is emphatically proclaiming Peter as the new shepherd, the visible shepherd of his flock.

92

c. In the Acts of the Apostles we read how the other apostles accepted the leadership of Peter.

When the time came to choose a member to replace Judas, Peter stood up before one hundred twenty people gathered together to announce an election. They accepted Peter's leadership in this. On Pentecost Sunday as the Holy Spirit in the narrative comes upon the apostles, it is Peter who gives the discourse under the influence of the Spirit. Peter became the first to work miracles in the name of Christ, and the first real missionary. When the time came to exempt the Gentiles from the traditions of the Jewish religion, Paul faced Peter in order to convince him that the Gentiles should not be bound by these laws. By choosing Peter as the one to convince in this case, Paul showed the position of leadership given to Peter in the eyes of the early Church.

d. From later letters of the early Church, we find that the bishops of Rome, Peter's successors, retain an honored position.

About the year one hundred, we already discover letters suggesting that the Bishop of Rome is held in high esteem. No special organization decreed this nor did Christ himself decree this. However, bishops of other areas would often consult with the Bishop of Rome before important decisions were made. The reason seemed to be based on the belief that an ancient apostolic community in Rome went back to Peter. The bishops of the early Church were carrying out a custom seemingly established during the time of the apostles. At a very early date, unity with the succession of Peter became a sign of being in unity with the whole Church.

e. The Catholic Church today accepts the Bishop of Rome as a true successor of the apostle Peter and as the visible head of the Roman Catholic Church.

Jesus Christ himself is considered the invisible head of the Church, the true shepherd and leader. The pope, as the visible head of the Church, should reflect the leadership of Christ which was a leadership of servanthood. The pope is at the service of the entire Church and as such holds a privileged position within the Church. Being pope does not guarantee holiness. A pope, as other members of the Church, must work toward holiness even though he is the visible head of the Church. Although the Church has been blessed throughout history with many holy men to serve as popes, the Church must also admit that some were far from the ideal of holiness the visible Church would hope to find in its leaders.

7. Is the pope infallible?

a. The Catholic Church teaches that the pope is infallible in matters that pertain to faith and morals.

If the pope were to announce to the world that it would rain all over the earth tomorrow, Catholics need not believe this. They need only respond to those matters which refer to faith or morals. Infallibility does not mean that the pope has knowledge of all truths. There are some matters of faith and morals which the pope does not know. However, when he proclaims as infallible matters of faith and morals and follows the required steps for infallibility, the pope is making an infallible statement.

b. Catholics believe that the pope is infallible in matters proposed for the Universal Church.

A pope cannot make a statement on faith and morals that pertains to only one area of the world. It must pertain to the whole Universal Church. What is infallible for one area must be infallible for all areas.

c. Catholics believe that the pope is infallible when he is acting from his special office as shepherd and teacher of all Christians.

When the pope speaks officially as pope, on matters of faith and morals and declares his statement as infallible, Catholics accept this infallible statement of faith. Only when he officially, from his position as pope, declares a statement to be infallible, need Catholics accept his position as infallible. If he were expressing an individual theological opinion to another person in a private conversation, Catholics would not have to accept this as an infallible statement.

d. The infallibility of the pope is the same infallibility possessed by the Church.

The pope is infallible to the degree that he reflects the infallible faith of the whole Church. He does not decide one day to make an infallible statement out of thin air, but rather listens to the Church as it is reflecting its faith. He enunciates the expression of this faith as well as possible. He and the Church proclaim that faith to the world as the faith of the infallible Church.

e. The college of bishops in union with the pope possesses this infallibility.

The college of bishops along with the pope also shares in reflecting the faith of a community. By coming together and sharing the reflection of the Catholic community at large and drawing up statements flowing from that faith experience, the college of bishops along with the pope, but not without him, can proclaim in an infallible way matters of faith and morals which must be accepted by the entire Church.

8. Can the Church ever change its teaching?

a. The Church may never change its basic infallible teachings about faith or morals.

As we look back through history, we note that the Church has always been guided in stating its infallible teaching either through councils or through papal statements. Christ has promised, ". . . know that I am with you always; yes, to the end of time" (Matthew 28:20). Under the guidance of the Holy Spirit, the Church has never had to change any of its basic teachings.

b. The explanation of these basic teachings may change since their explanations are limited by the language and world view which surrounds them.

As language changes and as we gain deeper insights into science and human nature we can sometimes explain things in a far better way than we could in the past. As we begin to understand more clearly God's hand in nature, we are more clearly able to explain basic teachings of the Church in such a way that they could seem different from previous explanations but which in reality explains the basic teaching more clearly. For example, in trying to explain the fact that God is the Creator of the world and that God created the world out of nothing, we could confuse the issue by trying to retain stubbornly the idea that God created the world in six days. The message has to do with God's power of creation out of nothing, not the fact that God created it in six days. As we understand the writings of the Scriptures in a clearer manner, we are more able to explain the basic doctrine that God is the Creator of the world.

9. How often do the pope and the college of bishops meet together?

a. The pope and the college of bishops meet together as the need arises.

The Church has no set law for a time when the pope and the college of bishops must meet together. Throughout history, popes have called all the bishops of the world together in order to determine how the Church can best serve in a particular age.

b. In the Church today, the pope meets with a "synod of bishops" every three years.

This synod of bishops consists of representatives from different countries throughout the world. These representative bishops speak on behalf of their own national conferences. In this way, the Church is able to continually meet the needs of the present day without calling all the bishops of the world together to answer this need.

c. A gathering of the bishops of the world in union with the pope is called an "ecumenical council."

The most noted council in our present age is the Second Vatican Council (1962–1965) called by Pope John XXIII. The council prior to this one was held one hundred years before and was called the First Vatican Council. In the early days of the Church, some of these councils were called by emperors, but throughout most of Church history popes have called these councils together under the guidance of the Holy Spirit. The Second Vatican Council in the Roman Catholic Church has ushered in many changes which we are experiencing in the Church today. Any document or decree that comes from such councils must be approved by the pope.

10. What names do we give to meetings among members of different beliefs?

a. Ecumenism refers to those activities among Christian communities whereby they come together for the sake of understanding, sharing, and praying toward unity.

There are many different Christian communities in the world today. Ecumenism is an attempt on the part of all members of these Christian communities to come together to share their understanding of the Christian message. Their hope and prayer is unity. Ecumenism is the challenge of sharing one another's belief in the Christian message and attempting to discuss that belief at an honest level. It does not mean "giving in" nor does it mean "giving up," but rather it means coming together, trying to listen, trying to understand, and trying to share in the Spirit of Christ, the message of Christ as each one lives and understands this message.

b. Interfaith refers to those activities among Christian communities and other communities who profess belief in God but who do not accept that Jesus is God.

Christians meet in a spirit of love, understanding, and prayer with those who accept belief in God, but who do not accept the belief that Jesus is God. The Jewish faith, as well as other world religions, accepts God as we do, but they do not accept the Godhood of Jesus. This difference should not drive us apart, but should make us open to a deeper understanding of and sensitivity to one another. In this openness, we hold firmly to the truths taught by the Church and strive to understand the faith of our brothers and sisters who do not accept the Godhood of Jesus.

c. In the spirit of ecumenism and interfaith we should respect the faith of our neighbor.

At the II Vatican Council, the Bishops sought to identify the "sole Church of Christ which in the creed we profess to be one, holy, Catholic and apostolic . . ." (Constitution of the Church, n.8) But in proclaiming this Church of Christ as the Catholic Church, the Bishops also realized that other Churches had certain elements that flowed from the true Church of Christ. They write:

This Church, constituted and organized as a society in the present world, subsists in the Catholic Church, which is governed by the successor of Peter and by the bishops in communion with him.

Nevertheless, many elements of santification and of truth are found outside its visible confines (Constitution on the Church, n.8).

Although they see the Catholic Church as the sole Church of Christ professed in the creed, they are quick to point to the beauty of Christ's Church found "outside its visible limits." Because of this statement, we could never allow ourselves to look down upon any other Church.

11. What does the Catholic Church believe about Mary the Mother of Jesus?

a. Mary has been named the Mother of the Church.

In calling Mary the Mother of the Church, the Church proclaims her spiritual motherhood over all the Church. In being the mother of Jesus, Mary was accepting the motherhood of all that Jesus stood for. She was accepting the spiritual motherhood of the Mystical Body of Christ here on earth. The Gospel of John portrays this acceptance on the part of Mary of this motherhood of the Church by the words of Jesus from the cross: "Seeing his mother and the disciple he loved standing near her, Jesus said to his mother, 'Woman this is your Son.' Then to the disciple, he said, "This is your mother" (John 19:26–27). Many see in these words a special call of Mary to become the mother of all people symbolized in the person of John. It is not simply that Jesus is telling John to take care of his mother after his death, but even more that Jesus is concerned for all people and making her the mother of all people. Because of this, the Church addresses Mary by this title "The Mother of the Church."

b. Mary is also called the Mother of God.

The Church teaches that Jesus is one person, even though he is human as well as divine. This is one of those mysteries that stand outside our experience. Because the Church proclaims that Jesus is one person and not two, the Church also recognizes that the mother of Jesus cannot be mother of the human Jesus alone. To accept this would be to accept two persons in Jesus instead of one person. The Church, in the early centuries, proclaimed that Mary is the Mother of Jesus and as such must also be called the Mother of God. We again speak of a mystery outside our experience. What the title "Mother of God" fully entails, we will never know until we reach eternity. In the meanwhile, we can safely say that this is the greatest title that could be given to Mary. With the Church, we give Mary the highest honor when we call her "The Mother of God."

c. The Church declared in an infallible statement that Mary was assumed body and soul into heaven.

When we speak of body and soul we simply mean that Mary's whole person was taken into eternal happiness. When we use the expression "assumed into heaven" we are simply using a scriptural sense of being taken up. What the doctrine of the Assumption of Mary really means is that Mary has been taken fully into eternal happiness. Her whole person now shares in Christ's resurrection and ascension. The meaning of this can never be fully understood in this life. The fact that Mary's whole person has entered into eternal happiness is meant as a sign for the rest of us that we too, like Mary, are called to this eternal happiness and that if we respond, we shall be taken with our whole person into eternity. In this way, Mary, as Mother of the Church, becomes the model for all people within the Church. Mary's assumption is one of the few official infallible statements made by the pope.

d. The Church has proclaimed in an infallible statement that Mary is the Immaculate Conception.

Since Mary was chosen to be the Mother of God, God freed her from all the chains of sin within her life. From the moment of her birth, Mary already shared, by God's special plan, in the gift of redemption. A Christian today shares this gift through the Sacrament of Baptism. Mary shared this gift without baptism. One of the inspired messages from the infancy narrative comes through the mouth of an angel, "Rejoice, so highly favored! The Lord is with you" (Luke 1:28). In these words, the author tells us that Mary is most blessed among all women, in fact, most blessed among all people. "O highly favored one" is not just a title, but actually a name given to Mary. We celebrate the feast of the Immaculate Conception on December 8.

12. How do Catholics honor Mary?

a. Catholics honor Mary by praying to her but never by worshiping her.

Only God may be worshiped. Whenever we pray in Mary's honor we are actually praising God through the person of Mary and thanking God for allowing one of God's creatures to be so highly favored. We honor God as we pray in Mary's name. By proclaiming our love and honor for one of God's favored creatures we are thanking God for the gift of God's mother, Mary. Mary does not have power equal to God nor is she divine. Mary is created just as we are. She is a model of what holiness can be in a human person on earth, and a model of God's love for all people.

b. We honor Mary by a special form of prayer called "The Hail Mary."

A popular Catholic prayer in honor of Mary is a prayer that has its roots in the infancy narratives. After the angel greets Mary and tells her that she is favored with God, Mary goes to visit her cousin Elizabeth who is with child. As Mary comes into the home of Elizabeth the Scriptures tell us, "Elizabeth was filled with the Holy Spirit. She gave a loud cry and said, 'blessed is the fruit of your womb' " (Luke 1:41–42). The Church has added the second part of the prayer of the Hail Mary asking Mary's special help in this life and at our death. The prayer is as follows:

Hail Mary, full of grace!
The Lord is with you.
Blessed are you among women,
And blessed is the fruit of your womb, Jesus.
Holy Mary, Mother of God,
Pray for us sinners,
Now and at the hour of our death. Amen.

c. Catholics honor Mary in a special way by a prayer called the "rosary."

The rosary consists of prayers that are recited while meditating upon a mystery of Christ's life. Catholics keep account of the prayers by following them upon beads called the "rosary beads." The prayer begins with the Apostles' Creed, followed by the Our Father, three Hail Mary's for the virtues of faith, hope, and charity and the Glory be to the Father. The person prays one Our Father, ten Hail Marys, and one Glory be to the Father, while meditating upon a mystery in the lives of Jesus and Mary. This is repeated four more times, each time meditating on a new mystery. (See the appendix at the end of this book for the mysteries of the rosary.)

d. The Church honors Mary in a special way through the prayers of the Church.

The Church honors Mary when it joins together in worship and sets aside certain days in her honor. These days point to some special mystery in the life of Mary. For example, we celebrate the feast of the Immaculate Conception on December 8, the Assumption of Mary on August 15, the Birth of Mary on September 8, and the Solemnity of Mary as the Mother of God on January 1. In these and other feasts that honor Mary, we are worshiping God in a special way for the blessings God has shown to Mary. In this way, we thank God for God's goodness in giving us Mary.

Conclusion

In the introduction to this chapter, we spoke of a priest who shocked his audience by inviting his Methodist friends to become Catholic. After his talk, one of the Methodist ministers told the audience that this priest would make a fine Methodist minister, since he liked to talk so long. The audience laughed, enjoying the friendly exchange between the minister and the priest that would have seemed almost impossible fifteen years ago.

The minister became more serious as he continued, "With all my heart I would like to share in faith with this wonderful priest. But even more! I would like to know about a faith that nourishes such people as my friend here. But before we share as one faith, we must pray, enjoy, and study together. We must share our insights and discoveries. And we must do it carefully and slowly. It would be a shame if we lost the gifts we all have to share because of our impatience to be one faith. The seed is in the ground. Now we must give it time to take root and grow."

In these few words, the audience caught a glimpse of the difficult road to unity. The love and desire for unity was present, but the need for understanding and discovery that come only in time will be its foundation.

For Scripture reflection and discussion concerning this chapter, see Journeying in His Light, *"Our Christian Family— Church."*

The Sacraments and Love

Introduction

As they drove home from the ball park, Tom and his fourteen-year-old son talked excitedly about the game that day. A car sped suddenly from a side street and rammed the side of Tom's car where Billy sat. The ambulance attendants found Billy slumped lifelessly in a bundle on the floor and his father breathing heavily with blood pouring from his nose and ears. The ambulance attendants put Tom and the two passengers from the other car into two ambulances and covered Billy's lifeless body. At the hospital, a doctor friend of the family worked on the three survivors, while Billy was left alone presumably dead. A short time after, Billy's mother along with some friends came in quietly to the hospital, sat down next to Billy's body and wept. As she sat there, she suddenly noticed an almost imperceptible twitch in Billy's face. A scream rang down the corridor, "He's still alive!" Attendants came running, hurrying, pushing back Billy's eye lids and rushed him off behind a curtain, the family doctor following them. After some time, the family doctor came downstairs to Billy's mother and sat next to her. He whispered, "Billy is going to be all right," and he burst into tears. For a moment, all the tension, all the fears, all the love came pouring out in those tears of the family doctor and friend. He patted Billy's mother on the hand and walked back into the emergency room.

1. Why is the Church concerned about signs and symbols?

a. Signs tell us something is happening or something should be happening, or they may simply give information.

A sign on a door could tell us that Joseph Smith is an "Attorney at Law," or a sign on the highway could warn us that the "Right Lane Ends 1000 Ft."

In the story in the introduction, we have a series of signs at work. The stop sign told the driver of one car that he should have stopped rather than run through an intersection. The stop sign could not make him stop. It simply informed him that he should stop. A twitch was a sign that Billy was still alive. The sign showed life. When the doctor came down to share the good news, his weeping was a sign of his love for Billy and his family. In all of these cases, nothing is said, nothing need be said. The sign told us that a stop should have taken place, that life was still going on, that love was in the doctor's heart. A central part of being human consists in the fact that a great deal of our day is spent sharing and responding to signs.

b. A symbol points beyond itself and has a deeper meaning.

As human beings, we have an ability to look beyond the immediate sign to its deeper meaning. When we are able to do this, we refer to such a sign as a symbol. For example, the tears of the doctor in the opening story tell us more than the external sign of drops of water staining his face. We can look beyond the tears and see in them an expression of the doctor's love for the child and the family. This ability to look beyond the signs to their deeper meaning is important to our understanding of the sacraments.

Because symbols have a far deeper meaning than signs, we can never use the expression that something is "just a symbol." In reality, a symbol has the power to move beyond a sign and to make present a far deeper meaning than any external sign.

One of our insights into the personality of Jesus comes through our human ability to look beyond signs. In one of the miracle stories found in the Gospel of Luke, Jesus raises a widow's son from the dead (Luke 7:11–17). We can marvel at the wonderful powers of Jesus, but we also read the deeper meaning of the healing—the compassion of Jesus. Luke writes, "The Lord was moved with pity upon seeing her . . ." (Luke 7:13). Because the author was able to look beyond the external signs of touching and healing, he was able to see the action as a symbol of Christ's loving compassion.

c. Jesus is a symbol of God's presence among us.

The life of Jesus tells us not only about himself, but it also tells us about an aspect of God's love and concern for all people. Jesus is God, and when he became flesh, he gave us an opportunity to truly meet and understand the presence of God in our midst. Revelation in the Scriptures not only tells us some deep mysteries about the nature of God, but it also tells us about the personal love and compassion of God for all people.

104

In the Gospel of John, Philip comes before Jesus and says to Jesus, "Lord, let us see the Father and then we shall be satisfied" (John 14:8). Jesus' reply shows that he is a symbol of God's presence here on earth. Jesus tells Philip, "Have I been with you all this time, Philip, and you still do not know me? To have seen me is to have seen the Father" (John 14:9). As we look back through the Scriptures we see the love of God reflected in the life of God's son, Jesus. We see the power and compassion of God, we see the forgiveness of God, we see the concern of God. In the gospel portrayal of Jesus, we see a symbol of God's presence in the world.

d. The Church is a symbol of Christ's continued presence in the world.

The New Testament book of the Acts of the Apostles tells us about the ascension of Christ and the message given to his followers on that occasion. We read, "They were still gazing up into the heavens when two men dressed in white stood beside them. 'Men of Galilee,' they said, 'why do you stand here looking up at the skies? This Jesus who has been taken from you will return, just as you saw him go up into the heavens' " (Acts 1:10–11). The episode marks the end of Christ's appearance in visible form on earth, and it looks forward to the day of the second coming of Christ. In the meanwhile, the Church must continue to make the world realize that Jesus still lives in the world through its members.

The New Testament continues to remind us of this presence of Christ in the Church. St. Paul speaking of the Church as the Body of Christ wrote, "Now you together are Christ's body; but each of you is a different part of it" (1 Corinthians 12:27). As we read earlier, when Paul was persecuting the Church, Jesus appeared to Paul. "He fell to the ground and then he heard a voice saying, 'Saul, Saul, why are you persecuting me?' 'Who are you, Lord?' he asked, and the voice answered, 'I am Jesus, and you are persecuting me' " (Acts 9:4–5). The Church has the mission to proclaim, live and share the gifts of Jesus Christ. In this way the Church is a symbol of Christ's presence here on earth.

e. The Church uses signs to bring about a deeper relationship between God and all people.

By using water, oil, bread, and other familiar items from life and by prayers, the Church, a visible channel for God's blessings, establishes a relationship with the individual, the community, and God. Because the Church gives these signs a meaning which extends far beyond their external appearances, we can properly call them symbols.

2. What is a sacrament?

a. One characteristic of a sacrament is that it is a sacred and symbolic action.

Because of his close relationship with the family, the doctor's tears in the introduction to this chapter expressed a feeling that already existed within the doctor. His tears did not make him love the child; they simply expressed a love that already existed. For the mother of the child, the tears conveyed a deep message. Through them, she knew of the doctor's love for the child.

In the sacraments, Christ uses symbolic actions which not only tell us of the love God has for us, but they actually bring about a change in the relationship between ourselves and God. God loves us, and through the external symbolic actions, such as, for example, flowing water and prayers prayed at baptism, we know of this love. In the very expression of this love, a change takes place. The symbolic actions not only express what is happening; they are making it happen. This is one aspect of a sacrament.

b. Another characteristic of a sacrament is that it consists in an intimate encounter with Christ.

Our lives are filled with intimate encounters. Whenever we meet someone whom we have come to love, we experience an intimate encounter. As we draw closer to a person, we become more informal and free in our expressions. We call that person by his or her first name (or nick name), and we tell that person details of our lives which we would not share with others. In time, a man and woman may decide to join together in marriage, and the intimacy which they once enjoyed now becomes a deeper intimacy. They share in life as husband and wife.

Our life is filled with encounters, but most of them lack the intimacy found in loving friendships. Even among friends, the depth of the encounter differs because the intimacy differs. A married couple share a deeper encounter (because of their intimacy) than two friends working at the same place. With Jesus, our encounter can become most intimate; we can actually become one with him.

Through a sacrament, we are called to the deepest type of intimacy. Through a sacrament, Jesus invites us to call out to God the Father in the same informal way that he himself addresses his Father. Jesus calls his Father, "Abba," which is properly translated "Daddy," and he invites us to do the same. Our intimate encounter with Christ in a sacrament is so deep that we become one with Christ. It consists in an encounter at its deepest level, an encounter not able to be reached through our human powers alone. In addressing God the Father as Abba, we have only one example among many of the meaning of the intimate encounter which we have with Christ in a sacrament.

A true encounter moves in two directions. It expresses a gift and a response. In a sacrament, God's care and concern comes to us through Christ, and it brings us closer to Christ and to one another in Christ. This intimate encounter with Christ is a second characteristic of a sacrament.

c. Another characteristic of a sacrament is that it is an action which comes to us from Christ and is celebrated through the Church.

In the past, some viewed sacraments as "things." Sacraments are not things, but living, symbolic "actions" by which Christ touches us in a most intimate manner. The sacraments come from Christ and are celebrated by the Church. These actions which make up the intimate encounter are truly celebrations of God's love given to us through Christ. In stating that the sacraments are symbols of God's love and care for us, we should not reduce sacraments to a single moment. Because they are actions, they touch every aspect of our lives. The time during which we celebrate this special encounter with Christ, that is, the period of celebrating the sacrament, is not a passing moment, but a new beginning whereby we deepen our relationship with God through Christ.

d. A sacrament has the threefold effect of recalling the past, bringing it into the present, and giving us hope for the future.

The sacraments have their roots in the death, resurrection, and ascension of Jesus. Each of the sacraments recalls what Jesus has done for us, and they bring this gift of Jesus' life into the present. Because this gift is always present and living, sacraments give us hope for a life lived in union with Christ. Although centuries have passed since Jesus' public ministry, the sacraments continually remind us that his ministry is still active and living in every one of us who shares in these gifts of the sacraments. Each sacramental celebration brings the past, the present, and the future together in Christ.

e. A sacrament can be defined as an intimate encounter with Christ, which comes to us through living symbols of God's loving care, and which is celebrated by the Church.

A sacrament is a mystery, and we will never fully understand its meaning. Any attempt to define a sacrament will always fall far short of the true mystery, but we must always strive to express the mystery in our limited way so that we can have some understanding of this great gift which comes from Christ.

3. Why do we refer to the presence of Jesus Christ and the Church as sacraments?

a. Jesus Christ is considered a sacrament in the broader sense because he gives us an image of the living God.

When Jesus told Philip that the one who sees him sees the Father, he was speaking of a visible presence of God the Father as shown through the presence of the Son, Jesus, here on earth. The life of Jesus not only pointed to the living God, but it brought about an intimate encounter with God for all people. Since there is only one God, and since Jesus is God, we conclude that Jesus not only tells us about God's presence here on earth, but that Jesus *is* God's presence. Just as a sacrament not only tells us about a presence, but actually brings about that active presence, so Jesus is not merely telling us that God is present; he is God's living presence among us. As human beings, we are able to look beyond the external, physical appearance of Jesus and understand his true meaning in our lives and in all of creation.

In the Gospel of John, we read the words of Jesus who proclaims this oneness with God. Jesus says, "Whoever puts faith in me believes not so much in me as in him who sent me; and whoever looks on me is seeing him who sent me" (John 12:44–45). With our human ability to look beyond the external signs, we recognize in the presence of Jesus the one who sent him.

b. The Church is considered a sacrament in the broader sense because it gives us a living image of Jesus' presence among us.

In the Church, we have Christ's living presence within the world. In his letter to the Corinthian community, Paul speaks of all members of the Church being united with one another as the one body of Christ. He tells them that they become one in Christ through the gift of baptism. Paul writes, "The body is one and has many members, but all members, many though they are, are one body; and so it is with Christ. It was in one Spirit that all of us, whether Jew or Greek, slave or free, were baptized into one body" (I Corinthians 12:12–13).

4. Where does a sacrament take place?

a. A sacrament takes place within the Christian community called Church.

To fully understand the sacraments, we must understand the idea of community as mentioned in the previous chapter on Church. The Church is the living symbol of the continued presence of Christ here on earth. Through this living community, Christ is able to reach out and touch each new person by certain symbols. A community called Church shares Christ's gifts through the sacraments and grows closer to Christ as each member shares more fully in the sacraments. Each sacrament becomes a community event, a community celebration, and no sacrament can be said to be a private encounter between an individual and God. Even when celebrated privately, the community shares in the richness of a deepened relationship with God. The gifts flowing from the sacraments enrich the community.

b. A sacrament takes place within a community worship service which is called "liturgy."

As members of the Church, through symbols and ceremonies, we join with Christ in worshipping God the Father. These symbols and ceremonies by which we join with Christ in the Church are called sacred liturgy. In other words, liturgy is the public worship of God the Father by Christ and his people through his Church. Liturgy in the Catholic Church includes all the sacraments. Through the sacraments we join more fully with Christ in worshiping God the Father. Even when celebrated privately, we refer to a sacrament as liturgy.

c. Because a sacrament is a community event, Catholics should strive to share in the sacrament at a time when the community is present.

A sacrament should bring joy, not only to the one celebrating the reception of the sacrament, but to the whole community. As each new member shares in a deeper relationship with God, the whole community shares in some way in that deeper relationship. The image of the Body of Christ brings this out when Paul writes ". . . if one part is given special honor, all parts enjoy it" (1 Corinthians 12:26). Proper liturgy demands that internal and spiritual joys should be expressed in some external form. If the community rejoices and grows through the celebration of sacraments by individual members, then the whole community should gather together to live the symbol of this sharing. Whenever possible, a sacrament should be celebrated when the greatest number of the community could come together to celebrate the sacrament.

5. How many sacraments are there?

a. There are seven sacraments through which we recognize God's continuous concern for our lives.

Although each one of us is a unique and individual person, we share much in common. We are born; we eat to live; we age, passing through different crises or phases of life as we do so; we face anxiety in life, sometimes guilt and failure; we are challenged to act in a responsible manner; we choose to marry or remain single; we choose to relate to God in our lives in many different ways; we suffer physical or mental pain; we face the inevitable fact that someday we will die, and we live in a large human family made up of relatives, friends, and people of other neighborhoods and countries whom we will never meet. God knows that we must face these and other aspects of life as we journey from birth to resurrection. The sacraments remind us that we are not making this journey alone.

The sacraments, by touching us at significant points in our lives, remind us that Jesus is always present to our life. Through the Sacraments of Baptism, Confirmation and Eucharist, we are initiated into the family of Christ. In these sacraments we are reminded of Christ's continual activity in our everyday life. Through the celebration of baptism, confirmation and Eucharist, a person becomes one of the faithful. For that reason, we call these sacraments by the name, "Sacraments of Initiation."

In the Sacrament of Reconciliation, we recognize that we can hurt our relationship with God, our neighbor, and ourselves and we seek to reconcile ourselves to God and the community through this sacrament. In the Sacrament of Marriage, we acknowledge the joys as well as the difficulties of family life, and we call upon Christ to be present in an active way within the family. In the Sacrament of Holy Orders, we recognize our call to be a worshipping community, and our need for order and leadership in worship and spreading the Word of God. In the Sacrament of Anointing of the Sick, we recognize that some of us will experience the pain of sickness or disease in our lives, and that we need the special help of God and the community in this time of anxiety.

b. Through these significant moments in our life God shows concern.

The power and help of the sacraments flow from these special moments into our daily lives. They affect everything we do. They tell us that God does not leave us alone on the earth but that God is continually working in, with, and through us. They remind us that we continually share in the power and gifts of Jesus Christ. Through these sacred symbols, the sacraments, Christ shares with us in a visible way, symbols of his continual, living presence.

6. What is the "Rite of Christian Initiation of Adults"?

a. The Rite of Christian Initiation of Adults, known by many as the "RCIA," refers to the process used by those people entering the Catholic Church.

In question five of this chapter, we mentioned that the Sacraments of Baptism, Confirmation, and Eucharist are called the "Sacraments of Initiation." When a person has shared in these three sacraments, that person is one of the faithful in the Catholic Church. Before adults share in these sacraments, however, they begin a journey or a process whereby they gradually enter into the understanding of Christ and his Church. During this journey, they pass through periods of sharing their own experiences, reflecting upon the Scriptures (with special emphasis on the Gospels) and the teachings of the Church. At certain stages along the way, these adults enter more fully into the daily life of the Church.

b. In the RCIA process, there are four periods and three stages.

In the early Church, the Christians used a Greek word meaning "to teach" to refer to the process used for those seeking to become members of the faithful. They used the name "catechumenate" and those who were going through the process were called "catechumens."

In *Journeying through the RCIA* (by William A. Anderson, Dubuque, IA: Wm. C. Brown Publishing Company, 1984), we find a short description of the periods and stages used in the RCIA process:

Period I: Precatechumenate: The journey begins long before the participants come together to share in the formal process. By the time they enter this period, the participants might already have become aware of the action of the Holy Spirit in their lives. During

111

this period, they share their experiences and ask questions about the Catholic family. They reflect upon the Scriptures and tell their own stories of faith in relation to the Scriptures. After an extensive period of time, they are ready to enter the first stage of their journey.

Stage I: Rite of the Catechumenate: The participants now arrive at their first step or stage on the journey as they seek to become members of the Church. Through a special rite, they ask to be accepted into the Catholic family and the Church accepts them as candidates. They are now called catechumens.

Period II: Catechumenate: The candidates begin a journey which takes them through a time of sharing and reflecting upon the Scriptures and the teachings of the Church.

Stage II: Rite of Election: When the Church is satisfied that the candidates have shown a sincere desire to become one with the community and have undergone a long period of instruction, it calls them to a new stage of spiritual preparation. At this time, the candidates commit themselves to such a preparation.

Period III: Enlightenment: During this time of spiritual preparation, the readings from the Liturgy of the Word for each Sunday become the basis for spiritual reflection for the candidates.

Stage III: Rite of Initiation: At this stage, the candidates enter the community of the faithful through the Sacraments of Initiation which are baptism, confirmation, and Eucharist. This rite is ordinarily celebrated during the Easter Vigil Liturgy.

Period IV: Mystagogia: Throughout the weeks which follow, the newly initiated meet together to share their experiences of the sacraments and the Church. During this period, they also select their service or activity toward the Christian community or the Church.

The periods and stages of the RCIA often appear too lengthy to some who believe that becoming a member of the Church should be a simple matter of only a few months. When we understand the great gifts and responsibilities involved in being a Christian, we can easily understand why any preparation should be long. Some of these gifts were named by Peter on the morning of the first Pentecost when he spoke to a large crowd of people gathered together in Jerusalem for the feast. Peter quotes from the Old Testament prophet, Joel, who tells of the changes that take place in those guided by the spirit. Peter tells us:

Instead this is what the prophet Joel spoke about:
"This is what I will do in the last days," God says: "I will pour out my Spirit on everyone. Your sons and daughters will proclaim my message; your young men will see visions, and your old men will dream dreams. Yes, even on my servants, both men and women, I

will pour out my Spirit in those days, and they will proclaim my message, I will perform miracles in the sky above and wonders on the earth below" (Acts 2:16–19).

c. This process is an adaptation of a process used in the early Church for those who wished to become members of the Catholic faithful.

In the early Church, a candidate, seeking entrance into the community of the Church, would pass through several stages of preparation before entering fully into the community. The Church today has reached back to its roots in its desire to prepare properly, adults seeking to share in the community of the Church. In planning the ritual for the various steps on the journey into full communion with the Church, the Church also looks for a renewal within the community, preparing itself to receive this new member. While the candidate is making his or her spiritual journey into the community, the community is urged to renew its commitment in faith and love to Christ and his Gospel.

7. What are sacramentals?

a. Sacramentals are blessings, prayers or blessed objects designated as sacred in a unique way by the Church.

Catholics perform many actions that are unknown in other faiths. As they enter the Church, they bless themselves with holy water. They wear blessed medals around their necks, keep blessed statues in their homes and finger "rosary beads" as they pray. The priest makes a motion of the symbol of the cross over a person who requests a blessing. On Ash Wednesday, Catholics stroll the avenues with a dab of black ash on their foreheads. On Palm Sunday, they come from Church with palm branches for their homes. Their celebration of sacraments is surrounded with anointings and prayers that do not directly affect the celebration of the sacrament. The Church calls these actions, blessings, prayers, and blessed objects "sacramentals." These include only a few of the many sacramentals in the Church. The purpose of a sacramental is to show, in a visible way, the continued action of Christ among us. They differ from sacraments in so far as they flow from the Church rather than from Christ. The sacraments come down to us from the life and message of Jesus Christ. In its holiness the Church places certain merit upon other visible actions to share the same message of Christ's continued presence and gifts among us. The sacraments are far more important than the sacramentals, but the sacramentals should serve to make the sacraments more meaningful to all of us.

113

b. *Sacramentals must not be used in a superstitious way.*

Because a person wears a blessed medal around his or her neck does not mean that he or she will be able to take risks with a hope of never being hurt. Sacramentals are ways of honoring the saints or sharing in special blessings from the Church. To use them in a superstitious way is to use them in a way never intended by the Church. For example, to feel that sacramentals would miraculously keep a reckless driver from having an accident is a false, superstitious use of a sacramental. We should treat sacramentals with respect, realizing that they have been set aside in a special way by the Church to bring about Christ's blessings through the Church.

Conclusion

When Billy grew to adulthood, he entered an overseas medical program to help the poor receive medical attention. The doctor who saved Billy's life proudly commented on his part in saving the boy's life. He felt that he had a share in the good work Billy was doing.

God is continually saving us in some spiritual way in our lives. When God offers gifts to us, God does not give them for ourselves alone. God wants us to share these gifts to build up the world. God sees in us an extension of the work of Christ here on earth. When we act, Christ acts; when we build, Christ builds; when we share, Christ shares. Through the sacraments God touches us in a very special, intimate way so that we may reach out and touch others with the gifts of Christ's love.

For Scripture reflection and discussion concerning this chapter, see Journeying in His Light, *"The Sacraments and Love."*

Sacraments of Initiation, Part 1: Baptism

Introduction

Many towns in the United States are named after families that originally owned the land and all the stores in the town. One town in the midwest, however, bears the name of the family that settled in the town with nothing but a wagon, a horse, and some scrap furniture. The family had originally intended to move on farther West, but the friendly welcome they received in the town soon changed their minds. The mother and father, along with the five boys ranging in age from thirteen to three, found a plot of land outside the town and began to farm the land. Within three years, the family suffered tragedies: first, the father was killed by a runaway horse, then rains completely washed away any hope for a harvest. The older boys went to work in town to raise enough money for more seed. The townspeople joined forces to bring food to the family so that they could save their money for seed. Within three more years, the boys had saved enough for more seed and had reaped a successful harvest. They, in turn, invited some of the poor of the town to come to their farm and take what they needed. As their farm continued to produce, an invitation went out once each year to all the poor of the town. The boys even began to plan extra plantings to care for the poor. Although the family never owned a store in the town and had very little invested in the town bank, the townspeople wished to preserve the memory and spirit of such good people. A special town meeting was called and the townspeople voted to change the name of their town to the name of this family. As a testimony to some good people who settled in that area, the name of the family still lives on in this small midwest town.

In this chapter, we reflect on the Sacrament of Baptism. Through baptism, we receive a new family name in memory of the Person of Jesus Christ who died and was raised that we might live. We receive the name

Christian through this sacrament, and once we receive this name, the world depends upon us to keep the memory and spirit of Jesus Christ alive in the lives of all people.

1. What is the Sacrament of Baptism?

a. Baptism is a sacrament that brings us into a new life in union with Christ and the Christian community.

To the members of the early Church, the manner of baptizing signified their belief in what was happening. The one being baptized would step down into a pool of water and be completely submerged in the water. He or she would then come out of the water (usually on the other side of the pool) as a symbol of his or her entry into a new life. This was considered an entry into the death and resurrection of Christ. In the letter to the Romans, Paul expresses the belief behind this practice when he writes:

For surely you know that when we were baptized into union with Christ Jesus, we were baptized into union with his death. By our baptism then, we were buried with him and shared his death, in order that, just as Christ was raised from death by the glorious power of the Father, so also we might have a new life. For since we have become one with him in dying as he did, in the same way we shall be one with him by being raised to life as he was (Romans 6:3-5).

Just as Christ entered a new life through his resurrection, so a person enters a new life in union with Christ and the Christian community through baptism.

b. Baptism is one of the Sacraments of Initiation into the Catholic Church.

At the outset of the baptismal ceremony, the sign of the cross is made on the forehead of the person entering the Church, and the presider, in the name of the community, welcomes the one being baptized into the community. Through the Sacrament of Baptism, a person becomes a member of the Christian community, and shares in the gifts and duties of the community. Because the community commits itself to the newly baptized at the time of the baptism, and because the newly baptized, in turn, commits himself or herself to the community, the Church urges that the ceremony take place in the presence of the assembled community.

116

In speaking to the Corinthian community, Paul reminds them that they all belong to the one body of the Church through their baptism. We read, "The body is one and has many members, but all the members, many though they are, are one body; and so it is with Christ. It was in one Spirit that all of us . . . were baptized into one body" (I Corinthians 12:12–13).

c. Baptism is a sacrament which brings us into the reign of God.

When Jesus began his mission, he proclaimed, "The reign of God is at hand! Reform your lives and believe in the Gospel" (Mark 1:15). With the coming of Jesus and his death, resurrection, and ascension, the reign of God became a living reality on earth. The people of the Old Testament saw God as reigning over all, but, with Jesus, this reign entered the world in a new way. Through union with Jesus, a person enters the reign of God.

When Nicodemus, a Pharisee, sought instruction from Jesus during the secret hours of the night, Jesus told him, "I solemnly assure you, no one can see the reign of God unless he is begotten from above" (John 3:3). Nicodemus asked if a person could then enter his mother's womb and be born again, but Jesus explained this new birth into God's reign in a special way. Jesus told him, "I solemnly assure you, no one can enter into God's kingdom without being begotten of water and Spirit" (John 3:5). In this text, Jesus is not speaking of life hereafter, but he is speaking of the reign of God which is existing on earth and which will reach its fulfillment in eternity. Unless a person is born of water and the Spirit, he or she does not enter this special union with Christ, known as the reign of God even on earth.

Although the Church reveals the presence of the reign of God on earth in a visible way, we cannot say that the Church and the reign of God are one and the same. The Church belongs to the reign of God on earth, but the Church does not exhaust the total meaning of the reign of God. Through baptism, a person not only enters the Church, but also the reign of God which is "at hand." Through their lives, baptized Christians make the reign of God a continual, living reality on earth.

d. Baptism is a sacrament by which all one's sins are forgiven.

Since baptism signifies a dying to one's old life and a rising to new life, it also signifies death to all sin which had control over our life in the past. In union with Christ, a person enters a new life of grace. In Paul's second letter to the Corinthians, we read, ". . . if anyone is in

117

Christ, he is a new creation. The old order has passed away; now all is new! All this has been done by God, who has reconciled us to himself through Christ . . ." (2 Corinthians 5:17–18). The use of water in the sacrament further underlines this idea of leaving the slavery of sin behind. Just as the Israelites passed from slavery to new life through the waters of the great sea, so we pass from sin to new life through the waters of baptism.

e. Baptism is a sacrament which draws us into a new covenant with God through Christ.

In the Old Testament, God made a covenant with Abraham, Isaac, Jacob, Moses, and other great leaders of ancient Israel. This promise was the hope and expectation of all the Hebrew people from the time of Abraham, and they looked toward the coming of the Messiah. Christians believe that the Messiah came in the person of Jesus Christ, and that union with Christ and his Church through baptism draws one into this covenant made with Abraham and his successors. In his letter to the Galatians, Paul tells us:

"You were baptized into union with Christ, and now you are clothed, so to speak, with the life of Christ himself. So there is no difference between Jews and Gentiles, between slaves and free men, between men and women; you are all one in union with Christ Jesus. If you belong to Christ, then you are the descendants of Abraham and will receive what God has promised" (Galatians 3:27–29).

Just as we have two parties to every covenant and certain promises and responsibilities on the part of both, we must recognize that the baptized not only share in the many gifts of Christ, but that they also have certain responsibilities to fulfill as Christians.

2. What is our responsibility as baptized Christians?

a. As baptized Christians, we are called to worship God the Father in the name of Jesus.

An expression commonly used in some areas is "the priesthood of the faithful." Through baptism, all Christians share in this gift of Christ's priesthood. We should not confuse the term "priesthood of the faithful" with the "ordained priesthood" which refers to those who have celebrated the Sacrament of Holy Orders. The priesthood into which all are baptized reminds them that they have a call to worship God in the name of Christ. The Church attempts to help the faithful realize this gift by urging them to active participation in worship, through singing, praying, and serving in specific ministries during worship. In becoming one with Christ, a Christian shares in the gift of Jesus' priesthood.

b. As baptized Christians, we are called to share in the mission of spreading the Word of God.

In the baptism of a child, the priest touches the child's ears and mouth, praying that the child will hear God's Word and speak God's Word. The duty of sharing this Word of God is given to the disciples and all the Church in Jesus' words at the time of his ascension. Jesus tells his disciples, "Teach them [all nations] to carry out everything I have commanded you. And know that I am with you always, until the end of the world" (Matthew 28:20). As people who hear and spread the message of Christ, we share in the gift of Jesus as prophet.

c. As baptized Christians, we are called to serve those in need.

Paul saw his mission as one which continued the service of Christ on earth. He writes, "In my own flesh, I fill up what is lacking in the suffering of Christ for the sake of his body, the church" (Colossians 1:24). Jesus showed his concern for others during his life, and he was willing to suffer for others. Paul recognizes that his own suffering continues the presence of Christ on earth in service to others. Jesus gave us an example of service in washing the feet of the twelve at the Last Supper, and he told a story of service in the parable of the Good Samaritan who cared for a man who was robbed and beaten. Jesus is considered a king, but his reign differs from worldly reigns. Jesus' kingship is shown in service. In writing to the Galatians, Paul tells them, ". . . remember that you have been called to live in freedom—but not a freedom that gives free reign to the flesh. Out of love, place yourselves at one another's service" (Galatians 5:13). Through service to others, we share in the gift of Christ as king.

d. Through the Sacrament of Baptism, a Christian must confront all divisiveness and sin in the world and work toward unity.

Just as Jesus came to confront the power of evil and to bring the world into one in himself, so the newly baptized must work toward the same goal. The Christian must continually make evil uncomfortable in the

119

world, never allowing an evil attitude toward life to overcome the message of Christ. Through his death and resurrection, Jesus overcame the power of evil in the world, and the Christian must use the gifts of baptism to continue this confrontation of evil.

In overcoming evil, the Christian continually works toward a unity of love in the world. The Christian realizes that all are called to be one in Christ, and with the assurance of Christ's guidance, the Christian must work toward this unity. In Paul's letter to the Ephesians, we read, "There is but one body and one Spirit, just as there is but one hope given to all of you by your call. There is one Lord, one faith, one baptism; one God and Father of all, who is over all, and works through all, and is in all" (Ephesians 4:4–6).

3. Who may be baptized?

a. All adults who have not yet shared in the Sacrament of Baptism and who believe that Jesus Christ is the Son of God become human and who wish to follow his message as lived through the Catholic Church, may receive the Sacrament of Baptism in the Catholic Church.

Before adults celebrate the Sacrament of Baptism, they must first profess their belief in Jesus Christ as the living Son of God, come as man, and now resurrected and ascended to the Father. They must also profess a belief in the Holy Roman Catholic Church and commit themselves to live out the teachings of Christ as reflected in the Church. The community renews its vows along with the candidates. When Peter finished preaching to the crowd on Pentecost, they believed that Jesus was the Messiah, and they asked Peter what they must do. Peter answered, "You must reform and be baptized, each one of you, in the name of Jesus Christ, that your sins may be forgiven; then you will receive the gift of the Holy Spirit" (Acts 2:38).

b. A person already baptized in another Christian faith who wishes to enter the Catholic faith cannot be baptized again unless there is a reasonable doubt concerning the fact of the first baptism.

If a person has shared in baptism in a Christian Church under the formula, "I baptize you in the name of the Father and of the Son and of the Holy Spirit" and has received sprinkling, pouring of water or immersion in water, then that person has celebrated a true baptism. In carrying out these words and using these actions, other Christian Churches are acting in unity with the message of Christ as understood by the Catholic Church. Once we receive the Sacrament of Baptism we cannot receive this sacrament a second time. A previously baptized person wishing to enter the Catholic faith must make a profession of faith before the community. In case of doubt, the priest confers this sacrament in a conditional way, that is, he adds the words, "if you are not already baptized, I baptize you in the name of the Father and of the Son and of the Holy Spirit."

c. Parents who are faithfully living out their baptismal commitment may have their child baptized in the Church.

At the time of the child's baptism, the parents take upon themselves the responsibility of sharing the faith with their child both by practicing the faith and by providing a Catholic up-bringing and education of the child. If the parents are not willing to fulfill this obligation, the minister of the sacrament should delay the baptism of this child. In conferring all sacraments, the minister must have some positive hope that the baptized person will understand and live out the calling of that sacrament. If the parents are baptized and show no concern in living out their baptismal vows, the minister may conclude that the child will not receive a proper education in the living out of the baptismal promises. In this case, the minister of this sacrament should delay the baptism.

d. Any child in danger of death may be baptized.

Although an adult in danger of death must show some desire to receive the sacrament, a child cannot show such a desire. In danger of death, a child should be baptized. In this case, the religious conscience of the parents should be considered.

4. Who may baptize?

a. In the Catholic Church the ordained minister is the ordinary minister of the Sacrament of Baptism.

Because baptism is a community event even when the major part of the community is not present, the ordained minister, as representative of the community, should confer this sacrament of initiation into the Church community. A priest or deacon, both ordained ministers, share this ministry of baptizing in the name of the Church. The minister of this sacrament is responsible for the proper preparation for the sacrament. Instruction or preparation should precede the celebration of this sacrament. Parents should plan far enough in advance so that the priest or deacon may arrange some time for instruction and preparation for this Sacrament of Baptism.

b. In danger of death, anyone may baptize.

If a person foresees that death may occur before the proper minister of the Church can arrive, that person may baptize. If the person in danger of death is an adult, he or she must make some sign of desiring the sacrament. A person may not baptize oneself. A simple way of baptizing is to pour the water on the forehead of the person to be baptized or on any part of the body that might be exposed while pronouncing the words, "I baptize you in the name of the Father and of the Son and of the Holy Spirit."

5. What happens to those who are not baptized?

a. If a person believes that Jesus Christ is God become human, that he shared his sacraments and message with us through the Church, and that we are obliged to receive the Sacrament of Baptism, that person has an obligation to receive the sacrament.

Jesus invites us to follow him. For those who recognize this invitation as coming through the Sacrament of Baptism, the sacrament becomes an obligation. To refuse this sacrament while realizing the obligation is to commit a serious sin against God. It is to turn down Christ's invitation "to come follow" him. For those who seem to believe that this sacrament is necessary, yet do not respond, we cannot easily judge their motivation, nor can we easily say that they have sinned. Perhaps their belief is not as strong as it appears on the surface.

b. A person who does not know Jesus Christ, or does not know or believe the necessity of baptism, but follows conscience as perfectly as possible is not obliged to receive the Sacrament of Baptism for salvation.

Many wonderful and good Jewish people will never share in baptism since their faith does not believe in the necessity of this sacrament. These people and others who lead a good life without seeing the necessity of baptism are not obliged to receive this sacrament. If these people truly believed in the necessity of baptism, they would most likely receive the sacrament. Some have called this "baptism of desire." In the early Church we read of cases where people who had not yet received the Sacrament of Baptism died for Christ. Some claimed that these people received "Baptism of Blood." Neither the baptism of desire nor the baptism of blood can be considered a sacramental baptism. The sacrament demands the signs of water and the saying of the words of baptism.

c. The Scriptures do not tell us what happens to infants who die without the Sacrament of Baptism.

As we mentioned earlier in the chapter, Jesus told Nicodemus concerning baptism, "I solemnly assure you, no one can enter into God's kingdom without being begotten of water and the Spirit" (John 3:5). The Church accepts this text as assuring the immediate entrance into heaven of a child who dies after baptism, since the child has committed no personal sin. The Scriptures, however, say nothing about the child who dies without the Sacrament of Baptism. In the past, the text "no one can enter into God's kingdom" seemed to exclude a nonbaptized child from the external happiness of heaven. But the Church now realizes that the kingdom of heaven is not just life hereafter, but life here on earth. To enter the community of the Church is to enter the reign of heaven here on earth. Because Christ could be referring to the Church in this text rather than life hereafter, we cannot speak of any rejection of a child who dies without the Sacrament of Baptism. Knowing a merciful and loving God, it is hard to accept a state of just natural happiness without God or even worse a state of eternal rejection. That these unbaptized children are invited to eternal happiness with God does not destroy the need for baptism. Baptism is celebrated that Christ may continue to work in the world through baptized Christians. Perhaps Scripture never intended to make such a strong statement about life hereafter as we have interpreted it.

6. What is a sponsor or godparent?

a. The Rite of Christian Initiation of Adults (RCIA) calls for a person to act as a sponsor on behalf of the Church.

As people make their journey into the faith, they will have many questions and a need to have some type of personal link with the parish family. Besides their relatives and friends who guide them in these areas, they should also have a sponsor, chosen by the parish family, to serve as a guide and spiritual companion during the period of catechumenate. The sponsor should have a good grasp of the Catholic Faith, have shown some involvement in the parish family and have an open manner of sharing personally with another. Besides acting as a companion during the discussion sessions, the sponsor accompanies the catechumens through the rituals of the RCIA, and can serve as a friend in introducing the catechumens to other members of the parish family. Some parishes have special sessions to prepare sponsors serving in this privileged role on behalf of the Church. The sponsor is called upon to witness to the readiness of those seeking membership in the Church.

b. Godparents are those who commit themselves to assisting the newly baptized, or (in the case of infants) parents of the newly baptized in their specific duties.

A person becomes a godparent through the special witness given at the time of the celebration of baptism. Although adults may choose to have their sponsors (chosen by the parish) as their godparents, many of them will have others from among their friends or relatives serve as godparents. Godparents for adults commit themselves to helping the newly baptized in their duty as Christians. Godparents for children do not commit themselves to the child, but to the parents of the newly baptized, stating that they are willing to help the parents in their duty as Christian parents.

c. Godparents and sponsors are to be Catholics in good standing and who have celebrated the three Sacraments of Initiation.

The godparents and sponsors should have a grasp of Catholic teaching; be living a life consistent with the faith and the responsibility of a godparent; be mature enough to fulfill this responsibility (a person sixteen-years-old or older is presumed to have the requisite maturity); be initiated with the Sacraments of Baptism, Confirmation and Eucharist; be neither the mother nor the father of the candidate; and, be canonically free to fulfill this office. Ordinarily, there are two godparents for a child, and one or two for an adult. At least one godparent is to be a Catholic and one who fulfills the requirements mentioned above. Another person, a baptized and believing Christian not belonging to the Catholic Church may serve as a Christian witness along with a Catholic godparent, if the parents so desire. In the ceremony, the godparents profess their faith with others, and promise to be witnesses to that faith.

7. Why is the sign of water chosen for the Sacrament of Baptism?

a. One of the uses of water in life is for cleansing.

In the Sacrament of Baptism, all sins of the adult candidate will be washed away. This symbol of cleansing from sin is considered a major symbol in the use of water in this sacrament. More recently the use of water has received its deeper scriptural meaning.

b. Water in the Scriptures often symbolizes sin or chaos or death.

In the beginning of the story of creation, we read that the world was a watery mass and everything was in chaos. Into this watery mass and chaos, God brought order by creating the world in six days. Later, in the same Book of Genesis, we read another story concerning water. God sends a flood upon a sinful world. Out of this water of the flood, new life emerges. From this sin comes a new creation in the person of Noah and his family. In the Book of Exodus, the people were caught in the chaos of slavery in Egypt, and God led them into the desert through the waters of the Red Sea. Christ begins his public life by going down into the waters, being baptized by John the Baptist. When Jesus hung upon the cross, the sign of new life occurred as the soldier ran a spear through his side, and blood and water flowed forth. Through these signs used in the Scriptures, the authors expressed the symbol of water as signifying death followed by new life. Water symbolizes sin, chaos, or death. Coming out of water shows an entry into a new life.

c. Water in baptism symbolizes a dying and rising with Christ.

In the early Church, people were baptized by stepping down into a pool of water. The deacon or deaconess would submerge the candidate and pronounce the words "I baptize you in the name of the Father and of the Son and of the Holy Spirit." A newly baptized person would then come out of the water sharing a new life, a new beginning. Baptism by immersion, that is, complete submersion in the water, is still used in the Church. Also used is the pouring of water upon the forehead of a person. It has the same symbol of dying and rising, going down into the water and coming out with a new life, life in union with Christ.

8.   How is the ceremony of baptism of a child performed in the Church today?

a.   The ceremony begins with a greeting by the minister, followed by a reminder to the parents and godparents of their obligations.

The parents, as primary teachers of the child, play a major role in the Sacrament of Baptism. They are reminded of their obligation of being parents of a Christian child. The godparents are reminded of their duty to give example to the child by their Christian way of life, to pray for the child, to help nurture the faith of the child, and to assist the parents in their duty as Christian parents.

b.   By the sign of the cross the Christian community welcomes the child into its presence.

The minister makes the sign of the cross on the child's forehead and invites the parents and godparents likewise to make the sign of the cross on the child. At this moment, the minister proclaims through prayer that the Christian community joyfully welcomes this child into its presence. We are reminded here that baptism is a community event, not merely a family event.

c.   An anointing with blessed oils on the breast of the child symbolizes the child's call to be Christ or the Anointed One.

Another name for Messiah or Christ is the Anointed One. By the use of the oil, the minister is proclaiming that this child shall be the anointed one or the new Christ in the world.

d.   The minister blesses the water to be used in the sacrament.

During the Easter Season, water blessed at the Easter Vigil should be used. This is to show that baptism is actually a Passover event, that is, a dying and a rising. Outside the Easter Season, the minister blesses the water at each ceremony. This symbolic use of water is a sign that the child is dying to its old life and rising to a new life in union with Christ.

e.   The parents and godparents along with the community present renew their baptismal vows.

Along with the community, the parents and godparents publicly profess their belief in God and their faith in the Church. When all have finished renewing their vows, the minister asks the parents:

Is it your will that N. should be baptized in the faith of the Church, which we have all professed with you?

Parents and godparents: *It is.*

f. The minister pours the water over the forehead of the child or immerses the child in the water and pronounces the words of Christ as given in the Scriptures.

At the moment of baptism, the minister calls the child by name and performs the baptismal rite as mentioned earlier.

g. After the baptism, the minister anoints the forehead of the child with the oil or sacred chrism.

Later on in life, the child will receive the Sacrament of Confirmation when the bishop uses the oil of sacred chrism to bless the child's forehead. The minister at this time shows the link between the Sacraments of Baptism and Confirmation. In the early Church, adults would come up out of the water after baptism, put on a white garment and come out into the church where the bishop would apply sacred oil. In time, bishops could not be present at all baptisms and this action of applying sacred oil became separated from the Sacrament of Baptism, namely, the Sacrament of Confirmation which we will speak of in a later chapter.

h. A white garment is placed on the child and a lighted candle is held by one of the parents.

The white garment or baptismal robe, as well as the lighted candle, symbolize that Christ has come into the world. The child has clothed himself or herself in Christ and the parents are told to keep the light of Christ burning brightly in the life of their child.

i. The minister touches the ears and the mouth of the child praying that the child will hear God's Word and preach God's Word.

Through the Sacrament of Baptism, we are called to discipleship. We are called to evangelize or to be a witness to Christ's message. Many have left this to the priest, ministers, or sisters in their particular Churches. But the duty to witness to the Gospel and to understand the gospel message comes to us through the Sacrament of Baptism.

j. The community joins along with parents and godparents in the prayer given by Christ by which we address God the Father in the most intimate way as "Our Father."

When Christ teaches the apostles how to pray he addresses God the Father under the Hebrew title of "Abba." The original meaning of this word could be translated more closely by the word "Daddy." It is an informal personal greeting of one's true father. Through the Sacrament of Baptism we now share so closely with Christ that we dare to say "Our Father" in a most personal relationship.

k. The ceremony ends with the blessing for the mother, then for the father and finally for all the baptized.

With words of thanks and a request for God's help in living as Christian parents, the minister blesses the mother and the father. The minister then asks that God bless all baptized Christians throughout the world that they may live more fully their baptismal calling to be Christ in the world.

Conclusion

The family in the introduction of this chapter moved into a town that welcomed them and eventually took their name. The sole reason for the change of the name was goodness and love. Jesus comes into our lives looking for a welcome. He never forces his way into our lives, but comes and, at times, waits. Through the Sacrament of Baptism, we welcome Jesus, and we begin to bear his name in the title *"Christian."* If the town that bore the name of this family ever forgot the spirit of the family and became self-centered and destructive, the family might wish that the town had not chosen to take their name. If we, as Christians, do not live up to the goodness, love, and sharing demanded in baptism, Jesus could wish that someone more deserving would have accepted his name through baptism. In the name and spirit of Christ, we receive his gifts and name at baptism and share these gifts in building God's world. This is our call in bearing the name of Christ.

For Scripture reflection and discussion concerning this chapter, see Journeying In His Light, *"Sacraments of Initiation, Parts 1 and 2."*

Sacraments of Initiation Part 2: Confirmation

Introduction

A playful five-year-old boy watched the smoke swirl up from his father's cigarette. He ran across the room to where his father sat, playfully cupped some of the smoke in his hands and ran off to the corner of the room with his treasure. He opened his hands in the corner and, to his surprise, he found no smoke in them. He immediately ran back to where his father sat smoking, cupped more smoke in his hands and slowly moved toward the corner as though he were carrying eggs. Again, he found no smoke when he opened his hands. He looked confused for a moment, but immediately ran off to play another game.

At times in our lives, we become like that playful five-year-old boy. We believe in God; we go to Church, and we try to treat our neighbor well. But events happen in life that try our faith and belief in a caring God. Like that child, we think we have our faith in the palm of our hands, but just when we open our hands to find it, it has eluded us. We believe in God, but where is God when an innocent child dies or a spouse dies? We believe in God, but why did we have to lose this particular job? We believe in God, but where is God in this world? The challenges come, and we open our hands looking for faith. Some of us find it, and some do not. To live as an adult Christian in the world takes more than courage, it takes a special gift of God. God shares a very special gift with us when God offers us the Sacrament of Confirmation. Christ is alive; Christ is loving; Christ is sharing—in us. The Sacrament of Confirmation enables us to open our hands and find our faith as well as witness to our faith. In confirmation, we live our baptism more fully.

129

1. What is the Sacrament of Confirmation?

a. Confirmation is one of the Sacraments of Initiation.

As we mentioned in the chapter on sacraments, the three Sacraments of Initiation are baptism, confirmation and Eucharist. Through these three sacraments, a person becomes one of the Catholic faithful. Through the Sacrament of Baptism, a person belongs to the community of the Catholic Church, but the Sacrament of Baptism is really the beginning of the journey into full sharing in the Church. Through confirmation and Eucharist, a person journeys into a deeper sharing in the gifts given by Christ to the Church.

In a document from the II Vatican Council, the Church insists that we recognize the Sacrament of Confirmation as one of the Sacraments of Initiation. The Church wanted this unity to be preserved when the new rite for confirmation was completed. In the Constitution on the Liturgy, we read, "The rite of Confirmation is to be revised . . . so that the intimate connection of this sacrament with the whole of the Christian initiation may more clearly appear" (II Vatican Council: Constitution on the Sacred Liturgy, No. 71).

b. The Sacrament of Confirmation emphasizes the full presence of the Holy Spirit in our lives.

In celebrating the sacrament, the presider prays that the newly confirmed person will receive the gift of the Holy Spirit. Although the Church recognizes that the ritual for the Sacrament of Confirmation draws us into a greater awareness of the Holy Spirit in our lives, we must be careful not to leave the impression that we are receiving the Spirit for the first time in confirmation. In the Sacrament of Baptism, we are baptized in the name of the Trinity (Father, Son, and Holy Spirit), and we have the Trinity dwelling in us. Through our baptism, we have received the gifts of the Spirit. Through confirmation, however, the Church pays special attention to these gifts of the Spirit and prays that we might enter more fully into a living unity with the Spirit. The emphasis on the gift of the Spirit coming to us at confirmation reminds us that the Spirit works in different ways at different times, and that all our human activities continually depend upon the activity of the Spirit in our lives.

c. The Sacrament of Confirmation confirms the presence of the baptismal gifts and calls us to live a Christian life in a responsible manner.

In reality, the Sacrament of Confirmation confirms the presence of the baptismal gifts in a person. In the past, we might have said that a person reaches a mature age and is then, as an adult, able to confirm one's commitment to God. This does not seem to have any foundation in history, even when the sacrament was part of the baptismal rite. A caution with such an emphasis lies in the danger that we might view baptism only as a sacrament of the moment, an entry into union with Christ and the community, rather than a life-long commitment to living a faithful Christian life. In baptism, we receive gifts of the Spirit which call us and enable us to witness to Christ in a mature manner in our daily lives. In confirmation we continue to share in these gifts of the Holy Spirit and the confirming or sealing means that this person continues to become a member of the community, sharing in its privileges and responsibilities for life.

d. The Sacrament of Confirmation emphasizes the unity of the Church in its mission.

When the bishop celebrates the Sacrament of Confirmation before the community, the rite reminds us that the Church reaches beyond our small community to the entire world. Even in cases where the priest confirms, the oil used for the anointing must be blessed by the bishop, thus, emphasizing unity. In witnessing in the name of the Church, the presider recalls that he does not speak for a small community of Christians, but for the universal Church. Because of this, a Christian is not free to preach his or her own message, but the message of Christ as given through the Church.

2. How did confirmation develop?

a. The early Church celebrated the sacrament now known as confirmation along with the Sacrament of Baptism.

The members of the early Church did not consider confirmation as a sacrament separate from baptism. The person was baptized, anointed by the bishop (confirmation) and brought to share in the Eucharist. The early records tell us how adults went through these steps to enter the Church community, and we must presume that the children somehow accompanied their parents through this process. In the early Church, whole families came into the community together.

The first records of the baptism of children are found in the early third century. A century later, the people of the world followed their emperor, Constantine, into Christianity and the baptism of children became more common. Many of the converts of this era became Christian for economic and political reasons, but many more sincerely became members of Christianity, and they would bring their children to the church for baptism.

The one being baptized would go down into a pool of water and the minister would submerge the person, using the words for baptism. The newly baptized would then come out of the water, put on a white robe, and come before the bishop and the assembled community. The bishop would place his hand on the head of the newly baptized, and anoint the person with oil, praying as he did so that the Holy Spirit would continue to work through the newly baptized. From these records, we realize that the bishop's action was not seen as something separate from the baptism, but as a continuation of the ritual of baptism.

b. By the fifth century, the role of the bishop became separated from the baptismal ceremony.

In the fifth century, the number of people entering Christianity was rapidly growing, and the bishops were no longer able to assist at every baptism. Another influence upon the number of baptisms, especially of infants, came from St. Augustine's teaching on original sin. St. Augustine claimed that a person needed baptism in order to enter eternal, spiritual happiness. Parents naturally wanted their children baptized as soon as possible. Eventually, the role of the bishop in the celebration of the Sacrament of Baptism changed.

The Christian Church of the East solved the problem by having the baptizing priest continue with the anointing ordinarily performed by the bishop. They saw this action and the celebration of the Eucharist as inseparable rites of initiation. The Christian Church of the West solved the problem by allowing the baptisms to take place without the presence of the bishop with the idea that the ministry of the bishop would take place at a later and more convenient time. Eventually, large crowds of people would gather whenever the bishop was present, and the bishop would lay hands on and anoint those who had not yet shared in this rite.

c. With the separation of the rite performed by the bishop from that of baptism, the rite performed by the bishop eventually came to be seen as the sacrament now known as confirmation.

Within the first thousand years after Christ, the rite performed by the bishop was gradually separated from the rite of baptism, and it received a new name, the "Sacrament of Confirmation." With the separation of the Sacrament of Confirmation from the Sacrament of Baptism, much study and discussion centered around the specific place that confirmation had in the Church. The conclusion was that the Sacrament of Confirmation is a special sacrament, flowing from baptism, but at the same time, distinct from the Sacrament of Baptism.

3. Who may administer the Sacrament of Confirmation?

a. The bishop ordinarily administers the Sacrament of Confirmation.

A bishop of a diocese has the right and duty to see to the confirmation of all members of his diocese. The auxiliary bishop (one who assists the bishop of the diocese) often helps the bishop in this duty and privilege. In places where there are a large number of people to receive this sacrament, the bishop may share with other priests the privilege of administering this Sacrament of Confirmation.

b. Adults who receive the Sacrament of Baptism or are received into the Church through a profession of faith are also confirmed at the time of entering the community.

The priest who baptizes or receives an adult into the Church through a profession of faith is also to confirm the new member of the community. Through this action, the adult immediately celebrates a full initiation into the Church at the time of professing communion with the Church. The Church shares this privilege of conferring confirmation with the priest for the sake of the new member and that person's full share in the community. If a child of grade school age is received into the Church and the child has not yet reached the acceptable age for confirmation as established by the bishop of the diocese, the priest may not confirm the child. But if the child has reached the acceptable age for confirmation, the child is baptized, confirmed, and celebrates first Holy Communion during the same Eucharistic celebration.

4. Who may be confirmed?

a. Before celebrating the Sacrament of Confirmation, a person must already have celebrated the Sacrament of Baptism.

The Sacrament of Baptism is the first Sacrament of Initiation and the sacrament which must be received before all others. Through the Sacrament of Baptism, the Holy Spirit establishes a new relationship with the new Christian. The Sacrament of Confirmation builds upon this gift of baptism. In order to share in a growth in the Spirit, a person must already have received the Spirit in one's life and be disposed toward this growth. In the Acts of the Apostles, we have a single incident which seems to say that baptism does not bring with it the gift of Spirit, but this incident must be read in relationship to other instances of Baptism in the Scriptures which speak of the gift of the Spirit at baptism. The incident, however, emphasizes the value of "laying on of hands," and is often used as an example of confirmation in the early Church. The Book of Acts tells us, "The apostles in Jerusalem heard that the people of Samaria had received the Word of God, so they sent Peter and John to them. When they arrived, they prayed for the believers that they might receive the Holy Spirit. For the Holy Spirit had not yet come down on any of them; they had only been baptized in the name of the Lord Jesus. Then Peter and John placed their hands on them, and they received the Holy Spirit" (Acts 8:14–17).

b. The candidate for the Sacrament of Confirmation.

In the United States, the bishop of each diocese is free to choose the age he feels most appropriate for this sacrament. In many dioceses of the United States, the age varies from late grade school to late high school. The Code of Canon Law states that a child must have reached at least the age of discretion, unless the conference of bishops determines another age. Outside the danger of death, it is required, if the person has the use of reason, that one be suitably instructed, be properly disposed and able to renew one's baptismal promises. In those dioceses which emphasize the call to adult Christianity as the basic meaning of the sacrament, the age for the celebration of the sacrament is usually somewhere between the end of the sixth grade and graduation from high school. In the Eastern Church children celebrate the Sacrament of Confirmation immediately after their baptism.

5. Who may be a sponsor for confirmation?

a. Sponsors must be baptized and confirmed Catholics who will help the candidates in the fulfillment of their Christian commitment.

Sponsors should help prepare the candidates for the sacrament and see that the candidates act as a true witness to Christ and faithfully fulfill the obligations that come with the sacrament. They accompany the candidates and present them to the priest or bishop for the reception of the sacrament. If the candidates are adults, they present themselves by name. Each sponsor must be a practicing, baptized Catholic who has celebrated the Sacraments of Baptism, Confirmation, and Holy Eucharist; be canonically free to carry out this office; has completed the sixteenth year; and may be either male or female for any candidate.

b. The godparents at baptism should, if possible, be chosen as sponsors at Confirmation.

Throughout the first part of this chapter, we spoke of the close link between the Sacrament of Baptism and the Sacrament of Confirmation. The liturgy should teach as well as share the blessings of Christ. The use of the same sponsors shows the close relationship between these two sacraments. Another reason for choosing the same sponsors arises from the sacraments themselves. Since confirmation is another aspect of initiation, the godparents in baptism should be the ones to continue the ministry of sponsoring in confirmation. Another way of showing a link between the Sacraments of Baptism and Confirmation occurs when the candidate chooses the same name for this sacrament as he or she chose or was given in baptism.

6. How is the Sacrament of Confirmation conferred?

a. The bishop or ordained priest places his hands on the head of those to be confirmed.

The gift of the Holy Spirit is often invoked in the Scriptures through the laying on of hands. The action of passing on the Spirit comes through this imposition of hands. The bishop or ordained priest makes a reference in prayer to the Sacrament of Baptism, showing the link between baptism and confirmation. He then prays that the candidate may receive the special gifts of the Holy Spirit:

> *Give them the spirit of wisdom and understanding,*
> *the spirit of right judgment and courage,*
> *the spirit of knowledge and reverence.*
> *Fill them with the spirit of wonder and awe in your presence.*
> *We ask this through Christ our Lord.*
> *R. Amen.*

b. The actual conferring of the sacrament takes place through the anointing with oil accompanied by the short prayer invoking the Holy Spirit.

The bishop dips his thumb in holy oils (a special perfumed oil known as *chrism*) and makes the sign of the cross on the forehead of the candidate to be confirmed. At the same time, he repeats the words:

> *N., be sealed with the Gift of the Holy Spirit.*
> The newly confirmed responds: *Amen.*

In this response, the newly confirmed is proclaiming acceptance of the hopes and of the responsibilities that this sacrament brings with it.

7. What are some ways of witnessing to the faith?

a. A person witnesses to the faith by openly professing and living out a belief in Jesus Christ.

Some people seem to apologize for their belief in God. We are called to profess openly our belief in Jesus through our life and through our words. We witness not only by speaking of Christ and his message but by living that message. For example, by treating our neighbor in a loving way, by reaching out to those in need, by accepting ridicule in the name of Christ, by being concerned for peace and justice throughout the world. Paul gave us an example of how we should witness to Christ when he said of himself, ". . . So I become all things to all men that I may save some of them by whatever means are possible. All this I do for the Gospel's sake in order to share in its blessings" (I Corinthians 9:22–23). When Paul found someone in need or someone who was weak, Paul acted as though he were the one in need or the weak person. For the sake of the Gospel, Paul shared in the sufferings and needs of all in order to help them.

136

b. We witness to Christ by speaking out against the social ills of our society.

Whenever a Christian sees the dignity of a human person destroyed by society, the Christian must speak out against these sins. A Christian must confront racism, poverty, and injustice. To be a witness is not to allow things to happen and say nothing, but rather to let our voice join with others so that we might all strive to raise up the human thinking of our society with the great concern for the dignity of God's human race.

In the Gospel of Matthew, we read a parable told by Jesus concerning the final judgement. In this parable, we learn that whatever is done to others is done to Christ. Jesus calls to heaven those who gave him food when hungry, drink when thirsty, shelter when homeless, clothing when naked, comfort when sick, and visits when imprisoned. He tells them that anyone who treated the least of his people in this way treated him in this way. For those who refused to treat those in need in this way, Jesus told them that they did not treat him in this way, and, therefore, they did not deserve eternal life. As we treat others, so we treat Jesus. This includes speaking up for the indignities heaped upon other human beings.

c. We witness to Christ when we reach out to our neighbor by daily acts of love.

Taking time to visit the sick and sharing with them a kind word, or taking time to sit down with a lonely person are ways of witnessing to Christ in the world. As we look through the Scriptures, we not only hear the message of Christ but we see the compassion of Christ. In the Sacraments of Baptism and Confirmation, we make Christ present in the world. The message of Christ and the compassion of Christ must continue in each one of us. Jesus called his disciples the light of the world, chosen to help others give praise to God through their actions. In the Gospel of Matthew, we read these words of Jesus, ". . . your light must shine before men so that they may see goodness in your acts and give praise to your heavenly Father" (Matthew 5:16).

8. Is the Church called to work toward justice in the world?

a. The Church is called to live and teach the gospel message of love of neighbor, and this love implies justice.

A Pharisee approached Jesus to ask which commandment of the law was the greatest. "Jesus answered, 'Love the Lord your God with all your heart, with all your soul, and with all your mind.' This is the greatest and most important commandment" (Matthew 22:37–38).

Justice demands that we recognize and respect the dignity and rights of our neighbor. When we do this, we are living out the call of Christ to "love our neighbor as we love ourselves." Shortly after Pope John Paul II was elected pope, he proclaimed that he would work to overcome oppression in the world. In his background, he could recall the indignity and lack of love that allowed leaders of governments to deprive people of their human rights. In his love and concern for all peoples of the world, Pope John Paul II echoed this goal to work for justice.

b. The Church has proclaimed its work toward justice as essential to its ministry.

In 1971, the third international Synod of Bishops met at Rome to discuss the issue of justice in the world. In a statement to the world, approved by Pope Paul VI, they described the work toward justice as a "constitutive element" in the Church's ministry. The expression "constitutive element" refers to a work that is essential or at the root of the ministry of the Church. The Synod of Bishops was stating that the work toward justice is not something extra the Church can undertake in the world, but rather that the work toward justice is on the same footing as celebrating the sacraments and preaching the Word of God. There is no more powerful way to remind all members of the Church that the work toward justice is essential to the ministry of the Church. To be true to the Church in living out its call, we must continually work toward justice in the world.

c. The Church is called to work toward social justice.

In our lives, we are surrounded by many outside influences that control our ability and ease in loving our neighbor. We live under certain political systems and organizations that often dictate custom, law, and even the use of our human rights. The economic structures of a society and its many organizations that control money and property often influence the rights of a just wage, good working conditions, or the ownership of property. Wherever we turn, we find ourselves living and working within systems and structures that we often do not even understand. When we speak of social justice, we refer to justice on these broader levels that control our lives. We are speaking of justice within a society rather than the simple idea of one person respecting the rights of another.

Because the Church is called to work toward justice for all people, the Church must work toward social justice. If the systems of government, the economic powers of business, and organizations act unjustly, the individual rights and dignity suffer. The Church must speak out against all social injustice and work toward justice on the social level. We are

138

social minded people, called to live together in society and to grow and enable others to grow through our society. Even on the level of social justice, the Church must recognize this ministry to seek justice as a "constitutive element" of its mission.

d. Working toward justice includes working toward peace in the world.

In a historic pastoral letter on peace, entitled "The Challenge of Peace: God's Promise and Our Response," the American bishops carefully considered the challenge of peace in our nuclear society. They presented the scriptural basis for peace and discussed those occasions when a just war would be possible. In this letter, they pointed out that some can accept the idea of a just war and rightly serve in the protection of one's country or the human rights of others, but others may choose, in conscience, to be totally opposed to a particular war, or to all war. They supported the right of conscientious objectors in the Church, and they went on to examine the situation of nuclear war. Because of the extensive damage of nuclear war and the inability to avoid killing thousands or millions of innocent lives, the bishops could in no way support nuclear war as acceptable in accordance with the just war theory. They proposed that all nations work toward a positive approach to peace which recognized the dignity of all life and the hope for peace which comes through prayer and trust in God.

Because of their stand against nuclear war, the bishops faced criticism from many who stated that they should not interfere in politics. The bishops, however, recognize their call to guide the moral consciences of those who wish to follow Christ. In the letter, the bishops state that they do not propose the considerations in the pastoral as laws to be followed, but as guidelines to help shape one's conscience.

In Matthew's Gospel, Jesus tells his listeners during his Sermon on the Mount, "Blest too the peacemakers; they shall be called sons of God" (Matthew 5:9).

9. What is Evangelization?

a. Evangelization consists in sharing the person and message of Jesus Christ with all people of the world.

In the Gospel of Matthew, Jesus directs his disciples to reach out to all people of the world to invite them into discipleship: "Go, therefore, make disciples of all the nations" (Matthew 28:19). The Church, as a source of the message and gifts of Jesus Christ, has the call to share these

139

blessings with the whole world. Evangelization is this call to share the good news of Jesus Christ with all people of the world. Pope John Paul I, during his short term as pope, proclaimed evangelization as a major call of the Church. Through our baptism and confirmation, we share in this special mission of the Church to "make disciples of all the nations." Through these sacraments, every Catholic is called to evangelization.

b. Evangelization reaches out to the unchurched.

Millions of people throughout the world have never heard of Jesus Christ. Some have heard the name, but know nothing else about Jesus. Many of these people claim no Church affiliation. The mission of the Church reaches out in a special way to these unchurched that they might hear and know the message of Jesus and the gifts shared through his life. The unchurched have a right to this knowledge and the Church has the privilege and duty of sharing this good news of Jesus Christ. In Paul's letter to the Romans, we have some very direct questions from Paul which challenge us in our sharing of the faith. Through the Sacraments of Initiation, we receive a gift worthy of being shared with others, but Paul asks us, "But how can they call to Him for help if they have not believed? And how can they believe if they have not heard the message? And how can they hear if the message is not proclaimed?" (Romans 10:14). All of us are called to share the message which we have received in faith from Christ.

c. The call to evangelization involves the whole community of believers.

The Church invites the unchurched to share in the family of believers. In this family of the Church, a new member should be able to recognize a deep concern for each member of the Church community. Included in this call to evangelization is a call to reach out to fallen-away members of the family. The Church should continually invite these non-practicing members home to the community.

Another aspect of the call to evangelization is the call to the Church community to live fully the good news of Jesus Christ that it preaches. When a family invites others to share in its family activities and celebrations, the family presumes that others will enjoy sharing with them. In the same way, the Church family should strive to live the good news of Jesus Christ in such a way that others will find support and joy in living and celebrating this good news with the community. The full call to evangelization consists not only in reaching out to the world, but also consists in reaching inward to examine and keep alive the living message of Jesus Christ within the community.

Conclusion

How surprised we would be if the child in the introduction ran to the corner of the room, opened his hands and let out a puff of smoke! We would not believe we saw the smoke, and if we did believe it, we might want to experiment ourselves to see if it is possible.

In the Sacrament of Confirmation, we open ourselves to surprises. When we do not stifle the Spirit in our lives, we shall always be open to the surprises of the Spirit. We must have confidence in the Spirit within us, and we must accept our call through confirmation to witnessing to Christ. Then the surprises begin to happen.

For Scripture reflection and discussion concerning this chapter, see Journeying in His Light, *"Sacraments of Initiation: Part 2."*

10

Sacraments of Initiation, Part 3: Eucharist

Introduction

When their mother celebrated her seventieth birthday, all ten of her children, ranging in age from the late twenties to the late forties, wanted to make this an occasion she would never forget. She had proven herself a loving mother, and her children, her sons- and daughters-in-law and her grandchildren crowded into a rented hall to celebrate her surprise party. Two of her daughters had lured her to the hall on the pretext that they were taking her out for a birthday dinner. From the moment she entered the hall till the party ended almost four hours later, the family centered all their attention on her, hugging her, singing to her, serving her, and presenting gifts to her.

At the end of the evening, when the family called for her to make a speech, she stood with a broad smile and said, "You have all been good to me, and given me many gifts. But the greatest gift of all is that you all love each other, and you joined together to share your love with me. I have been blessed."

In this chapter, we will be studying ways of showing our love for God. In recognizing God's great love, we want to share in that love and to celebrate it. God, like the mother in the story above, loves a party, a celebration, and God's joy abounds when the family comes together to celebrate that love. This chapter tells us about celebrating with God as a loving family.

1. Why do people worship?

a. Some people worship out of fear.

In ancient times, if a community suddenly experienced a tragic flood or a mighty storm, they would seek to ward off the anger of the gods by offering the best of their animals for sacrifice. They hoped that these sacrifices would appease the gods: the storm gods, the wind gods, the sun

143

gods, or whatever unknown god was causing this disaster. They worshiped these gods, even in time of peace, fearing that if they forgot about the gods, they would suffer a new disaster. In the Church today, there are people who worship God out of fear of going to hell. They go to Church not because they love God, but because they fear that at death they will suffer eternal damnation, eternal unhappiness.

This need to worship out of fear may be necessary for some as they begin to approach God. There is, however, another type of fear, a reverential fear, which is actually a result of love. The Old Testament tells us that the ". . . fear of the Lord is the beginning of wisdom" (Psalm 111:10). The fear addressed here is a reverential fear, such as one would have in the presence of a great leader or a loving parent. This type of fear makes a person aware of the greatness of the person in whose presence he or she stands. Such a fear leads to worship out of love, rather than out of fear of what a person might do to us.

b. Some approach worship as a debt to be paid.

For some, the motive in this form of worship comes very close to worshipping out of fear. God has been good to us, and we must repay God as though we are returning a favor. Because God has given us great gifts in our lives, we have an obligation to return the debt, to thank God for these gifts. In the Old Testament, the psalmist calls out to God and says, "How shall I make a return to the Lord for all the good he has done for me?" (Psalm 116:12). Throughout the Scriptures, we are reminded of God's great love by providing for us, and our need to respond to that love.

c. Some worship God fully out of love.

Through the love shown by God throughout the Old Testament, through the loving words and actions of Christ in the New Testament, and through the gifts in their lives, people recognize God as a loving and compassionate God. The experience of a loving and compassionate God leads people to want to worship this God, to want to be able to say, "I love You." In the letter to the Hebrews, the author expresses the love and gift of Christ who became a member of our human family and offered us a way of reaching out to God in love. The author writes.

Our high priest [Jesus] is not one who cannot feel sympathy for our weaknesses. On the contrary, we have a high priest who was tempted in every way that we are, but did not sin. Let us be brave, then, and approach God's throne where there is grace. There we will receive mercy and find grace to help us just when we need it (Hebrews 4:15–16).

2. Why is the scriptural image of a "memorial" important to our understanding of Christian worship?

a. Our ability to remember is basic to our humanness.

As human beings living together in a concerned society, we must have the ability to remember. Our whole life is shaped by our memories of our families, our friends, our memories of shared joys and tragedies, our recollections of birth and death. Someone once said that we are a story people. We play a part in the large story of life, and we look to the future because we recall the past, and shape our identities according to our memories. If we were to lose our memory, our story would end, because we would have nothing upon which to build the present and the future.

Historical religions such as Catholicism and Judaism depend very much upon their memories of God and the people with whom God related. We recall the promises of the past and we look with hope to the future because of these promises. Without our ability to remember, we would lose our identity as a people of God. In the psalms, we read about a man in exile in Babylon who asks God to curse him if he ever forgets his true home, Jerusalem. He writes, "If I forget you, Jerusalem, may my right hand be forgotten! May my tongue cleave to my palate if I remember you not, If I place not Jerusalem ahead of my joy" (Psalm 137:5–6). The people of Israel remembered that Jerusalem was their true home, and they prayed that they would never become so content with Babylon that they would forget their true homeland and the true meaning of Judaism. To forget Jerusalem would be to forget their link with God as the people of God.

b. Each year, the Jewish people recall the living memorial of their Passover from slavery to the promised land.

Each year Israelite families would gather together to celebrate the great feast of the year, the Passover feast. They would recall that God had chosen them as God's special people, had freed them from the slavery of Egypt, had guided them through the desert, and finally had led them into the promised land. In loving gratitude, they remembered the gifts that God had given them, and realized that God still guided their nation. On the Passover feast each year, they reenacted in a prayerful way a living memorial of an event that had taken place in past history, but the blessing of which still flowed down to the present moment. They would sacrifice a lamb to God in the temple, then take some of that lamb home to eat and share in the festival meal. This reminded them of the Israelites of

145

Egypt, who killed the lamb, offered it to God and painted the lamb's blood on their doorpost that the angel of death might pass over them. The family would celebrate this feast on the night called the greatest of all nights because it commemorated the Passover from slavery to the freedom of the promised land. The family would sing psalms of praise and thanksgiving to God for the gift of the Passover. They celebrated a memorial of thanksgiving for God's protection in the past and guidance in the present.

In the Book of Exodus, we read that God directed them to commemorate this event each year so that the people would not forget what God had done for them. We read:

You and your children must obey these rules forever. When you enter the land that the Lord has promised to give you, you must perform this ritual. When your children ask you "what does this ritual mean?" you will answer, "It is the sacrifice of Passover to honor the Lord, because He passed over the houses of the Israelites in Egypt. He killed the Egyptians, but spared us" (Exodus 12:24–27).

This memorial event was not just a recalling of what happened in the past. The Israelites believed that the event was happening in the present in some way, as though the event and God's blessings remained timeless. In the passover ritual celebrated today, one of the youngest in attendance asks the question, "Why *is* this night different from every other night?" The significance is that they do not ask, "Why *was* this night different?" For those celebrating the Passover Meal, the night of the celebration, "this" night, is, even now, different from every other night.

c. At the Passover feast, Christ offered the Church a new living memorial of thanksgiving.

In his Gospel Luke explains the feast of the Passover as celebrated at the Last Supper. At this Passover, Jesus offered himself in place of the lamb and offered a new memorial to the apostles. "Then he took some bread and when he had given thanks, broke it and gave it to them, saying 'This is my body which will be given for you; do this as a memorial of me.' He did the same with the cup after supper, and said, 'This cup is the new covenant in my blood which will be poured out for you' " (Luke 22:19–20). In the words, "Do this as a memorial of me," the Church sees Christ as offering to the apostles and their followers the gift of continually sharing in this new memorial. Just as Jesus changed bread and wine into his Body and Blood, so the Church believes that this gift and power are shared in the Church. The Church believes that even today this bread and wine become the Living Presence of the Body and Blood of Jesus during the Eucharistic Liturgy.

146

d. Jesus realized the great act of faith needed to accept this teaching.

In the Gospel of John the author tells how Jesus fed five thousand men in the desert. After he had fed them, the author shares a discourse on the bread of life which is the gift of Jesus' living memorial. Jesus realizes their need for faith and says,

I am telling you the truth: if you do not eat the flesh of the Son of Man and drink his blood, you will not have life in yourselves. Whoever eats my flesh and drinks my blood has eternal life, and I will raise him to life on the last day. For my flesh is the real food; my blood is the real drink. Whoever eats my flesh and drinks my blood lives in me, and I live in him (John 6:53–56).

A few seconds later, he says, "This then is the bread that came down from heaven; it is not like the bread your ancestors ate, but then later died. The one who eats this bread will live forever" (John 6:58). In this text, the author is showing the insights of the early Church into the message of Jesus. The response of the people reflects the need for faith in the early Church. Many of his followers heard this and said, "This teaching is too hard. Who can listen to it." Without being told, Jesus knew that they were grumbling about this, so he said to them, "Does this make you want to give up?" (John 6:60–61). Without the gift of faith, the fact that Jesus gave his Body and Blood under the form of bread and wine was indeed difficult to accept. As a result of this revelation, we read in the Gospel of John "Because of this, many of Jesus' followers turned back and would not go with him anymore" (John 6:66). To believe that Jesus would actually share with us his Body and Blood, under the form of bread and wine, simply must rest on the gift of faith.

e. Christ, through his death, resurrection, and ascension, offers us a living memorial by which we express our love for God in a perfect manner.

In his life, Jesus became obedient unto death even to death on the cross. Because of this confrontation of evil and his acceptance of obedience to death, God showed pleasure in Jesus by highly exalting him. God the Father was pleased with Christ's offering. Through the resurrection and exaltation of Jesus, that offering of Christ became our offering. Every time we share in this living memorial of Christ's passion, death, and resurrection, we, the Church, worship God the Father. It is the most perfect way of worshipping God the Father and expressing our love for God. Paul writes, "Every time, then, you eat this bread and drink this cup, you proclaim the death of the Lord until he comes" (I Corinthians 11:26).

147

f. The name the Catholic Church gives to the celebration of this living memorial is the name Eucharist which comes from the Greek meaning, "To give thanks."

Not only does the Church receive the gift of Christ to his Father, but the Church also celebrates this gift as a living memorial of thanksgiving. Many refer to this celebration as the Mass, but it is more truly called a "Eucharistic (thanksgiving) Celebration." By the gift of this Eucharistic Celebration, we are thankful for all of the gifts of Christ, but most especially the gift of being able to worship God the Father in so perfect a manner and of being able to express our love for God as a community.

3. Why is the scriptural image of a "meal" important to our understanding of the Eucharistic Celebration?

a. In the time of Jesus, an invitation to a meal was considered an invitation into a person's life.

During the time of Jesus, invitations to meals were not given lightly. When people gathered for a meal, they ordinarily gathered with their "own kind of people." In a sense, the people could have said, "Show me whom you eat with, and I'll tell you what you are." Because of this attitude, the people of Jesus' day made their judgments of Jesus based upon the people with whom he ate. Many of the stories found in the Gospels center around Jesus' dining with sinners, tax collectors, and Pharisees. Each one of these meals had a significant message to teach.

In a story found in Luke's Gospel, Jesus invites himself to dine with a man named Zacchaeus (Luke 19:1–10). The underlying message of the story is that Jesus is inviting himself into the life of Zacchaeus, and this tax collector accepts Jesus into his life through an immediate change in his attitude. He repents of his past sins and seeks to reconcile himself with those whom he has hurt. This story offers a good example of the deeper meaning of inviting a person to a meal during Jesus' day.

b. Jesus chose a meal as the setting for the Eucharistic Celebration.

When two friends meet who have not seen each other for some time, they often decide to discuss old times over a meal. At a meal, people come together in friendship, trust, and relaxation. According to the

Scriptures, Jesus offers the Eucharist at a meal, a very special meal. At a Passover supper, Jesus offered his Body and Blood under the form of bread and wine. When Paul writes to the Corinthians, he reminds them of the love and sharing that should take place at the Lord's Supper. He tells them to be considerate of each other, as they gather for this meal: "So to sum up, my dear brothers, when you meet *for the Meal,* wait for one another" (I Corinthians 11:33). In a veiled way, the author of Luke tells how two disciples of Jesus recognized him after the resurrection at a meal that could easily be the Eucharistic Celebration. Scriptures read, "Now while he was with them at table, he took the bread and said the blessing; then broke it and handed it to them. And their eyes were opened and they recognized him; but he had vanished from their sight" (Luke 24:30–31). Immediately the disciples rushed to Jerusalem to tell the eleven about this experience of Jesus. And the simple narrative ends with the words, "Then they told their story of what had happened on the road and how they had recognized him at the breaking of bread" (Luke 24:35). Today, we celebrate a Eucharistic Meal by preparing bread and wine and sharing that bread and wine as the Body and Blood of Christ. Another reference for this Eucharistic Celebration is the expression, "The Lord's Supper." Again in Paul's letter to the Corinthians. "When you hold these meetings it is not *the Lord's Supper you are eating,* since . . . everyone is in such a hurry to start his own supper" (I Corinthians 11:20–21).

c. By telling us about the meals in which Jesus shared during his life, the Gospel writers are also telling us more about the Eucharistic Meal.

As we read about Jesus and the meals he shared during his life, we learn about our sharing in the Eucharistic Meal. Jesus did not dine just with good people; he dined with tax collectors and sinners. During a meal, Jesus heard the Pharisees complain to his disciples about their master eating with tax collectors and sinners, and Jesus told them, "People who are in good health do not need a doctor; sick people do. . . . I have come to call, not the self-righteous, but sinners" (Matthew 9:12,13). The Eucharistic Meal does not invite just those who are living close to God, but it calls those who are sinners that they might find love and change their lives.

During a meal, Jesus castigated the Pharisees for seeking places of honor, and for tending only to themselves and not to others. The message tells us that the Eucharistic Celebration allows no room for class distinction or for self-seeking. All come together as one for the sake of praising God.

149

4. Why is the scriptural image of "sacrifice" important to our understanding of the Eucharistic Celebration?

a. The idea of "sacrifice" had many different meanings in the ancient world.

The basic notion behind sacrifice was a people's belief in a higher and more powerful force over creation. The ancient pagans would offer an animal or a portion of their crops, seeking to praise or appease their gods. The ancient Israelites offered animals or food to God to praise God and to thank God for blessings received. The reason food or animal sacrifice was offered to God (or the gods) was that they were central to the life of the people. In this way, the sacrifice was seen as a sharing of one's life with God. The image which a people had of their gods would often determine the type of sacrifice and the meaning behind the sacrifice. The pagans, for instance, often sought to appease angry gods, while the Israelites more often wanted to praise God who was a loving God. In offering their sacrifice to God, the people of Israel recognized that their own life was fragile, and they acknowledged their dependence upon God through their offering.

A religious sacrifice as found in Israel is called a "cultic" sacrifice, and it connotes a religious context in which a priest acts as a mediator, making the offering on behalf of the people. The people of Jerusalem would bring their offering to the temple, and the priest would offer their sacrifice to God on behalf of the people by killing the animal upon the altar of sacrifice. The offering was then made sacred, and a portion would be taken home by the people for a sacred meal.

The priests of the Old Testament protected the idea of a cultic sacrifice which involved some type of blood offering. The prophets and wisdom writers would often remind the people of another type of sacrifice, the sacrifice of their own will to that of God's will. They told the people that God is pleased with their blood offerings, but God also wants them to live a life worthy of the chosen people of God. We read in the psalms, "Not for your sacrifices do I rebuke you, for your holocausts are before me always. . . . He that offers praise as sacrifice glorifies me" (Psalm 50:8,23). In the New Testament, we see Jesus following these prophets and wisdom writers when he tells the Pharisees, "If you understood the meaning of the text, 'It is mercy I desire and not sacrifice,' you would not have condemned these innocent men" (Matthew 12:7).

b. The sacrificial meal was a sign of unity with God.

Because the meal held such an important role among the Israelite people, it was natural that the sacrificial meal became the place where people were most conscious of God in their midst. At the Passover meal, the people of Israel celebrated with God by sharing together the lamb offered in sacrifice. During the meal, the life of the Israelite nation was again joined with the presence of the living God in the midst of people. In this meal, the triple idea of meal, sacrifice, and memorial bonded the lives of the people of Israel with that of God. It is in the context of a sacrificial meal that Catholics bond their lives with that of Christ.

c. The sacrifice made by Jesus was to offer his will totally to the will of God the Father.

The Last Supper is found in the context of the passion narrative. Its place in the Gospels has a message for us; it reminds us that the Eucharist comes to us in the context of the sacrifice of Jesus' life for the sake of all people. In this offering of himself, Jesus draws us into the new covenant sealed in his own blood. In the Gospel of Matthew, we read:

> "While they were eating, Jesus took a piece of bread, gave a prayer of thanks, broke it, and gave it to his disciples. 'Take and eat it,' he said; 'This is my body.' Then he took a cup, gave thanks to God, and gave it to them 'Drink it all of you,' he said; ' this is my blood, which seals God's covenant, my blood poured out for many for the forgiveness of sins. I tell you, I will never again drink this wine until the day I drink the new wine with you in my Father's kingdom' "
> (Matthew 26:26–29).

When we read this passage, we see many of the characteristics of "sacrifice." Jesus is offering his life for us; he is broken and killed. But, this has a deeper message. It is the act of choosing to follow the will of God which makes Jesus' sacrifice perfect. It is the offering made in praise of God which makes the gift a true sacrifice.

In the letter to the Hebrews, the author lets us hear the words of Jesus when he says, "You do not want sacrifices and offerings, but you have prepared a body for me. You are not pleased with animals—burned whole on the altar or with sacrifices to take away sins. Then I said, 'Here I am, to do your will, O God" (Hebrews 10:5–7). In the agony in the garden, Jesus shows that it is the obedience to the will of God that is his true sacrifice. "Father," he said, "if you will, take this cup of suffering away from me. Not my will, however, but your will be done" (Luke 22:42). Because of this obedience of Jesus, Paul is able to write in his

151

letter to the Philippians, ". . . it was thus that he humbled himself, obediently accepting death, death on a cross! Because of this, God highly exalted him . . ." (Philippians 2:9–10). Christ did not come into the world to be sacrificed as an offering of appeasement to a hurt God, but he came to follow the will of God, wherever that will would take him. The will of God was that Jesus would overcome the power of sin in the world, and Jesus obediently followed this will, even to death on the cross. In his obedience to God's will, Jesus brought us salvation, and became for us, the perfect sacrifice. In his sacrifice, Jesus did what no Old Testament sacrifice could do; Jesus offered himself fully.

d. In our sacrificial meal, we all share in this gift given to the Church by Christ.

In the New Testament, we do not have the same cultic priesthood found in Israel. The ordained priest of the Catholic Church does not offer a sacrifice on behalf of the people, but he shares in the one sacrifice of Jesus Christ along with the people. The ordained priest presides at the assemblies and performs a major role in the celebration of the Eucharist, but all people worship as one in the name of Jesus Christ.

As we share in the Eucharistic Sacrifice, we offer our lives as one with that of Jesus. In sharing in the sacrificial meal, we are also sharing in the life and attitude of Jesus Christ. Just as Jesus was obedient to the will of God, even unto death, so we too proclaim our willingness through this sacrifice to be like Christ, obedient to the will of God, even if it should lead us to death.

5. What is the role of the Christian community in the celebration of the Eucharist?

a. The community celebrates a common memory.

When the community gathers for worship, it recalls its common heritage which has the life and message of Jesus at its center. The "memorial" for the Church is not an individual memory, but it is one that recalls how God first chose a people of God, a community, and prepared that community for the coming of the Christ. The "memorial" remembers Jesus and the Twelve, and how this message spread from the early, small community of Jerusalem to a community of people reaching to the ends of the earth. When each of us enters community, we hear about Christ shaping his community of followers and the memorial of his Body and

Blood which Jesus left to the community. We begin to realize that the memorial of the Church is not primarily a memorial of a particular apostle or follower of Jesus, but it is a memorial of a community accepting Jesus and his message, spreading that message, and welcoming new members into the community. Christ redeemed the community of all people, left a living memorial to the community, and invited us to share in the community and its living memorial.

b. The community celebrates a common ritual meal.

At the Last Supper, Jesus did not sit down with a group of individuals, but he sat down with a community, and he offered his body and blood "for you," meaning for the community. The community gathering together to celebrate the Lord's Supper is an important aspect of the living memorial, as is the presence of Jesus among us as in the Eucharistic presence. As we gather today for the Eucharistic meal, we do not gather merely as individuals praising God, but as the family, a community, worshipping in Christ's name. Because a meal involves giving and sharing, we should not assist with our mouths closed, but we should join in the praying and singing to the best of our ability. Some members will take part in serving the community as readers or distributors of the Eucharist. Just as we read about Jesus' eating with sinners and tax collectors in the Scriptures, so we can expect sinners to join in our community banquet, and we should accept all with the hope that our community meal will eventually lead them to a change of life, as it changed the lives of so many others in the Gospels.

c. The community celebrates a common sacrifice.

In speaking about our unity with one another and with Christ and his sacrifice, Paul writes, "Is not the cup of blessing we bless a share in the blood of Christ? And is not the bread we break a sharing in the Body of Christ? Because the loaf of bread is one, we, many though we are, are one body, for we all partake of the one loaf" (I Corinthians 10:16–17). Paul recognizes that the call of the community to be one with Christ includes a share in the sacrifice of Christ. He later writes, ". . . I beg you through the mercy of God to offer your bodies as a living sacrifice holy and acceptable to God, your spiritual worship" (Romans 12:1). Although the community realizes that Jesus' sacrifice brought us salvation, we must still share that salvation with others. Because we are one with Christ, we must continue to act in Christ's name. Paul sees his ministry as linked to Christ's life and sacrifice when he writes, "In my own flesh, I fill up what is lacking in the sufferings of Christ for the sake of the Body, the Church" (Colossians 1:24).

When we gather as a community to celebrate the Eucharist, we recall the sacrifice of Christ not only as an event which took place in the past, but we believe that it is taking place in the present. It is the one, living sacrifice of Christ. Through our celebration of the Eucharist, we join our hearts with that of Christ, and we make our sacrifice one with his. The community shares in the one loaf, the one cup, the one sacrifice of the one Lord, and enables the living sacrifice of Christ to become more visible in the world today.

6. How is the Eucharistic Celebration Divided?

a. In the first part of this celebration, the assembly celebrates the Liturgy of the Word.

When people love each other, they share some of their deepest feelings with each other. They dare to share details about themselves that they would never share with any other person. In the Liturgy of the Word, we listen to God's Word. Through these readings, God is revealing many of God's deepest secrets to us. Through the Liturgy of the Word, we come to know God a little more deeply. In the New Testament, we read that Jesus would often go into the synagogue, read a section from the Scriptures and explain the Scriptures to the people. The Liturgy of the Word flows from the synagogue service, a service of sharing in the Scriptures.

b. In the second part of this liturgy, the assembly celebrates the Liturgy of the Eucharist or the sacrificial meal.

After listening to the Word of God and getting to know God a little more intimately, the community now prepares to share this sacrificial meal. During this part of the liturgy, the bread and wine are prepared for the sacrificing meal; the bread and wine become the Body and Blood of Christ. The community shares in this gift by celebrating Communion.

7. How is the Liturgy of the Word celebrated?

a. The Liturgy of the Word begins with a short period of preparation or introduction.

As the presider (priest) approaches the table of the Lord, the assembly joins together in singing a gathering song. The presider makes a special reverence to the Lord's table, the altar, which symbolizes Christ.

The altar should occupy the central position in the Church. The presider then moves to a chair separated from the altar which is commonly refered to as the presider's chair. During the Liturgy of the Word, the presider does not return to the altar. The presider, along with the assembly, signs himself with the sign of the cross. After a short greeting and litany, the assembly joins in a prayer of glory and praise to God. The presider calls the assembly to prayer with the words, "Let us pray," pauses for a few moments of silent prayer, and then prays a prayer especially chosen for that day. Through these introductory rites, the assembly deepens the experience of community and is now prepared to hear God's word.

b. Readings from the Scriptures and a psalm between the readings form the main part of the Liturgy of the Word.

On Sundays and special feast days, the congregation listens to three separate readings. Ordinarily, the Church chooses the first reading from the Old Testament. A responsorial psalm ordinarily follows, consisting of one of the psalms from the Old Testament, with the people responding at certain intervals. As a second reading, the Church chooses a reading from the Acts of the Apostles, the Letters, (Epistles) or the Book of Revelation. A third reading, the most sacred reading of all, comes from the Gospels. The assembly stands during this reading. In the course of three years a major part of the Bible will have been read during the liturgies on Sunday. If a person chooses to celebrate the liturgies during the week, that person will hear a major part of the Bible every two years. Through these readings we come to know God and to understand God's message more fully.

c. The homily also plays an important role in the Liturgy of the Word.

The homily consists of a message ordinarily shared by the presider of the Eucharistic Liturgy. The homily explains the readings and shows how their message touches God's community even today. The presider is urged to share a homily at all liturgies, even liturgies celebrated with a small group of people throughout the week. Ordinarily, a short period of silence follows the homily.

d. The profession of faith and general intercessions complete the Liturgy of the Word.

The assembly prays together a profession of faith. This profession of faith had its birth at the Council of Nicea in 325 when people were denying that the Son of God was equal to God the Father. In this profession of faith, we proclaim that Jesus Christ is the Son of God and equal to the

155

Father. The assembly then prays the general intercessions. In these prayers, the assembly prays for the particular needs of all people throughout the world. During the general intercessions, we must be careful not to make it a time of merely mentioning our own personal concerns. The Church reaches out to embrace all people in the world and in the general intercessions we should express a consciousness of this universal outreach. We can attach our personal concerns to universal concerns. An example of this would be, "For all those suffering from sickness throughout the world, especially for . . . (name person)." We should avoid prayers of thanksgiving in the general intercessions, since the entire Eucharistic Liturgy is a liturgy of thanksgiving.

8. How is the Liturgy of the Eucharist divided?

a. The Liturgy of the Eucharist begins with the preparation of the gifts of bread and wine.

The presider returns to the Lord's Table for the first time since he reverenced it at the beginning of the celebration. Members of the assembly join in the Eucharistic Celebration by bringing to the altar gifts of bread and wine. The presider than praises God for God's goodness in sharing these gifts which are used in the sacrificial meal. In the preparation of the wine, the presider adds a small amount of water and prays that just as the Son of God came to share in our humanness we, too, by the blessings of his death, resurrection, and ascension may share in his divinity. The presider invites the assembly to pray that this sacrifice will be acceptable to God the Almighty Father. He then prays a short prayer over the gifts.

b. The Eucharistic prayer begins more properly with a prayer of thanksgiving and an acclamation on the part of the people proclaiming God's holiness.

The presider then invites the people to lift up their hearts in a prayer of thanksgiving to God the Father. The presider thanks God the Father for the gifts God has given through Jesus Christ and prays that the whole world may continually proclaim the glory of God the Father. The assembly responds to this prayer, called the *preface,* with an acclamation taken from Isaiah, a prophet of the Old Testament. They pray:

Holy, holy, holy Lord, God of Hosts, Heaven and earth are full of your glory. Hosanna in the highest. Blessed is he who comes in the name of the Lord. Hosanna in the highest.

This is the first of several acclamations that the assembly will pray together.

c. *The presider takes the bread and wine and prays the words attributed to Christ at the Last Supper, "This is my Body . . . this is my Blood . . . do this in memory of Me."*

Catholics believe that at the moment the priest proclaims the words, "This is my Body," over the bread and "This is my Blood," over the wine, he is proclaiming that the Body and Blood of Jesus is now fully present in the Eucharist under the forms of bread and wine. We refer to this part of liturgy as the "Institution Narrative."

d. *The assembly proclaims an acclamation of faith in Christ and continues to pray for all people throughout the world.*

The assembly again proclaims an acclamation of faith in the death, resurrection, and coming again in glory of Jesus Christ. The Church prays for the pope, bishops, priests, and all living and deceased throughout the world. To show the special place of honor held by Mary, the Church honors her in the liturgy.

e. *The Eucharistic prayer properly ends with the "great Amen" of the assembly.*

The presider holds up the Body and Blood of Jesus Christ to the people and praises God the Father in these words; "Through him (Jesus), with him (Jesus), and in him (Jesus), in the unity of the Holy Spirit, all glory and honor is yours, almighty Father, forever and ever." At this point, the assembly exclaims its "great Amen." The "great Amen" professes a belief and an acceptance of the Eucharistic gift of Christ.

f. *The assembly prays the Lord's Prayer and shares a greeting of peace with each other as they prepare for the celebration of the Eucharist.*

Through the gift of baptism, we are able to pray to the Father in a very special and intimate way. To show this special intimacy and to show our oneness in worship, we pray together, "Our Father who art in heaven. . . ." The presider then prays a short prayer for peace and invites the assembly to share a greeting of peace with one another. This

157

greeting of peace flows out of the Lord's Prayer by which we seek forgiveness for our sins and promise to forgive those "who have sinned against us." As a sign of peace, we shake hands or exchange a kiss with the people around us saying, "The peace of the Lord be with you." The people then join in a short litany, "Lamb of God, who takes away the sin of the world have mercy on us. . . ."

g. *The members of the assembly celebrate the reception of the Eucharist, or Communion as it is called, under both kinds, bread and wine and are sent forth to share their gifts with all people.*

The General Instruction of the Roman Missal states: "The sign of Communion is more complete when given under both kinds, since in that form the sign of the Eucharistic Meal appears more clearly. The intention of Christ that the new and eternal covenant be ratified in his blood is better expressed, as is the relation of the Eucharistic Banquet to the heavenly banquet" (#240). We are here encouraged to share in the Eucharist under the forms of bread and wine. During the Communion Celebration, the assembly should sing a song of praise together as a visible sign of unity in sharing the "one sacrifice." The presider closes this portion of the liturgy by asking God's blessings on those who have shared in the banquet of the Lord. The dismissal rite follows upon the closing prayer. If any announcements are to be made, they should be made after the closing prayer and before the dismissal rite begins. The presider blesses the community "In the name of the Father, and of the Son, and of the Holy Spirit," and sends them forth to "Go in peace" to share the love and service celebrated in the Eucharistic Liturgy. The assembly prays the final, grateful response in the words, "Thanks be to God." The Eucharistic Liturgy is ended.

9. Why do Catholics believe so strongly in celebrating the Eucharistic Liturgy together on Sunday?

a. *Along with the early Church, the Catholic Church celebrates Sunday as the day of Christ's resurrection.*

The joys and gifts of Christ's resurrection affected the early Church so deeply that it celebrated the day of Christ's resurrection in place of the Jewish Sabbath. Whenever the assembly came together on Sunday, it celebrated Christ's resurrection and all the gifts that flowed from the resurrection. Today the Church joins with the early Christian community in celebrating each Sunday as a little Easter.

b. In celebrating each Sunday as the day of resurrection, Catholics strive to make Sunday a special day in their week by sharing more fully in the perfect act of love, the Eucharistic Liturgy.

If we love a person, we strive to understand how to express that love more perfectly. If our love is truly deep for a person, we wish to be with that person often, and certainly at least once a week. If a Catholic believes that the Eucharist is the best possible manner in which to express love for God and that the Sunday obligation is also an obligation to the community and if a Catholic does not respond to these beliefs, the Church believes that this person is committing a serious sin. In the early Church, many saw the day of resurrection as beginning around sundown the day before. The Church, keeping this vision in mind, has allowed the community to share in the Eucharistic Celebration on Saturday evening as well as Sunday morning. Due to the many different hours that some people work in our society, this privilege also becomes a necessity. Besides Sundays, many Catholics share in the Eucharist each day during the week. However, the community comes together in a special way on Saturday evening or Sunday to express in a visible form the living, loving Body of Christ, worshiping God in this Eucharistic Liturgy.

10. What are some regulations concerning the Eucharist?

a. Catholics in serious sin should ordinarily refrain from receiving the Eucharist.

God shares the sacraments with us that we may be able to live more fully as a true image of Christ. The Eucharist should not be seen as a reward for being good, but rather as a help enabling us to reflect Christ by our life. Even if a person has many minor faults or sins, that person should still celebrate the Eucharist to seek God's help in overcoming these faults or sins. When people approach Christ in the Eucharist, they are not proclaiming their goodness to the community, but rather their need for God's help in their lives. People in serious sin, who have had an opportunity to reconcile themselves with God and the community and have not done so should not receive the Eucharist. A person in serious sin should first celebrate the Sacrament of Reconciliation, which we shall treat in the next chapter.

b. Before the celebration of the reception of the Eucharist, Catholics should fast for one hour.

In general a person should fast one hour from food or drink before the reception of the Eucharist. This fast does not include medicine and water. In case of sickness, a person should try to fast for approximately fifteen minutes, if possible, but even this could be dispensed with if it becomes difficult. This fasting gives the person an opportunity to prepare in some small way for the celebration of the reception of the Eucharist. By fasting, a person shows special reverence for the Eucharist.

c. A Catholic who has been initiated in the Eucharist must receive Communion at least once during the Easter season each year.

Catholics refer to this as the Easter Duty. The Easter Season begins with the first Sunday of Lent and ends on Trinity Sunday, which occurs approximately sixty days after Easter. The fact that an obligation has been placed on Catholics to receive Communion once a year during the Easter Season is one of the sad events of Catholic history. Because people lost the true value of celebrating Communion, this law had to be made. When people stopped receiving Christ in the Eucharist, the Church had to make the law in order for them to share in this great gift. The Spirit was lost so a law took its place. Today, most Catholics respond by celebrating the reception of the Eucharist as often as they celebrate the Eucharistic Liturgy. Hopefully, this Easter Duty law will gradually drop from usage as Catholics realize the great value and privilege of celebrating the reception of Christ in the Eucharist.

11. What do Catholics do with consecrated bread and wine left over from the Eucharistic Celebration?

a. If any of the consecrated bread is left after the celebration of the Eucharist, the priest places this consecrated Bread in a special container called a tabernacle. If consecrated wine is left, it is consumed by the ministers of the Eucharist or by some of the assembly.

As Catholics enter the church, they have the custom of genuflecting (touching the floor with the right knee) and as they do this, turning toward the tabernacle, if it is in the place of worship. The tabernacle contains consecrated bread not consumed during the celebration of the

Eucharist. In some churches, this tabernacle is in a room by itself, called the Blessed Sacrament chapel. Often during the day, Catholics will come to church to pray to Jesus Christ in his Eucharistic presence in the Blessed Sacrament. The act of genuflecting is a special act of reverence for the presence of Jesus in the sacramental form of bread. Catholics genuflect before they enter their seat if the Blessed Sacrament is in the place of worship, or as they pass in front of the Blessed Sacrament. This custom has no basis in Scripture, but has simply developed as a Catholic practice (see appendix).

b. If someone is sick, a priest or another minister of the Eucharist may bring the Blessed Sacrament to this person.

Sick people cannot always come to the church to share in the Eucharistic Celebration. A priest or a minister of the Eucharist may bring the Eucharist to them at home or in the hospital. In this way, a sick person is able to share in the Eucharistic Liturgy with the assembly.

c. Benediction of the Blessed Sacrament is a special service given by the Church to honor the sacramental presence of Christ.

While the community shares in prayers and songs of praise, the priest places the Blessed Sacrament in full view of the people. The consecrated bread is ordinarily placed in a glass container which is surrounded by ornate decorations and placed high enough on a stand on the altar for all to see. Benediction of the Blessed Sacrament flows from the Eucharistic Celebration. "Benediction" means God's blessing. This, also, has no basis in Scripture, and is simply a form of worshiping God given by the Church. Although Benediction of the Blessed Sacrament is a high form of worship, it can never claim to be a greater form of worship than the Eucharistic Liturgy. In fact, the Church forbids Benediction of the Blessed Sacrament immediately following the celebration of the Eucharistic Liturgy. The Blessed Sacrament may be exposed immediately after the Eucharistic Liturgy when adoration shall continue for several hours or days.

12. What is the liturgical year?

a. The liturgical year is the celebrating and entering into the major events of Christ's life by the Church through a twelve month cycle.

In our own day, we are familiar with the calendar year that begins on the first of January and continues to the end of December. The Church also has a type of calendar year. The first day of the Church's calendar year begins four Sundays before the celebration of Christmas. This is late November or early December. The Church year also follows a twelve month cycle and during this time, we move from a period that prepares for the birth of Christ to a period that celebrates Christ's continued presence in the Church. The central feasts of the liturgical year are the feasts of Christmas and Easter. The whole liturgical year centers around these two feasts. For each of these feasts, we have a period of preparation, the feast itself, and the celebration of the mysteries that flow out of these feasts.

b. The period of preparation for the feast of Christmas is called Advent.

Four Sundays before the celebration of the feast of Christmas, we celebrate the season of Advent. During this season, we look forward in three ways: we look forward to a celebration of the birthday of Christ; we look forward to a new spiritual birth of Christ in our lives on Christmas day; and we also look forward to the second coming of Christ. During Advent, we place ourselves in union with the people of the Old Testament by longing for the coming of Christ. We remember that there was a time when people did not fully understand Christ and the meaning of Christ in their lives. With the people of the Old Testament we share their spirit of hoping and longing for the coming of salvation into the lives of God's people. During the season of Advent, we do penance in preparation for the Christmas season. We try to better our lives so that we might be more fully prepared to celebrate the birth of Jesus. During this season, the presider will wear violet vestments during the Eucharistic Liturgy as a sign of penance and hopeful preparation.

c. After Advent, we celebrate the feast of Christmas itself, and the events that flow from this feast.

After the four weeks of Advent have been celebrated, we joyfully come to the feast of the birth of Jesus on December 25. The Church celebrates the joy of this season by directing the presider to wear white vestments in the celebration of the major feasts of this season. Throughout the Christmas season, we celebrate a solemn feast in honor of Mary, the Mother of God. The Feast of the Manifestation of Jesus to the world as shown through the visit by the Magi in the infancy narrative is also celebrated during this season. The number of Sundays celebrated in the Christmas season depends upon the date of Easter which changes each year. This season leaves us at the doorstep of Lent.

d. On Ash Wednesday, six and a half weeks before Easter, the season of preparation for Easter begins the Lenten season.

The season of Lent is a strongly penitential season. Christians put themselves in union with the suffering Jesus, remembering his passion and death, but always looking forward to a joyful resurrection. During this season, Catholics enter more fully into the preparation period of making certain sacrifices. These sacrifices aim toward living the Christian life more fully, such as praying better or more consciously reaching out in love to others in their need. These sacrifices also consist in staying away from certain pleasures which are allowed to each of us. For instance, during this time, many Catholics will fast from certain food or drink. Whatever penance one might choose, the whole purpose is not to make one feel bad, but rather to look forward to the celebration of the joyful coming of Jesus through the celebration of his resurrection. The climax of the season comes during the last week of Lent when we celebrate Holy Thursday, the Lord's Supper, and Good Friday, the crucifixion of Jesus. On Holy Saturday, the Church waits in silent expectation of Christ's resurrection. The vestments worn during the Eucharistic Liturgy during this season are again violet to remind us that we are in a season of penance.

During the season of Lent, the Church obliges Catholics to fast from food and abstain from meat on Ash Wednesday and Good Friday. The general norm for fasting is that the two small meals eaten on that day should not equal the normal big meal of a person's day. The one big meal may also be eaten on that day, but no food should be taken between meals. On Fridays during Lent, the Church obliges Catholics to abstain from meat. The obligation for fasting with the Church involves everyone from eighteen to the beginning of their sixtieth year. The obligation for abstaining from meat involves those who are fourteen years of age and older. If a person has a good reason for not following these obligations, the person is excused.

e. After the celebration of Lent, the Easter season bursts upon us with the joy of Christ's resurrection and its meaning in our life.

On Easter Sunday, the Church rejoices that Christ, who has died has now been raised and has brought us into a new life. The vestments again become the white vestments of joy to symbolize the great gift shared with all people through the resurrection and exaltation of Jesus Christ. During this season, the Easter candle, a symbol of the light of Christ in the world, will be lighted in all the celebrations. A major feast that occurs during the Easter Season is the Feast of the Ascension which celebrates Christ's ascension, complete union with the Father and the Spirit, and the message that we should now carry his work out to all the world. We then celebrate the Feast of Pentecost when Jesus fulfilled his promise to the apostles. Since Pentecost is the Feast of the Holy Spirit, the Church uses red vestments to symbolize the flame of God's love which is the work of the Holy Spirit. The Church celebrates the Feast of Pentecost as the day when the Holy Spirit began to move the apostles to go out and share Christ's message and to draw all people into the community called Church.

f. After Pentecost we continue to celebrate the guidance of the Holy Spirit in the Church.

On the Sundays following Pentecost, we celebrate the presence of the Church as it now follows the guidance of the Holy Spirit. These Sundays after Pentecost will take us to the final Sunday before the beginning of the new liturgical year. On the last Sunday of the liturgical year, the Church will again look to the final coming of Jesus and remind us that Jesus is our final and eternal hope. Throughout these Sundays, the Church celebrates as though it were on a journey, a pilgrimage toward God. During this season, the presider will wear green vestments, a color symbolizing hope. As long as the Spirit is continually working in the Church as Christ has promised, there is always hope for a better world and hope for an eternal joy for all people.

Conclusion

In the introduction to this chapter, we spoke of our desire to express our love for God. Once we discover the great goodness and love of God for us, we want to return that love. But we feebly look for ways to express our love in a satisfying way. As God has done so many times in our lives, God shares with us a gift to satisfy this desire. Through the Sacraments of Initiation, baptism, confirmation and the Eucharist, we join with Christ in calling out to God in a most perfect way, "I love you." Through these sacraments, we have become part of the family. Even better, we have become one with Christ. In the image of the Son, the family of God calls out with the voice of Christ to proclaim to God, "We love you." This is the great gift of the Sacraments of Initiation.

For Scripture reflection and discussion concerning this chapter, see Journeying in His Light, *"Sacraments of Initiation: Part 3."*

1. What is conscience?

a. Conscience is a judgment by which a person decides whether a particular action agrees or disagrees with a fundamental way of thinking.

On the day that Tom cheated his neighbor, he felt bothered about it. His conscience had reminded him that he had acted contrary to his continual desire to do a good job for his customers. His conscience felt better as he headed home after working on the car because he had corrected his fault and had worked more in accord with his continual way of thinking.

Whenever any of us act against our fundamental way of thinking, our conscience immediately reminds us that something is wrong. We are bothered. In the life of a Christian, any action or sin against God or neighbor should immediately trigger our conscience to remind us that we are sinning. By continually sinning, we gradually quiet our conscience so that we no longer allow ourselves to be bothered by our sins. As this happens, our fundamental option or way of thinking is also changing to a direction that accepts sin rather than God.

It is hard to imagine a person with no conscience. A parent who hurts a child should normally feel a pang of remorse and wrong doing. However, for a person with no fundamental ability to love, conscience could easily be a stranger to that person's life. For most of us, conscience plays a major part in life.

b. For our conscience to form correct judgements, we must become aware of our Christian responsibilities.

A Christian forms a correct conscience by striving to understand the message of Christ and his Church. Tom's basic direction in life lies in being fair to his customers. We do not know how Tom formed this way of thinking, but it certainly lives out the goodness demanded by the Christian message. Within our lives, we have certain human responsibilities that affect our conscience. A parent who hurts a child will ordinarily feel a pang of conscience, whether that parent is a Christian or not. A Christian, however, should feel a pang of conscience when he or she strives to hurt even an enemy. Christ told us to love our enemies. As a Christian accepts and reflects on the message of Christ, a Christian is forming conscience in line with this message. The message of Christ becomes the fundamental way of thinking. This is a Christian conscience.

11

Reconciliation— A New Beginning

Introduction

Because Tom worked so well on all types of cars, the owner of the car shop had named him head mechanic. Over the years, Tom's reputation had gained many new clients for the owner. But on this Friday before the Labor Day weekend, even Tom had to admit that he could never finish all the cars by closing time. In a moment of weakness and weariness, Tom decided to take a short cut on an oil change ordered by his neighbor. In a few moments, Tom had poured enough oil in the engine to bring the gauge to the "full" mark, and drove the car out to the lot as though he had changed the oil. He knew his neighbor would never check to see if he actually had done the job. He would simply take it for granted.

Later that evening, as Tom drove home in a far better mood, his neighbor shouted as he passed, "Thanks for taking care of my car today, Tom." After supper, Tom thought of his neighbor's car and finally became disturbed enough to walk down to his neighbor's house to confess what had happened. Tom offered to change the oil in the driveway of his own house and to check the car for other possible repairs, all free of charge. The neighbor was surprised, but pleased that Tom had offered to work on the car. When Tom had finished, he promised his neighbor that the next oil change would also be free of charge. The neighbor insisted that Tom have a piece of his son's birthday cake and a cup of coffee before he returned home. By the time he started home that evening, Tom realized that his neighbor had not only accepted his apology, but had even accepted his friendship by inviting him to share in his son's birthday celebration. Tom felt better the second time he returned home that evening.

165

c. Conscience does not consist merely in "feeling" that an action is wrong.

Even though we try hard, we find some demands of the law of Christ difficult to accept. Some are able to reach a point of "feeling" no wrong in hating or hurting a neighbor who has spoken or acted against them. The basic direction of a person's life may be to live out Christ's message, and the very acceptance of that message enables the person to know that certain actions are contrary to this basic direction, even though the person may never "feel" that it is wrong or sinful.

2. What is a temptation?

a. A temptation is an attraction to choose a thought or action contrary to the love of God or neighbor.

A temptation consists in an invitation to sin. In the story of Christ's temptation in the desert by the devil (Luke 4:1–2), we see the devil inviting Jesus to perform certain actions that would be contrary to his mission. Instead of suffering and dying to show his messiahship, Jesus could simply have accepted the alluring solutions offered by the devil. Jesus rejected these temptations and won the battle against Satan. Temptations are an important part of our lives. Through temptations, we face the challenge of evil and the chance to conquer evil in the name of Christ.

b. Temptation is not a sin.

Christ, who committed no sin, was tempted. Only if a person accepts a temptation and intends to put the temptation into action does the temptation become a sin. When Tom felt the urge to cheat his neighbor, he committed no wrong. When he accepted the temptation and cheated his neighbor, Tom then committed a sinful action.

c. At times of temptation we call upon God through prayer.

We shall never be tempted beyond our powers. When we recognize our weakness in temptation, we should call upon God for help. When St. Paul speaks of asking God to remove some physical weakness, God speaks to him and says, "My grace is enough for you: my power is at its best in weakness (2 Corinthians 12:9). By praying at moments of temptation, we will find that God's grace is sufficient for us. Through prayer and continual good actions, we are able to overcome temptations.

3. Can God alone forgive sins?

a. *God alone has the power to forgive sins.*

Throughout the Old Testament, the People of God constantly called upon God for the forgiveness of their sins. David sinned with Bathsheba, the wife of Uriah. Uriah was a soldier who served the Israelite nation in war and who refused to enjoy the pleasures of his home while his army was in the midst of battle. David had Uriah placed at the head of the army that Uriah might be killed in battle. After the death of Uriah, David took Bathsheba as his wife. When Nathan, the prophet, prodded David's conscience and reminded him of his sin, David responded, "I have sinned against (the Lord)." Nathan answered David, "*(The Lord) for his part, forgives your sin; you are not to die!*" (2 Samuel 12:13).

In certain Old Testament rituals, the people would seek forgiveness for their sins through some specially chosen sacrifice. Although the priest offered this sacrifice to God in the name of the people, God, not the priest, forgave the sins of the community. The priest simply turned the offering for sins over to God, asking God's forgiveness for the community. For the people of the Old Testament, sin was an offense against God and only God possessed the power to forgive sins.

b. *Jesus Christ, who is God, came forgiving sins.*

A Pharisee had invited Jesus to dinner but did not perform the customary ritual of cleansing before the meal began. A woman, known to be a sinner, came to Jesus with perfumed oil and, with her tears and the oil, washed his feet and dried them with her hair. We read in the gospel: "Then (Jesus) said to her, "*Your sins are forgiven*" (Luke 7:48). At this meal, Jesus professed his ability to forgive sin. We read about a paralyzed man who was lowered through a roof in order to be cured. Elsewhere, the Scriptures continue,

> *Seeing how much faith they had, Jesus said to the paralyzed man, "My son, your sins are forgiven." Some teachers of the Law who were sitting there thought to themselves, "How does he dare talk like this? This is blasphemy! God is the only one who can forgive sins!" At once Jesus knew what they were thinking, so he said to them, "Why do you think such things? Is it easier to say to this paralyzed man, 'Your sins are forgiven', or to say, 'Get up, pick up your mat, and walk?' I will prove to you, then, that the Son of Man has authority on earth to forgive sins." So he said to the paralyzed man, "I tell you, get up, pick up your mat, and go home!" While they all watched, the man got up,*

168

picked up his mat, and hurried away. They were all completely amazed and praised God, saying, "We have never seen anything like this!" (Mark 2:5–12).

The Gospels tell us that Jesus came forgiving sins, and, at times, he even performed miracles as a sign of this power to forgive sins.

c. Jesus passed this power on to the Church.

Although God alone has the power to forgive sins, God shares this power with others. After the resurrection of Jesus, we read in the Gospel of John that Jesus shared this power with the apostles: "As the Father sent me, so am I sending you." After saying this, he breathed on them and said, "Receive the Holy Spirit. For those whose sins you forgive, they are forgiven; for those whose sins you retain, they are retained" (John 20:21–23). In the writings of the early Church, the apostles forgave in the name of Jesus Christ. They also shared this power with others. Although God alone has the power to forgive sins, God chose to share this power with certain members of His Church. The minister of the sacrament, the ordained priest, acts in the name of Jesus Christ, and also in the name of the community.

4. What is the Sacrament of Reconciliation?

a. Reconciliation is a sacrament by which a person renews a love relationship with God and the community.

Whenever we sin we weaken our deep relationship with God and the community. We no longer approach God as openly and freely as before. A need to reconcile ourselves with God and others becomes important. Through the Sacrament of Reconciliation, we are able to renew this love relationship. Reconciliation consists not only in confession of our sins, but also in a deep conversion of our whole life toward God. In the introduction Tom not only confessed his fault, but he also offered his neighbor a greater gift than the offense. By offering work free of charge, he sought to reconcile himself with his neighbor. In the same way, when we sin, we seek to reconcile ourselves with God and the community. We do not look at our sin and merely tell God we are sorry. We strive, in the future, to become an even better person. Another name given to this sacrament is the Sacrament of Penance. The idea of reconciliation, however, includes the idea of confessing one's sins, performing an act of satisfaction, and living out a change in life which draws God more deeply into our life.

169

A parable, known to many as the parable of the "Prodigal Son," has all the elements of true reconciliation, and it offers a warning to those who think they are following Christ by merely following his rules and not his Spirit. In this parable, found in the Gospel of Luke (15:11–31), a son takes his inheritance and squanders it on a sinful way of life. When the son repents of his sinfulness, he returns to profess his unworthiness before his father, and to ask his father's forgiveness for his sins. The father forgives him immediately, and orders a celebration for his son, a repentant sinner who has returned home. The father in the story refers to God who readily forgives anyone seeking forgiveness. Luke tells us that the father caught sight of his son at a distance and ran out to meet him. The message tells us that God is as anxious as the father to welcome repentant sinners. The elder son, who kept all the rules, becomes angry with the father who so readily forgives his sinful son. We discover in him a person who follows all the rules, but who has not grasped the spirit of the father. The elder son also needs reconciliation for his hard and unforgiving nature. The parable not only tells us that God is willing to share in reconciliation with us, but it also reminds us that we should be quick to reconcile ourselves with those who sin against us, as the father in the parable did.

b. Through the Sacrament of Reconciliation, a person makes peace with the community.

As was mentioned in an earlier chapter, through our baptism we are baptized into Christ which is the Church or the community of Jesus' people. We are so closely joined together in this community that our own sins affect the whole community. Paul writes "If one part is hurt, all the parts are hurt with it; if one part is given special honor, all parts enjoy it" (I Corinthians 12:26). Even our so-called private sins affect the whole community. Because we hurt the community by our sins, we seek forgiveness of the community by making peace through its representative. The ordained priest acts in the name of Jesus Christ, and also in the name of the community. Through this sacrament we not only reconcile ourselves to God but we also reconcile ourselves to the community.

c. In the Sacrament of Reconciliation, a sinner celebrates God's forgiving love.

God's love is always an inviting love. In the Sacrament of Reconciliation, we celebrate God's call for our return to God's love and our response to that call. In our need for reconciliation, we recognize more fully our need for God's help and God's love. We also recognize and accept God's love for sinners. Because of God's love, we celebrate our

170

return to God through the Sacrament of Reconciliation. In the parable of the "Prodigal Son," the occasion of the son's confession of sins becomes the occasion for a celebration. The father says, "Let us eat and celebrate because this son of mine was dead and has come back to life. He was lost and is found," and Luke tells us simply, "Then the celebration began" (Luke 15:23–24).

d. Through the Sacrament of Reconciliation, we receive help to live a better life.

By examining our conscience before the individual celebration of the sacrament, we pinpoint those areas of our life where growth must take place. We admit our need for help, and through the Sacrament of Reconciliation, not only are our sins forgiven, but also we share in the blessings of God which enable us to live a better life. Through the Sacrament of Reconciliation, we promise in our weakness to strive to draw closer to God, and God responds to our desire for conversion by sharing special graces or helps in order that we may live a new life. Paul writes, ". . . God, in Christ, was reconciling the world to himself, not counting men's transgressions against them . . ." (2 Corinthians 5:19).

e. Through the Sacrament of Reconciliation, even good people draw closer to God.

To celebrate the Sacrament of Reconciliation, we need not be in the state of sin. What is necessary for this sacrament is that we be able to recognize a sinful condition in life. This sinfulness does not mean that we must have committed a specific sin between the last celebration of this sacrament and the present celebration. It simply means that we recognize weak and sinful tendencies and recognize a need to draw even closer to God by celebrating this Sacrament of Reconciliation. Because of the special helps given to live a new and better life, we should periodically avail ourselves of this sacrament.

Whenever we are in serious sin, we should participate in this sacrament as soon as possible. The Church has established as law that any Catholic in the state of serious sin shall confess at least once a year. For those who continually strive to live close to God, such a law is never necessary.

5. How is the Sacrament of Reconciliation celebrated?

a. The rite begins with the reception of the penitent.

The reconciliation room is ordinarily a small room with at least two chairs, a small table and a divider. The penitent may confess in privacy if he or she wishes. The penitent may also choose the chair opposite the priest in order to converse more fully concerning one's spiritual failures and hopes. The priest greets the penitent. Both together make the sign of the cross. The priest then prays a short prayer by which he invites the penitent to trust in God's love and mercy. The penitent answers, "Amen."

b. A short reading of the Word of God follows the reception of the penitent.

The priest or the penitent may read or recite from memory a passage of Scripture which speaks about God's mercy and the need for a change of life. The purpose of the reading is to enable both priest and penitent to reflect upon the loving mercy of God and to try to understand that love more perfectly. The penitent may choose a special reading that relates to some point the penitent wishes to emphasize in this celebration of the sacrament.

c. Encouraged by this Word of God, the penitent then confesses how he or she has failed the Lord and the community by sin.

The penitent expresses failures as well as hopes for the future in the celebration of this sacrament. During this time, the priest gives assistance and advice. The priest and penitent should not make this time for lengthy spiritual counseling or spiritual direction. If more time is needed, the priest and penitent should establish another specific time for continuing this direction.

d. The priest assigns an appropriate act of satisfaction for sin.

God's gift is one of forgiveness. It is unconditional and free. The purpose of satisfaction is to bring about a loving reconciliation between oneself and others, or even oneself and the Church, and to aid the person in becoming the one God is calling that person to be. The priest may suggest an action or suggest some appropriate prayers to help the penitent carry out new hopes for the future.

e. The penitent prays a prayer of sorrow (contrition).

The priest invites the penitent to express in prayer an act of sorrow for sin. The penitent may do this in his or her own words or use a formal prayer. We commonly refer to this prayer as an "Act of Sorrow (Contrition)." These words simply sum up and express verbally the sorrow which has already taken place (see appendix).

f. The priest prays the prayer of absolution.

The priest then extends his hand over the head of the penitent, and prays the prayer of forgiveness or absolution. Placing a hand over or on the head of the penitent is an ancient gesture of invoking the Holy Spirit. In the prayer of absolution, a priest proclaims the gift of reconciliation existing between God and all people. This gift was accomplished by the death and resurrection of Jesus Christ. An important part of the reconciliation rite is the sending of the Holy Spirit among us for the forgiveness of all sins. The priest, in the name of Christ and as a member of the Church, prays "through the ministry of the Church" for pardon and peace, and absolves the penitent. The words of absolution read:

> God, the Father of mercies,
> through the death and resurrection of his Son,
> has reconciled the world to himself
> and sent the Holy Spirit among us
> for the forgiveness of sins;
> through the ministry of the Church
> may God give you pardon and peace,
> and I absolve you from your sins
> in the name of the Father, and of the Son, ✦
> and of the Holy Spirit.

The penitent answers: *Amen.*

g. Priest and penitent praise God and the celebration is ended.

Acknowledging God's great mercy in the sacrament, the priest and penitent share a brief dialogue of praise of God. The priest prays the prayer:

> Give thanks to the Lord, for he is good.

The penitent concludes: *His mercy endures forever.*

Then the priest dismisses the penitent who has been reconciled, saying:

> The Lord has freed you from your sins. Go in peace.

6. What is communal reconciliation?

a. Communal reconciliation consists in a service by which the individuals of a community come together to recognize the social nature and harm of sin.

In a communal celebration of the Sacrament of Reconciliation, the community shares publicly in a preparation for the Sacrament of Reconciliation. The reading of the Word of God ordinarily read in the reconciliation room is now shared with the entire assembly. A brief homily usually follows the Word of God. The priest or priests then go to different areas to be used for the celebration of this sacrament. The penitents individually confess their sins, receive an act of satisfaction, and are absolved by the priest. They will often remain until all have celebrated the Sacrament of Reconciliation and all will pray in thanksgiving and give praise for God's love and mercy. This may be done in word or song. Through this communal celebration we realize that the sacraments are community celebrations as well as the fact that all sins are offenses against the community.

b. Communal reconciliation at times includes "general absolution."

Due to a large number of penitents and a lack of sufficient confessors, the Church allows the priest to confer "general absolution" upon members of the community if the penitents are forced to be deprived of sacramental grace or Holy Communion for a long time through no fault of their own. The priest should do all in his power to see that the people are properly disposed for this sacrament, and that they understand what is happening. Keeping in mind the spirit of reconciliation and the desire to use all means of deepening a relationship with God, the Church requires those in serious sin to discuss that particular fault at a future celebration of reconciliation. Reconciliation is more than forgiveness. It involves a new direction or conversion in life, and such direction becomes more firm when openly discussed in this sacrament.

7. What is necessary for the reception of this sacrament?

a. The penitent who shares in the celebration of this sacrament must have sorrow for sins.

In order for a person to celebrate this sacrament worthily, the penitent must be able to express some sorrow for sins. This sorrow for sins

174

does not demand that a person come to the sacrament in tears nor with a deep, emotional feeling of sorrow. This sorrow can be a simple statement that a person seeks reconciliation for having offended God and the community. Sorrow does not necessarily express itself in tears but more in a change of life.

b. The penitent who celebrates this sacrament must also have the intention of never sinning again.

Overcoming sin and weakness is a lifetime task. God understands this, and God is ever present. God is always ready to renew the love relationship. The penitent should approach this sacrament with confidence and trust in God. To continue to confess sins that have already been forgiven in this sacrament is to show a lack of trust in the celebration of this sacrament. Once a sin has been confessed in this sacrament there is no need to confess that sin again. God has already invited us to share more fully in God's life.

Conclusion

Ever since Tom confessed his guilt to his neighbor, Tom and his neighbor have become the best of friends. Tom's gratitude to his neighbor for accepting his simple apology and for accepting the extra work on his car has helped Tom to realize the value of forgiveness. Not only has Tom's neighbor accepted the apology, but the neighbor has accepted Tom in a full and better way. This is a true sign of reconciliation.

Whenever we sin, we can turn back to God and the community and seek to draw closer to them in a new and better relationship. God is always accepting our friendship, always accepting our reconciliation. Each time we turn towards God, God does not bring us back into an old friendship but rather brings us into a new and deeper friendship. In this new friendship, we realize God's love for us and our love for God.

For Scripture reflection and discussion concerning this chapter, see Journeying in His Light, *"Reconciliation—a New Beginning."*

12 Marriage and the Family

Introduction

Marie sat at the kitchen table, speaking with her mother about plans for the anniversary celebration. In only three months, Marie's mother and father would celebrate fifty years of marriage. While they talked, Marie noticed her mother relax just a slight bit when she heard the front door open and knew her husband had returned from his daily walk to the park and back. She reflected on the silent communication that existed between her mother and father after all these years of marriage. She would notice at other times a slight tension while she spoke with her father in the living room, especially if the kitchen seemed too silent for too long. But the sound of a pan banging in the sink would ease the tension as she noted that same slight relaxation in her father. She had learned of the concern that existed between her parents for each other, and how the sound of a door opening or a pan banging in the sink communicated that all was well. Through fifty years of struggling, adapting, and even arguing with one another, the two had gradually welded into one.

At the anniversary celebration, the four children, the ten grandchildren and eight great grand-children stood as a living reminder of what their marriage had brought to the world. In their love and their family, Marie was able to understand the great ideal of marriage in God's creation. She smiled as she whispered to herself, "I guess God does know what He is doing."

1. How did the Sacrament of Marriage develop?

a. Throughout the Old Testament we see a gradual growth of the understanding of marriage.

Many of the ideas of marriage in early Old Testament times came close to those of their pagan neighbors. A man could have more than one wife. A man could divorce his wife, but the wife could not divorce her husband. A man committed adultery by going out with another man's wife, but a married man could have intercourse with a woman who was not married and not commit adultery. In later Old Testament times, a deeper religious understanding of marriage was gradually developing. We read in Genesis,

> *Then the Lord God made the man fall into a deep sleep, and while he was sleeping, He took one of the man's ribs and closed up the flesh. He formed a woman out of the rib and brought her to him. Then the man said, "At last, here is one of my own kind—Bone taken from my bone, and flesh from my flesh. 'Woman' is her name because she was taken out of man." That is why a man leaves his father and mother and is united with his wife, and they become one (Genesis 2:21–24).*

In this reading, we see that God is the author of marriage and that marriage comes from the very basis of God's creation. At the moment of marriage, the man and woman grow so close together that they actually become one flesh. About four hundred and fifty years before Christ the author of the book of Malachi cried out in prophecy, ". . . (the Lord) stands as witness between you and the wife of your youth, the wife with whom you have broken faith even though she was your partner and your wife by covenant. Did He not create a single being, that has flesh and the breath of life" (Malachi 2:14–15). God no longer accepts sacrifice from these chosen people because God is unhappy with the one who has broken faith with his wife with whom he is one flesh. Malachi even went on to say, "For I hate divorce, says the Lord, the God of Israel" (Malachi 2:16). Statements such as Malachi's stand out in stark contrast against the thinking of the people of the Old Testament, even to the coming of Christ. Like John the Baptist, the voice of Malachi on this point in the Old Testament could be called the voice of one crying out in the desert. With the coming of Christ, his voice would be heard more clearly.

b. Jesus brought a new awareness to the understanding of marriage.

In the Gospel of Matthew, we read that the Pharisees came to question Jesus about divorce. By the time Jesus had finished speaking, even the disciples wondered if they could carry out this law of Christ.

> *Some Pharisees came to him and tried to trap him by asking, "Does our Law allow a man to divorce his wife for whatever reason he wishes?" Jesus answered, "Haven't you read the Scripture that says that in the beginning the Creator made people male and female? And God said, 'For this reason, a man will leave his father and mother and unite with his wife, and the two will become one. Man must not separate, then, what God has joined together.' " The Pharisees asked him, "Why, then, did Moses give the law for a man to hand his wife a divorce notice and send her away?" Jesus answered, "Moses gave you permission to divorce your wives because you are so hard to teach. But it was not like that at the time of creation. I tell you, then, that any man who divorces his wife for any cause other than her unfaithfulness, commits adultery if he marries some other woman." His disciples said to him, "If this is how it is between a man and his wife, it is better not to marry." Jesus answered, "This teaching does not apply to everyone, but only to those to whom God has given it"* (Matthew 19:3–11).

The fact that the disciples portray surprise at the words of Jesus shows that he is sharing with them a new teaching contrary to their way of thinking. Jesus points to marriage in this passage as a permanent union between a man and a woman. Elsewhere in the Gospel of Matthew, the Sacrament of Marriage is shown to be so sacred that even a person's innermost thoughts must respect the marriage of others. "You have learned how it was said, 'You must not commit adultery.' But I say this to you: 'If a man looks at a woman lustfully, he has already committed adultery with her in his heart' " (Matthew 5:27–28). Through the life, death, and exaltation of Jesus, marriage is raised to the high dignity of a sacrament.

c. The letter to the Ephesians compares marriage to Christ and his Church.

In the letter to the Ephesians we read,

> *Men ought to love their wives just as they love their own bodies. A man who loves his wife loves himself. (No one ever hates his own body. Instead, he feeds it and takes care of it, just as Christ does the Church; for we are members of his body.) As the Scripture says, "For this*

reason a man will leave his father and mother and unite with his wife, and the two will become one." There is a deep secret truth revealed in this Scripture, which I understand as applying to Christ and the Church. But it also applies to you: every husband must love his wife, as himself, and every wife must respect her husband (Ephesians 5:28–33).

This letter portrays the high regard the early Church had for the Sacrament of Marriage. To compare the union of a husband and wife with the union of Christ and his Church is to use the highest comparison possible in the opinion of Christians. Just as Christ is his Church, the two become one flesh and share in this great union of Christ's love.

2. What is the purpose of Marriage?

a. One purpose of marriage is to share in God's co-creative work of bringing new human life into the world.

One of the great gifts of God's creation resides in the gift of being able to give birth to a child. Because this event happens in our world every day, we often overlook the amazing miracle of birth. We can never forget that God has shared this gift with us: "God created man in the image of Himself, in the image of God He created him. . . . Be fruitful, multiply, fill the earth and conquer it" (Genesis 1:27–28). In sharing this gift, God allowed a man and a woman to take part in the highest privilege of creation, namely the privilege of sharing as co-creators in bringing new life into the world. Not only does the privilege lie in giving birth to a child, but also in helping form the child for life. Christ reminds us through the Church of this privilege and obligation of the family. Marriage has as a primary purpose the bearing and rearing of children.

b. Another primary purpose of marriage is the development of mutual love between the husband and wife.

The development of love stands at the foundation of God's creation. Love should flourish in the family, and the love of a husband and wife shares first place in marriage along with the birth and education of children. Through sexual sharing, the husband and wife deepen their love for one another and bring to that sharing a complete giving of themselves in love. Through their daily life together, through joys and tragedies that they must face together, a husband and wife develop their love for each other. The commitment of marriage allows for trust and intimacy in which mutual love can continually grow. For this reason, mutual love is also considered another primary purpose of marriage.

3. What is a Christian marriage?

a. A Christian marriage is a sacrament in which a baptized man and a baptized woman pledge their love and faithfulness to each other through a special covenant.

Throughout the Old Testament, a key theme of covenant is often portrayed as a marriage between God and the nation of Israel. As was mentioned in an earlier chapter, a covenant differs from a contract. A contract usually refers to some work or action to be performed and concluded within a set period of time. A covenant, however, consists in a full personal commitment of one person to another for as long as the two live. When a man and a woman enter into marriage, they share in a deep personal covenant. The baptized man and woman share in a sacramental covenant which we call a sacrament.

b. A Christian marriage is one which most fully reflects the love of Christ for his Church.

In the Sacrament of Marriage there are really three people sharing together: the baptized man and woman along with Christ. Paul referred to the Sacrament of Marriage as a reflection of Christ and his Church. In the Sacrament of Marriage, Christ enters most fully into the covenant. Before God, and the community, and with the power shared by Christ's resurrection, two people fully commit themselves to each other for life, and Christ blesses this union by sharing the blessings and helps of a sacrament. The husband and wife enter into a deep relationship with each other and also into a deeper and more intimate union with Jesus Christ himself, as is the case in each of the sacraments, through Christian Marriage.

4. Does the Catholic Church believe in divorce?

a. The Catholic Church does not allow divorce and remarriage.

If a person is truly married and has sought a legal divorce with the state, that person is not free to marry again. The Church takes strictly the words of Christ as found in the Scriptures, "But from the beginning of creation God made them male and female. This is why a man must leave father and mother, and the two become one body. They are no longer two, therefore, but one body. So then, what God has united let no man separate" (Mark 10:6–9). In the eyes of the Church, marriage is a full giving of one's complete self to another for life. Once two people have entered this covenant, even if they separate, the covenant continues to exist. Later, in the same chapter of Mark, we read, "He (Jesus) said to them, 'The man who divorces his wife and marries another is guilty of adultery against her. And if a woman divorces her husband and marries another she is guilty of adultery too' " (Mark 10:11). Even if a legal divorce should take place, Jesus does not accept this as a sign that the covenant has ended. In Mark, we read that a man or woman who separates and marries again commits adultery.

b. For a serious reason the Catholic Church does allow divorce or separation without remarriage.

There are times when people are better off separated than together. If a person suffers a violation of his or her human dignity within marriage, then this person certainly may seek a separation. However, even if a legal divorce is obtained, the person does not have the right to marry again. In the eyes of the Church, if a person is divorced and remarried he or she may not share in the sacraments. The Church continues to invite the individual to share in worship. A divorced person who has remarried should not turn against the Church, but rather should continue to pray along with the Church that God will offer guidance and strength. A divorced person who has not remarried is ordinarily permitted to share in the sacraments. If a person has any doubts about his or her situation, he or she should consult the parish priest or parish associate(s) who deal with such situations.

c. An annulment consists in a declaration by the Church that no marriage ever existed.

In some cases, the Church will study the beginnings of a marriage to establish whether or not the marriage actually took place. There are certain demands a person must fulfill in order to enter a true marriage. A couple must have the intention of having children if they are physically able to do so. They must be a mature couple, capable of making a full commitment to each other. Reasons for annulment can be physical or spiritual. A divorced person should consult a priest or some other person in the Church who has knowledge of marriage laws to look into their marriage for a possible annulment. Some marriages that eventually break up have their root cause of the break up dating back to the beginning of the marriage.

5. What is necessary for a true (valid) marriage?

a. For the Sacrament of Marriage, a man or woman must be of mature age.

Ordinarily the Church requests permission of parents for anyone under eighteen years of age. However, when speaking about maturity we must speak about more than age. A person can be immature at the age of twenty-one or twenty-five. The one witnessing the marriage in the name of the Church must often make a judgment concerning the maturity of the individuals entering this sacrament. In order for a person to make a commitment for life, that person must be mature. Immature people do not have the full ability to make a life-long commitment.

b. There can not be a previously existing valid marriage.

Since the Church does not recognize divorce, a person who has previously married and who has received a legal divorce cannot enter the Sacrament of Marriage in the Church. The only exception to this rule would be a case where the previous spouse has died. If a previous marriage has been invalid, that is, if it has not fulfilled the demand for a true marriage, then a declaration of nullity must be received from the Church. A declaration of nullity simply declares that a previous marriage never existed.

c. A person entering marriage must be capable of sharing sexually.

The ends of marriage consist in procreation of children and in the mutual love between a husband and wife. Marriage is the sharing of one's full sexuality with another. For those who are physically capable, procreation is a necessity for a true marriage. In all marriages, people must be capable of sharing sexually. If a person does not have this capability, the person has a physical impediment to marriage. Sexual sharing is a symbolic sign of two becoming one and fulfills at least one of the primary ends of marriage, namely, mutual love between husband and wife. A lack of this symbolic sign makes a person incapable of celebrating this sacrament.

d. A person must freely intend to enter a lifelong commitment.

When entering marriage, the couple commit themselves to each other for life. If they enter the marriage with definite openness to divorce and if certain conditions are not fulfilled, that marriage is invalid. If a person is forced into a marriage commitment, that person has not entered a true marriage. A marriage must be entered into freely and knowingly.

e. In order to enter into marriage, two people must not be closely related to each other by blood or marriage.

A brother may not marry a sister nor may close cousins marry each other. After the death of a partner, a brother-in-law may not marry a sister-in-law unless a special dispensation is granted. In all cases of any relationship, a person should confer with a priest before planning marriage.

6. What steps must a person take in order to enter marriage?

a. Before two people enter marriage, they must arrange with the priest for a period of premarriage dialogue.

Some dioceses demand that a couple confer with the priest before they even set a date for their marriage. During the preparation period, certain papers must be filled out in preparation for the marriage. The couple also should attend marriage preparation sessions. At these sessions, a married couple, a doctor, a priest, and others will share in preparing a couple for their marriage. Along with these instructions, the parish priest or a representative will continue to work with the couple to prepare for the marriage. During this time, they will discuss matters that closely touch upon the life of a married couple. They will speak of communication in love, of pregnancy and child-bearing, of sexuality, finances, religion, and the ceremony itself. In some dioceses, special preparation is demanded for teenage marriages. In such cases, teenagers should give themselves a sufficient amount of time before planning to enter marriage.

b. When a Catholic marries another not of the Catholic faith, certain dispensations must be sought from the Church.

A person seeks a dispensation for marrying a nonbaptized person or a doubtfully-baptized person or a person baptized in another Christian Church. In such a marriage, the Catholic party promises to continue to

184

practice the faith and to share that faith with his or her children. The partner must be aware of this promise although the partner is not requested to sign any promises. Ordinarily the Church freely grants such a dispensation once the promises are known and agreed to.

c. The names of those entering the Sacrament of Marriage are usually announced on three consecutive Sundays before the marriage takes place.

Three weeks before a marriage takes place, the names of the persons to enter marriage, as well as the parish in which they live, will be read in church or printed in the bulletin. The name for this announcement is called "Banns of Marriage." The purpose for reading the banns is to give people an opportunity to come forward if they know of any reason why the marriage should not take place, and also to announce to the Christian community that a marriage is to be celebrated. This is required only for the wedding of two Catholics, but is recommended for weddings where only one party is Catholic.

d. The Sacrament of Marriage should take place within the Eucharistic Liturgy.

As with most of the sacraments the appropriate place for the celebration of the Sacrament of Marriage is within the Eucharistic Liturgy. The priest or minister, after the homily, will receive the marriage vows from the man and woman entering this sacrament. Although it is strongly urged that people share this sacrament within the Eucharistic Liturgy, people may celebrate the sacrament at another time. Even in the case of mixed faith, the Eucharistic Liturgy may also be celebrated.

7. Who is the minister of the Sacrament of Marriage?

a. The bride and the groom are the proper ministers of the Sacrament of Marriage.

In the Sacrament of Marriage, a baptized man and a baptized woman use their baptismal priesthood. They confer the sacrament upon each other. Because they have already celebrated the Sacrament of Baptism, they are able to celebrate this sacrament. If one of the parties has not celebrated the Sacrament of Baptism the two people still enter a true marriage, but not a sacramental marriage. The marriage does not become sacramental until both parties have celebrated the Sacrament of Baptism. In this case, however, we still have a true and valid marriage.

b. Where one or both parties entering marriage are Catholic, they must exchange their marriage vows in the presence of an ordained minister of the Catholic Church.

Although the bride and groom are the proper ministers of the Sacrament of Marriage, Church law requires that an ordained minister, whether a bishop, priest or deacon, ask for and receive the consent of the parties entering marriage if one, or both, are Catholic. Two people who have not been baptized in the Catholic Church or who have not professed faith in the Catholic Church may validly marry before a minister or a state official with the legal right to contract marriages.

c. A minister of another faith may be invited to participate in a marriage where only one party is Catholic.

With the permission of the bishop of the area and the consent of the appropriate authority of the minister of another church, a minister may be invited to participate in a marriage where one party is not Catholic. The minister may share in additional prayers or words of greeting. The ordained representative of the Catholic Church, that is, the ordained priest or deacon must accept in the name of the Church, the vows of those entering marriage.

d. In exceptional cases, a dispensation may be granted for the minister of another faith to accept the vows of marriage in the name of the Church.

In some cases, a person of another faith may have a close relationship with a minister of the same faith. A dispensation may be received granting permission to a minister of another faith to act in the name of the Church in receiving the vows of those entering marriage. However, such a dispensation demands a special reason. In a case where a minister of another church accepts the marriage vows, a Catholic priest may also take part by reading certain prayers, sharing blessings or giving exhortations.

8. Why is sexual intimacy allowed only in marriage?

a. A result of sexual sharing is new life which is nourished most perfectly within the family.

One of the major purposes of marriage, as was mentioned earlier, is to share as a co-creator with God in bringing new life into the world. Through a special gift of God, a man and a woman are able to share in such a way that they conceive life. The ideal of sexual sharing should be open to the continuing care and development of this new life. The new life is most perfectly developed within the family which properly demands marriage and full commitment between a man and a woman. Through the Sacrament of Marriage, God shares special helps with a man and woman in the rearing of their children.

b. Sexual sharing is a high expression of mutual love and commitment between two people.

In God's plan, sexual sharing becomes a deep, loving communication between two people. In the introduction to this chapter, Marie noted how her parents communicated without words. They experienced each others' feelings and presence. In life, we communicate through words, actions, and even by silence. When two people meet, they communicate their love to each other through sharing intimate details about their lives. Before the community, in the marriage ceremony, they communicate their trust and commitment to each other by the exchange of the marriage vows. In their sexual sharing, this communication should continue. True sexual sharing does not consist in one body sharing with another body, but rather one person communicating love and pleasure with another person. When the angel in the infancy narrative told Mary that she was to conceive a son, Mary used an expression in common use in that day to describe the sexual act. Mary's response was, that she did not *know* man. In the Scriptures, the expression "know" refers to sexual intimacy, and it carries with it the idea of communication. Even in our own day, we use an expression for sexual sharing that includes communication. We call sexual sharing "intercourse." When two people share together sexually, it should include a deepening of their communication of trust and love with one another. Outside of marriage, the true meaning of sexual communication is lost and a full loving sexual sharing can never be achieved because two people lack the deepest form of communication, namely a lifelong commitment to one another.

c. Sexual sharing without full communication becomes destructive.

True sexual sharing is primarily directed toward giving and sharing. A continual sharing sexually outside of a deep commitment very often leads to a deep frustration. The act itself tends toward a deeper desire for communication and a desire to live and share together.

Love is so closely tied in with sexual sharing that a person who shares in the depth and commitment of marriage will often deepen in love towards one's partner. On the other hand, to share this act outside of marriage robs a person of a true ability to experience genuine love in this marriage act.

d. The Scriptures often speak of the dignity of sexual sharing in marriage.

Throughout the Old Testament, we read certain images in which God relates to the people of Israel as a husband to his wife. At times the Israelites are like an adulterous wife. They turn to other gods; they prostitute themselves, and God punishes them for their unfaithfulness. In the New Testament, Christ continually points out that a person who shares sexually with another who is married commits adultery. He even says that a person who looks with lust on a woman commits adultery. In this way, Christ is telling us of the great dignity of sexual sharing within marriage. Paul writes to the Corinthians:

You know that your bodies are parts of the body of Christ. Shall I take a part of Christ's body and make it part of the body of a prostitute? Impossible! Or perhaps you don't know that the man who joins his body to a prostitute becomes physically one with her? The Scripture says quite plainly, "The two will become one body" (1 Corinthians 6:15–16).

In this writing, Paul proclaims that sexual sharing makes us one with our partner in this sexual act. If we share with a prostitute, we become one with that prostitute. If we share with another outside of marriage and outside of love, we become one with lust. Through a true sexual sharing in marriage, we become one in love with the person with whom we share as well as with God.

9. What sexual sins could a person commit?

a. When an unmarried man and an unmarried woman share sexually outside of marriage, they commit the sin called fornication.

Fornication occurs when a man and a woman, both unmarried, share sexually without the full, exclusive, life-long commitment that comes through marriage. As with any great gift that comes from God, the gift of sexual sharing leads to certain responsibilities. It demands an exclusive, life-long love that shares in all the joys and difficulties involved in married life. Sexual sharing is directed toward a deep expression of love and commitment to one another, and the commitment to rearing children that flows from this expression of love. Through marriage, the couple commit themselves before God and the community to each other and their children. Fornication is sinful, because it seeks sexual gratification

188

without facing any of the responsibilities involved. Even if two people agree as "mature" adults to this mutual sexual sharing outside of marriage, they still "use" each other for their sexual gratification. It is using a great gift of God in a selfish and destructive way.

Where two people are planning to marry each other, they are still called to the ideal that flows from marriage, namely that a true, life-long commitment does not take place until marriage itself. Engaged couples, deeply committed to each other, may break off their engagement with the right to commit themselves to another marriage. Although they see themselves as exclusively committed for life in their own eyes, engaged couples do not reach this stage until they have committed themselves to each other before God and the community through marriage. Otherwise, marriage would have no greater meaning than the engagement.

b. Adultery occurs when a married person shares sexually with another person who is not a spouse.

In the act of adultery, one or both parties may be married. When they are sharing sexually with a person other than their own husband or wife, they are breaking the commitment they made to their spouse before God, namely not to share in such an intimate, committed way with another. They have sinned against the exclusive nature of marriage and have sinned against God and their spouse. Adultery is often a sign that a marriage is "in trouble." Not only does it destroy family life, but it also points to the fact that the family life has already started to break down. Some people show by adultery that they lack the maturity necessary for a fully committed marriage. If both parties in a marriage have faced the adultery of one or the other party, they should seek help in adjusting to "new beginnings" in correcting the problem. The very situation that led to adultery could still be existing and must be faced for a long-lasting solution.

c. Masturbation consists in turning self-gratification in upon oneself.

Masturbation consists in giving sexual pleasure to oneself. In the past, every action of masturbation was considered sinful. Many hold the opinion today that some acts of masturbation do not have full consent of the will. In many cases, they become habits that are extremely difficult to overcome. Often, masturbation becomes part of a growth process, a searching for sexual identity that one may go through in adolescence. If it continues into later life, it should be a matter of concern since it becomes a sign of sexual immaturity and perhaps a sign of escapism. People who have a habit of masturbation may not actually be committing sin. Simply to accept, however, and not work against it in some way could easily become a major weakness or sin in a person's life.

d. Homosexuality exists when a person's sexual desires tend toward a member of the same sex rather than a member of the other sex.

When the Scriptures speak against homosexuality, they often refer to a sin committed by people who could share sexually with the other sex but who choose to share sexually with the same sex. Homosexuality, in itself, does not immediately place a person in a condition of sin. There have been many insights into the question of homosexuality, and many attempts to try to understand it. In cases of morality, we ordinarily apply the same norms for a homosexual that would apply for sexual sharing between a man and a woman. Just as it is wrong for a man or woman not married to each other to share sexually, so it is wrong for a homosexual to share sexually with a person of the same sex. Both these cases are contrary to the nature and meaning of marriage.

Note: In all acts mentioned in this question (9), we must remember that we are speaking about actions that are contrary to the usual order of God's creation. We can never judge the degree of sinfulness of any person who performs these actions. The degree to which habit, psychological need, or life situation affects the freedom of the will should not be overlooked. People who continually find themselves unable to overcome any one of these actions should seek the guidance of an understanding confessor. The confessor will ordinarily suggest another type of counseling where he feels this is needed.

10. When is birth control permitted?

a. If a person does not have a serious reason for practicing birth control that person should not practice birth control.

By birth control, we mean that the person controls the number of children the person will bring into the world. Some people would like to have an extra car in the garage, or like to raise their standard of living by several levels beyond a level which is really necessary. In order to reach certain material success, they are willing to give up the idea of having children or to limit themselves to one child. In this case, birth control becomes sinful due to the selfish motive. Some sincerely feel in conscience that they cannot contribute to an overpopulation of the world. They may choose, for this reason, to limit the number of children. No one is allowed to practice birth control in marriage unless there is some good reason for choosing to control the number of children.

b. Natural birth control is allowed by the Church for special reasons.

In planning their family, parents may use natural means of birth control. A married woman shares sexually with her husband only on those days when she knows she ordinarily would not conceive. There are several methods of Natural Family Planning.

c. Parents should show a mature responsibility in planning and rearing their family.

The Catholic Church does not say that every parent should give birth to a child whenever the sexual act takes place. Often, parents may decide how many children they can properly care for within their family. They consider their capability as well as their financial status and try to decide, to the best of their ability, the number of children they could reasonably rear. Having a large number of children is not necessarily the sign of a good Catholic family.

11. What are some forms of natural birth control?

a. One method, which does not seem to work for most, is known as the Rhythm Method.

This method involves charting the days between the menstrual periods. For most women, the time between periods is somewhere between twenty-eight and thirty-three days. Ovulation usually takes place fourteen days before menstruation. If a woman is consistent in the days between her period, she can determine when she and her husband can share sexually, and when they must abstain. With this method, a couple must abstain a specific number of days before and after the estimated ovulation period. The problem with this method is that stress, sickness (even a cold), tiredness, change of diet, or any number of causes can change the cycle without the woman's knowing it.

There are other natural methods used which enable a couple to determine when the woman is most likely and least likely to conceive. The two most common methods which have proven effective are the Sympto-Thermal Method and the Ovulation Method, sometimes called the Billings Method. Training in these methods is held in many areas of the country, and a couple can ordinarily learn from the parish priest or from the Office for Family Life in the Diocese where it will be held.

b. The Sympto-Thermal Method bases its program upon the changes in the woman's body around the time of ovulation.

A shift in the woman's basal temperature will take place shortly after ovulation. On the third day after this shift in the basal temperature, the infertile phase will begin. The method demands a daily tracking of the woman's temperature throughout her cycle. Besides the shift in temperature, the method looks closely at certain symptoms which take place in the woman's body as, for example, changes in the cervical mucus discharge, pain which identifies ovulation, and changes in the shape and texture of the cervix.

c. The Ovulation Method identifies the changes in the mucus discharge throughout the cycle, thus identifying the infertile, the less fertile and the most fertile phases of a woman's cycle.

Right after her period, the woman will ordinarily enter a "dry phase," which means that she has no mucus discharge from the cervix. These are infertile days. This is followed by a mucus discharge which is at first sticky, more cloudy, but which soon becomes clear, slippery and able to be stretched without breaking. The final day of this last situation is called the peak, and ovulation usually occurs one day after the peak. In this method, the fertile period is determined to last from the beginning of the mucus discharge until the end of the third day after the peak. The woman is then considered infertile from the fourth day after the peak to the beginning of her next menstrual period.

d. Besides being helpful to families at a period when they do not wish to conceive a child, the Sympto-Thermal Method and the Ovulation Method are also helpful to families who wish to have children.

By knowing when the woman is most likely to conceive, a couple can share sexually at that time with a greater hope of conception taking place. The methods are not strictly birth control methods as they are methods of learning and understanding the woman's body. Whether or not a couple wishes to conceive a child at a designated time, the understanding of the gift and workings of one's body offer us a greater insight into God's creation.

e. The use of Natural Family Planning demands sacrifice on the part of the couple.

They will have certain phases during the cycle which will not allow for sexual sharing if they wish to avoid the conception of a child. The ability to make such a decision and abstain at will is a human and mature decision. Because marriage belongs only to the human family, it naturally requires sacrifice and dedication. Both spouses should enter the training for the use of any of these methods, since both will be making the decision together. The woman should not be the only one who keeps track of the days when the couple may or may not share sexually. The value of using one of these methods lies in its avoidance of possible dangers from taking pills or placing objects within the body.

Some confuse the Sympto-Thermal Method and the Ovulation Method with the Rhythm Method. These are not other forms of the same method, but are scientifically studied and researched methods of Natural Family Planning which have proved at least as effective as the pill in controlling birth. The methods simply learn about the body God gave women, and they call upon the love God gave to the husband and wife joined together in marriage.

Note: The answer to this question is taken from *Journeying toward Marriage* by Rev. William A. Anderson (Dubuque, IA: Wm. C. Brown Company Publishers, 1985).

12. When is birth control not allowed?

a. Church authority has often taught that artificial or contraceptive birth control is contrary to God's law.

By artificial or contraceptive birth control, we refer to pills or devices used to interfere with the conception of a child. Marriage is directed toward the giving birth and rearing of the child as well as toward the mutual love between the husband and wife. In the eyes of the authority of the Church, anything that interferes with either of these in an artificial way is contrary to the idea of marriage as found within our very nature. The use of artificial or contraceptive birth control methods brings about a direct interference in the conception of a child. By nature, a woman passes through periods when she cannot conceive. To set up situations where the woman is continually, or for a time, not able to conceive a child, or to make use of devices that hinder the possibilities of fertilization are seen to act beyond this law within the nature of the human act of marriage. In 1968, Pope Paul VI wrote a special letter to the entire world that affirmed the view that artificial birth control is contrary to the teaching of the Catholic Church.

b. Those in authority in the Church must continually call its members to the ideal of living a full, Christian life.

Like Christ, Church authority must present nothing less than the ideal. Pope Paul VI called the world to the Christian ideal of peace when he proclaimed before the United Nations, "No war! Never again!" Pope Pius XII, during the second world war, also recognized the call to the Christian ideal of peace. But when the ideal was not reached, he established certain norms for a "just war." In regards to artificial contraception, Church authority again calls all Christians to the ideal. But Church authority is also conscious of the problem.

In a document from the Second Vatican Council, we read:

The Council realizes that married people are often hindered by certain situations in modern life from working out their married love harmoniously and they can sometimes find themselves in a position where the number of children cannot be increased, at least for the time being. . . . (The Church in the Modern World, n. 51)

Although the document goes on to state that only those means approved by Church authority may be used, it recognizes the high degree of virtue demanded in rejection of the artificial means of birth control.

. . . in cases like these it is quite difficult to preserve the practice of faithful love and complete intimacy of their lives. But where the intimacy of married life is broken, it often happens that faithfulness is imperiled and the good of children suffers: then the education of children as well as the courage to accept more children are both endangered. (The Church in the Modern World, n. 51)

The problem is well stated in this document.

Many Bishops' Conferences throughout the world accepted the teaching of Pope Paul VI, but they reminded us that we could never judge the conscience of couples practicing artificial birth control. The judgement of conscience exists between the penitent and the confessor. Along with the Pope, Bishops' Conferences have been unanimous in inviting those who find themselves in this situation to make continual use of the strength which comes from the sacraments.

c. Direct abortion is never allowed and always sinful.

Abortion is the direct killing of a fetus or embryo, or causing the occasion that would bring about this death. To kill the fetus or embryo while in the womb or to cause an ejection of such before it is able to live outside the womb is abortion. This also includes pills or devices

194

used to keep a fertilized egg from implanting itself in the womb. The Catholic Church considers life to be present from the moment of conception. Any act which directly kills the embryo or fetus is considered a violation of a person's right to life. As Christians, we have the obligation to speak out in the name of the unborn, since they do not have the voice to speak out for themselves. If we remained silent, these lives would continue to be quietly destroyed with no dissenting voice to defend their right to life.

d. Indirect abortion may be permitted.

A woman who discovers after becoming pregnant that she has a cancerous womb may have that womb removed, even though it will lead to the death of the embryo or fetus. The intention behind the removal of the womb is the saving of the life of the mother. Through this operation, the embryo or fetus will die, but this is not the intent of the operation. An indirect abortion occurs when the primary intent of any action is to save the life of the mother. This primary intent can not consist in directly killing the fetus or embryo.

13. What obligations do parents have toward their children?

a. Parents have the obligation of rearing children in the Catholic faith.

Whenever we have something good to share, we wish to share it with those we love. A person who shares in all the gifts of the Catholic Church should desire to share these gifts with those close to them, most especially members of their own family. At the baptism of the child, the parents accepted the responsibility of rearing their child in the practice of the faith. Through the Sacrament of Marriage, the family is joined together by God for the sake of helping each member grow closer to God. The parents, by their life and example, are expected to teach the child as the child grows toward maturity. The parents will also share in preparing the child for the sacraments throughout the child's early life.

b. Parents must show love and respect for their children.

A child does not become the possession of a parent. A parent has the privilege of sharing life with the child and guiding that child in life. However, once that child is born, the child is an individual who depends very much upon the parents. As a child grows, the parents should share with the child all that is needed for a healthy growth through life. The parents should be open, at a certain point in life, to allow that child to walk freely when the child has reached a mature age.

c. Parents should show children the dignity of family life.

A child learns not just by being told things, but by the way the parents act. Parents, who show love and respect for one another and who show love and respect toward the child, will fill that child with a loving formation in family life. Parents shall share time with each other and time with their children that all may be able to grow in deeper love and respect for one another.

Conclusion

After some years, Marie's father died and her mother moved into a small apartment a few doors down from Marie's house. When Marie visits her, she tells Marie to cherish her husband and give time to her children. Marie sometimes resents the fact that her mother treats her like a child who needs directions about loving her husband and rearing her children. But then Marie remembers that her parents were really successful parents. They never had the riches that built new homes or bought new cars, but they had love. Their marriage was a true success. They had their tragedies, their doubts, their fights, and their joys. And through it all, they always had each other.

For Scripture reflection and discussion concerning this chapter, see Journeying in His Light, *"Marriage and the Family."*

A Ministry of Service

Introduction

Father Damian came to Hawaii in 1864 to work in the missionary fields. By 1873, he had heard about the leper colony at Molokai that lacked any type of medical or spiritual help. Knowing that he might never again be accepted among the "normal" people of the Islands, Father Damian still volunteered to go to this colony. Leprosy was the dreaded disease that condemned people to a slow death on the Island of Molokai, away from their families and friends. Father Damian brought the joy of Christ into those drab lives. He began by cleaning up the church building and painting some of its walls with bright colored paints. The dark colony soon came back to life under the enthusiasm of Father Damian. Father Damian took care of their spiritual and physical needs and brought to that colony a glimmer of hope. In the spirit of Christ's service to his people, Father Damian saw his life as one of continual service to the people of Molokai. He served the lepers for fifteen years, and suffered with leprosy for the last three years of his life. He saw his disease as a gift from God. Not only did he serve the people, he now shared in their suffering. He had become one of them, a castaway leper on the colony of Molokai.

1. What is ministry?

a. Ministry is a special call to serve in the name and spirit of Jesus Christ.

Jesus Christ traveled across the land of Palestine, preaching the Good News of the reign of God and healing spiritual and physical ills. He had nowhere to lay his head, but neither did many of the people he served. At the Last Supper, he gave a further sign of his service by washing the feet of the apostles. Throughout his life, Christ gave an example of the type of ministry he calls us to live. His was a ministry of servanthood.

He allowed himself to be led to the cross, to be crucified and even to die as part of his ministry to confront evil. Christ was the obedient servant. Through our baptism, we received a call to follow the example of Christ and to serve in the name and spirit of Christ.

b. Ministry is a special call to serve as a member of the Church.

We are members of Christ's body and, as such, we are members of his Church. After Christ's resurrection and ascension, the apostles began to share his ministry with others. In the name of Jesus, they cared for the poor, cured the sick and preached the message of the reign of God. The Acts of the Apostles proclaim the call of the disciples to serve as ministers in many different ways. The Acts tell how some in the Church shared in the ministry of preaching and the ministry of serving. As the early Church saw new needs arise, it would call upon its members to fill those needs. As a member of the Church, Christians reached out to others and to one another. They recognized their ministry as a special call to serve as a member of the Church. Through the Sacrament of Baptism, we are called to ministry as members of the Church. Paul speaks about the various ministries given by Christ, and he reminds us that they are given for the buildup of the Church, the Body of Christ on earth. Paul writes, "It is he (Christ) who gave apostles, prophets, evangelists, pastors, and teachers in roles of service for the faithful to build up the Body of Christ . . . " (Ephesians 4:11).

c. Ministry is a special share in the gifts of the Holy Spirit.

In calling us to ministry, Christ does not call us to act alone. In the Gospel of John he tells his apostles, "I will not leave you orphans" (John 14:18). Christ continually shares his gifts with us through the power of the Holy Spirit. These gifts enable us to carry out our ministry as Christ and the Church would have us carry it out. Paul writes of the gifts of the Holy Spirit that help us to live our call to ministry.

There are different kinds of spiritual gifts, but the same Spirit gives them. There are different ways of serving, but the same Lord is served. There are different abilities to perform service, but the same God gives ability to everyone for their particular service. The Spirit's presence is shown in some way in each person for the good of all. The Spirit gives one person a message full of wisdom, while to another person the same Spirit gives a message full of knowledge. One and the same Spirit gives faith to one person, while to another person he gives the power to heal. The Spirit gives one person the power to work miracles; to another the gift of speaking God's message; and to yet another, the

198

ability to tell the difference between gifts that come from the Spirit and those that do not. To one person he gives the ability to speak in strange tongues, and to another he gives the ability to explain what is said. But it is one and the same Spirit who does all this; as he wishes, he gives a different gift to each person (1 Corinthians 12:4–11).

Some refer to their special gifts of the Spirit as "Charisms."

d. All baptized Christians are called to ministry in Christ.

Through our baptism, we are all called to ministry. When Christians reach maturity, they have an obligation to share their ministry with others. A passive Christian, looking to save his or her own soul with no concern toward serving others, is not fully responding to the baptismal call of sharing the light of Christ with others. Paul, writing to the Colossians, tells us that we were baptized not only into Jesus' death, but also into his life, and it is this living presence of Christ which we are called to share through our ministry. Paul writes, "In baptism you were not only buried with him but also raised to life with him because you believed in the power of God who raised him from the dead" (Colossians 2:12). Through our baptism, we are called to minister to the worshipping community, and to minister to those outside the worshipping community. We are meant to hear the Word of God and to share it by word and action.

Paul goes on to remind us of the virtues involved in our ministry. He writes, "You are the people of God; He loved you and chose you for his own. So then, you must clothe yourselves with compassion, kindness, humility, gentleness and patience. . . . Christ's message in all its richness must live in your hearts. Teach and instruct one another with all wisdom. Sing psalms, hymns, and sacred songs; sing to God with thanksgiving in your hearts. Everything you do or say, then, should be done in the name of the Lord Jesus, as you give thanks through him to God the Father (Colossians 3:12, 16–17).

2. What is the ordained ministry?

a. The ordained ministry refers to bishops, presbyters, and deacons.

Through our baptism, all of us share in the one priesthood of Jesus Christ, and can properly be called priests. Through our gifts of priesthood, we worship God, the Father, "in . . . with . . . and through . . ." Christ, and in this way share in the highest form of worship. In the early Church, the ordained minister was not called a "priest" but rather a "presbyter." The ordained ministry included the bishops, presbyters (priests), and deacons. Since we are all priests through our baptism, a more exact term for the ordained priest would be presbyter.

b. The ordained ministry is a special call to the service of the Word of God.

Ordained ministers are especially called to share Christ's message with all people. In order to share fully in this call to ministry, they should become familiar with the Word of God and be able to communicate that Word in as clear and understandable a way as possible. Through their writing, preaching, and living, the ordained ministers should reflect the Word of God in such a way that others will see in them a living reflection of this Word of God.

c. The ordained ministry is a special call to the service of worship and celebration.

The ordained minister receives special gifts to share the sacraments given through Christ's resurrection. In the name of the Church, the ordained minister confers certain sacraments upon other members of the Church. He invites them into the community and shares with them the gifts of the community. The ordained minister calls the assembly to worship, and leads the assembly in worshipping God the Father in the name of Christ.

d. The ordained ministry is a special call to leadership through service.

The reign that Jesus came to preach is far different from any earthly reign. The way to this reign is a way of service. Christ came as a servant king. The ordained minister is also called to lead the way, but to lead the way as a servant to the people. The ordained minister is called to leadership within the community, but a leadership that flows out of service and a leadership that shows itself most perfectly when it is serving members of the community. Christ gave an example of this service when he washed the apostles' feet at the Last Supper. After Jesus washed the feet of the disciples, he told them, "Do you understand what I have just done to you?" he asked. "You call me Teacher and Lord, and it is right that you do so, because that is what I am. I, your Lord and Teacher, have just washed your feet. You, then, should wash one anothers' feet. I have set an example for you, so that you will do just what I have done for you. I am telling you the truth, no slave is greater than his master, and no messenger is greater than the one who sent him. Now that you know this truth, how happy you will be if you put it into practice" (John 13:12–17).

e. The ordained ministry is a special call to service through consecration to God.

A person enters the ordained ministry through a sacrament called Holy Orders. It is a special commitment and consecration by which the ordained minister is dedicated to minister with the people of God. Some see celibacy as included in this dedication to serve as Jesus served. Celibacy means that a person agrees to live in the world without marrying. In the case of the ordained priesthood of the Western Rite, celibacy is required before the Church ordains its priests. The practice of celibacy began around the fourth century and eventually became the law for the entire Western Church around the twelfth century. Because celibacy is Church law, the Church may dispense from this law when needed. This has been done, for instance, in cases where a married minister of another denomination (such as the Episcopal Church) seeks to join the Catholic Church, and further seeks, after a period of preparation, to become an ordained priest in the Catholic Church.

3. What are the different orders of ordained ministry?

a. One of the ordained ministries is the order of bishop.

The early Church gradually singled out the bishop as having the office of sharing in a high-priestly service to the community. A bishop shares in certain powers or charisms which other ordained ministers do not share. Only a bishop may administer the Sacrament of Holy Orders. He ordinarily confers the Sacrament of Confirmation.

b. Another ordained ministry is the order of presbyter (ordained priest).

With the bishop, the presbyter shares the duties of proclaiming the Gospel: celebrating the Eucharist and other sacraments. A presbyter does not share in the power of conferring Holy Orders. A presbyter belongs to a group (or order) of presbyters throughout the world. In this way, he shares in a type of collegiality with all presbyters throughout the world.

c. Another ordained ministry is the order of deacon.

With this ordination the deacon receives the privilege of celebrating certain sacraments and sacramentals in the name of the Church. The deacon may baptize, preach, witness marriages and funerals, and preside in the name of the Church at certain ceremonies. A deacon does not preside at the Eucharistic Liturgy nor have the power to forgive sins. In the early centuries, the order of deacon shared many varied activities ranging from liturgical roles to leadership roles within the community.

4. How is the office of deacon developing today?

a. A person who has been ordained a deacon and intends to move on to the ministry of presbyter is commonly called a "transitory deacon."

The title, "transitory deacon," is an unfortunate title for a deacon who wishes to be ordained a presbyter. When a person moves from one order to the next, the person does not erase the previous ordination. Even though he becomes a presbyter, the order of deacon still remains with those ordained to this order. Each order, once conferred, is permanent. The term "transitory" became necessary to distinguish such a person from a "permanent" deacon, which is another unfortunate title.

b. A person who is ordained to the diaconate with no intention of going on to the ministry of presbyter is commonly called a "permanent deacon."

All deacons, whether wishing to go on to the order of presbyter or not, are actually "permanent" deacons. When speaking of "permanent deacons" today, we are speaking of those who intend to serve in the ministry of ordained deacon with no intention of becoming a presbyter. The ordination to this office in the Church as a special and life-long ministry was found in the early Church and has been revived in our present day. This order includes people of mature age, married as well as single, who will have a particular work or profession other than serving as deacon. Through the Church, they share in the special charism of their ordination and reflect the presence of the Church in the world. They share all the duties of deacons as mentioned in the previous question.

5. What are some other special ministries within the church?

a. The Church has established the ministries of reader and acolyte and has invited lay Catholics to share in this ministry.

At one time, only those who were candidates for ordination would share in certain ministries within the Church. In recognition of the priesthood shared by all people at baptism, Pope Paul VI has opened the ministry of "reader" and "acolyte" to lay Christians along with those preparing to receive ordination. Through the institution of reader, a person is committed to reading the Word of God, with the exception of the Gospel, at liturgical celebrations. The reader is also called to prepare others for the proper reading of Scriptures and to instruct the faithful for the worthy reception of the sacraments. Through the institution of acolyte, a person is called to assist the deacon or priest at liturgical celebrations and to see to the proper preparation for service at the altar. In addition, the acolyte is to have a good grasp of Eucharistic theology. The acolyte distributes the Eucharist at liturgy and brings the Eucharist to the sick.

b. Laity should share in only one special ministry within a single liturgy.

The reader should be concerned solely with reading the Word of God and should not distribute the Eucharist at the same liturgy. Nor should the lay distributor of the Eucharist distribute the Eucharist at more than one celebration on any given day. The reason the Church makes these requests in worship is to avoid confusion of ministries as well as to protect the special value of each ministerial function. The ministers should share fully in the service in which they are ministering.

c. Laity share in the responsibility of ministering in the name of the Church to those in need.

The laity witness to Christ through a multitude of ministries such as teaching religion, planning and guiding parish programs, caring for missions in a diocese, and assisting in many pastoral activities within the parish. These are only a few of the many ministerial and pastoral activities of the laity. A major call for all members of the community is the ministry to the sick, the shut-in, and the poor. In general, the whole Christian community is called to visit the sick, support the needy, heal the ill, clothe the naked, and join their voices and hearts in worship of God. This call to ministry flows from the Sacrament of Baptism, and it is shared in equally by all the baptized. Each one, in this way, and in accordance with his or her own condition or office, contributes to the building up of the Body of Christ.

6. How did the ordained ministry develop?

a. In the Old Testament, a priest was a mediator between God and the people of God.

In the Old Testament, we do not find an ordained ministry. We read that God set aside the family of Levi as the family of priests of ancient Israel. All the males born into this family would serve the rest of the tribes of Israel as their priests. Their function would be to offer to God in the name of the people the gifts and sacrifices the people of God brought before the altar. They would often receive the gifts from the people and offer them to God in the name of God's people. In this way, the priests functioned as mediators between God and the people.

b. The New Testament portrays the ordained minister as one who serves.

The apostles were the first ordained ministers of the early Church. They served in the name of Christ by bringing Christ's blessings to the people and joining with the people in worshiping God, the Father. They really showed no specific sign of acting in the same sense as priests in the Old Testament. They did not take the people's offering and place it before God. They preached the message of Jesus and they shared the gifts that Jesus shared with them.

c. By the end of the first century, there was a structure of orders in the Church.

By the end of the first century, we see bishops as separate from presbyters and presbyters as separate from deacons. Apparently, in the early Church, only bishops made up the ordained ministry. The eventual need to share some of their powers led to the establishment of the orders of presbyter and deacon. Through the imposition of hands and praying of a specified prayer, the bishop shared with others some of the powers of his office. After the first century, the distinction between bishop, presbyter, and deacon became more clearly defined and separated. The structure we know today developed through centuries of living and reflecting on the gifts of Christ to his apostles and to his Church.

7. How is the liturgy of the ordination of presbyter celebrated?

a. The Sacrament of Holy Orders should take place within the context of the Eucharistic Celebration.

The Eucharist is the source of the ordained ministry as well as the aim of the ordained ministry. Ordination should take place before the community because the ordained minister is a person called forth from the community to serve the community.

b. A person is called to a special ministry by the bishop.

In the ceremony, the candidate for ordination is called by name by the deacon of the Eucharistic Liturgy. The deacon calls out, "Let those who are to be ordained come forward." As each name is called, the person responds, "I am ready and willing." The bishop then asks if they are worthy and a presbyter answers in their name, "I testify that upon inquiry among the people of God and upon recommendation of those concerned with their training, they have been found worthy." The bishop then responds, "We rely on the help of the Lord God and our Savior, Jesus Christ, and we choose our brothers here present for the office of presbyter." At this point, the people as a group share their approval either by applause or by responding together, "Thanks be to God" or both.

c. The bishop then questions the candidates who are to be ordained.

The bishop asks the candidates if they are willing to share with the bishop in caring for the Lord's flock. He asks if they are willing to share and celebrate the sacred mysteries, if they are resolved to preach the Word worthily and with wisdom, and finally asks if they are willing to consecrate their lives to the salvation of all people. To each of these questions the candidates respond, "I am."

d. At this point in the ceremony, the candidates promise obedience to the bishop.

The bishop asks if they are willing to be obedient to their Ordinary. The candidates respond, "I am." The bishop then prays that God who began the good work in these candidates may bring it to fulfillment.

e. Ordination takes place when the bishop and presbyters lay hands on the head of the candidates, and the bishop prays a special prayer for ordination.

The bishop puts both hands on the heads of each of the candidates. Then all presbyters present impose hands on the heads of the candidates. After this, the bishop prays for God's help and aid in this ceremony. In his prayer, he recalls God's special gifts to the people of the Old Testament, especially in the priesthood of Levi. He prays that God grant the dignity of presbyter to these candidates who, in turn, join with other ordained ministers in sharing Christ's message.

f. The bishop now brings the newly ordained into the community of presbyters by symbolic actions.

The newly ordained now receive the presbyter's garments for Eucharistic Celebration. Their hands are anointed and they are presented with a chalice in which wine and water have been poured and a paten on which rests bread to be consecrated. The bishop and all presbyters present give a sign of peace that symbolizes a welcome into the Order of Presbyter. As the liturgy continues the newly ordained with the bishop celebrate the Eucharist.

8. What are religious?

a. Religious are people who consecrate themselves to God by vows or promises of poverty, chastity, and obedience.

Christ proclaimed that the reign of God was here among us. Accepting this reality of Christ's presence in the world and Christ's wish to share this reign, men and women dedicate themselves through special vows to living out and sharing this presence of Christ's reign. They become a living sign of this reign on earth, while at the same time reminding us that the full experience of this reign is yet to come. With love of God, and with a living hope that love and service will reach fulfillment in the eternal reign of God, religious accept a life of service to all people.

By the vow of poverty, religious commit themselves before God to share in common their material possessions. The purpose behind the vow is to free them of all attachment to riches of this world, and to remind them of the one great possession, Jesus Christ. By the vow of chastity, religious forego the right to marriage that they might more readily show the world the continual presence of Christ and the willingness to belong to all who call upon them for the sake of the Gospel. By obedience, religious offer themselves to the service of the Christian community. They commit themselves to serve the Church as this call comes to them through their community. Through these vows, religious commit their lives to God.

b. A religious is a person who ordinarily lives a common life within a religious community.

In vowing poverty, chastity, and obedience, the religious person seeks to live together in community with others. The vows enable the person to live this life more fully. A religious community ordinarily is founded for a specific work which may change as times and needs change. Today many different communities with a variety of ministries serve in the name of the Church.

c. A nun or a sister is a woman who belongs to a particular religious community.

A woman who commits herself to God by the vows of poverty, chastity, and obedience is commonly referred to as a sister or a nun. Sisters and nuns also live together in community and share in common life. They may be called to teaching school, doing social work, hospital work, working in the mission field, coordinating religious education, or ministering in a parish. Sisters and nuns have responded to the many needs in the Church today.

d. A Brother is a man who lives the religious life.

A man who vows poverty, chastity, and obedience and who consecrates himself to God through a specific community is referred to as a brother. Brothers also engage in various activities and ministries within the Church. They may serve as teachers, hospital assistants, administrators, and religious educators or in other ministries to which they are called.

9. Do presbyters belong to religious communities?

a. Some presbyters belong to religious communities.

When a presbyter vows poverty, chastity, and obedience in a certain community, we refer to that person as an ordained religious priest. Communities of presbyters in the Church usually have a specific function or mission as a community. One community may be dedicated to teaching, while other communities may be dedicated to preaching or serving in mission fields. The presbyters who belong to these communities are usually assigned by the superior of their religious community. For pastoral appointments, recommendations are made to the bishop by the superior, and the bishop officially makes the appointment in his diocese.

b. A presbyter who serves in a particular diocese with a promise of obedience to the ordinary of that diocese is referred to as an ordained diocesan priest.

At the time of his ordination, a presbyter promises obedience to the Ordinary of the diocese and to his successors. The ordained diocesan priest usually serves in one diocese and accepts various appointments within that diocese. He does not belong to a religious community and is responsible for his own welfare.

Usually presbyters of the Latin Rite, whether religious or diocesan, do not marry. The law that forbids marriage for presbyters in the Western Church became a law of the Western Church about ten centuries ago. Before that time, presbyters were permitted to marry.

Conclusion

Father Damian had accepted the ministry to the lepers, and as a true presbyter of the Catholic Church, he led the people to Christ by service. He brought the Word of God to these people, but he also brought the compassion of Christ into his work. He could look to Christ who became like us and Father Damian could rejoice because he became like the people he served. Through his life, Father Damian showed the world what the ordained ministry involved. He shared in a sacred privilege and he used that sacred privilege to show us an image of Jesus Christ who came in service to all people. In the exaltation of Jesus, we looked back into his life and saw what this exaltation cost. Because he served so well, most remember him as "Damian the Leper." In both cases, these titles tell of their exaltation.

For Scripture reflection and discussion concerning this chapter, see Journeying in His Light, *"A Ministry of Service."*

14 Anointing of the Sick

Introduction

Virginia had never experienced sickness like this before. As she lay in the hospital bed, she looked anxiously to the doctor who was hurriedly examining her. The doctor finally stopped examining and said, "Virginia, we think you have had a slight heart attack. It really isn't serious, but we would like to keep an eye on you. Rest now."

It was only then that Virginia realized that the nurses and doctor had taped strange, round objects to her body. She knew that someone in another room was sitting by the monitor keeping an eye on the rhythm of her heart. She relaxed with a sigh, thanking God that it was no worse.

Throughout the rest of the day, a nurse occasionally stopped in, smiled and asked if she needed anything. A nun with a bright, broad smile stopped by to pray with her. A priest had stopped by, and, as peacefully as one could imagine, had administered the Sacrament of the Anointing of the Sick. It was a pleasant experience to celebrate that sacrament. For years she had dreaded the moment a priest would stand over her "with the oils," but the experience was far different from her fearful expectations.

Virginia felt that she could never forget the kindness, gentleness and blessings of all the people who shared her sickness. They made her feel very much at home, despite her illness. She told a friend some weeks later, "I suddenly understood what a healing touch of kindness and concern really was!" Virginia watches her diet and works a little more carefully now, but she still claims that those days in the hospital were the most pleasant days of her life.

1. How does the Church respond to sickness in the world?

a. The Church urges that we work with charity toward relieving the pain and suffering of a sick person.

Paul reminds us that when one member of the Body of Christ suffers, all members suffer along with this one member. When any person is suffering here on earth, the whole of God's creation suffers along with this person. The Church urges that we use every means to alleviate the suffering of this person, and to overcome the sickness of this person. It encourages the use of scientific means to draw a person back to health. It encourages all of us to treat the sick person with kindness and love, realizing that we are this suffering member. A person who is ill is encouraged to accept the illness as sharing in the suffering of Jesus Christ. However, the acceptance does not mean an acceptance of an illness that can be cured, but rather the acceptance of pain that often accompanies an illness even during the healing.

b. The Church urges that family and friends see themselves as a reflection of the Church in caring for those close to them.

The Church reminds the family and friends of the sick, as well as those who care for the sick, that they have a special share in the ministry of comfort. It is their task to strengthen the sick with words of faith and to pray with them. In case of sickness which keeps a person at home for some period of time, the family should consult the priest so that he may respond to the needs of the person during the period of sickness.

c. The Church urges the priest to view visiting and care of the sick as an important part of his ministry.

The priest as a representative of the concerned Church, should show concern and visit the sick. The Church reminds the priest of his pastoral duty. In a case where sickness has kept a person at home, the priest should arrange to bring the Eucharist to this person. The Eucharist may be brought by the priest or by the lay minister of the Eucharist.

d. All Christians are reminded to care for the sick with love and kindness.

Although the Church reminds the priest of his pastoral duty to care for the sick as a representative of the Church, the Church also encourages all its members to reach out in charity to those who are sick. Each member of that community should show a deep concern for other members of that community, especially for suffering members. The priest should not be the only one within a parish to visit or care for the sick. The members of that community should concern themselves with the sick of that community, and should see to it that they themselves respond to the sick person's needs by caring for the sick, helping the family or simply reminding the sick that they are in their prayers. All who show compassion for the sick participate in Christ's healing ministry. In writing to the Philippians, Paul tells them how much their support meant to him in his hardships. He writes, "In my life in union with the Lord, it is a great joy to me that after so long a time you once more had the chance of showing that you care for me. . . . I know what it is to be in need and what it is to have more than enough. . . . I have strength to face all conditions by the power that Christ gives one. But it was very good of you to help me in my troubles" (Philippians 4:10,12,13–14). Paul trusted in the strength which came from Christ, but he admitted to the Philippians that their support meant a great deal to him.

e. In case of serious sickness, the family should call the priest to celebrate the anointing of the sick.

The Church urges that all people be made aware of the meaning of the Sacrament of the Anointing of the Sick and that they call upon a priest to celebrate this sacrament in certain cases of sickness. Families should remember that a person need not be in danger of immediate death to receive this sacrament. The introduction to the rite states that "great care and concern should be taken to see that those faithful whose health is seriously impaired by sickness or old age receive this sacrament."

2. What is the Sacrament of the Anointing of the Sick?

a. The Sacrament of the Anointing of the Sick is a sacrament by which the Church continues the concern of the Lord himself by sharing with the sick special sacramental gifts passed on from Jesus Christ.

Throughout the Gospels, we read of Christ's continued concern for the sick and dying. He would reach out to the sick and cure them. He would look upon them with kindness and share a healing. In a story found in the Gospel of Luke, a leper comes to Jesus and states boldly, ". . . Lord if you will to do so, you can cure me" (Luke 5:12). Although Jesus recognizes the presence of suffering and sickness in the world, he expresses a basic desire of God that all people will be healed. Jesus answers the leper as though he were answering all people, ". . . I do will it. Be cured" (Luke 5:13). In the curing of the leper, Jesus is offering us an example of our need to cure others in whatever way we are able. The Sacrament of the Anointing of the Sick continues to show this loving concern of Christ for those whose health is seriously impaired.

b. Through this sacrament, the Holy Spirit shares the blessings of health, trust in God, and strength against temptation.

Through this sacrament, the Church shares with a person a new strength to bear suffering bravely and even to fight against suffering. At times, a return to physical health may follow upon the reception of this sacrament. We should keep in mind that the sacrament always ministers to the whole person. It strives to bring about a deep inner healing as well as the forgiveness of sins when necessary.

c. The beginnings of this sacrament are shown in the New Testament.

In the Gospel of Mark, Jesus draws aside the twelve apostles and sends them off two by two with instructions for their missionary journeys. During these missionary journeys we read in the Scriptures,

"They cast out many devils and anointed many sick people with oil, and cured them" (Mark 6:13). At this time, we see the use of oil even by the twelve apostles as they are sent out by Christ.

In the Letter of James, we read about a custom of the early Church of praying over the sick and anointing them with oil:

Is there anyone who is sick? He should send for the Church elders, who will pray for him and rub olive oil on him in the name of the Lord. This prayer made in faith will heal the sick person, the Lord will restore him to health, and the sins he has committed will be forgiven (James 5:14–15).

Through this Letter of James, we find a basis for this Sacrament of the Anointing of the Sick.

212

3. Who may receive this Sacrament of Anointing of the Sick?

a. Any person whose health is seriously impaired by sickness or old age should receive this Sacrament of Anointing of the Sick.

The priest makes a judgment regarding the health of a person being seriously impaired and the judgment should be based on the spiritual and physical condition of the person. The priest should encourage the faithful whose health is seriously impaired to celebrate the sacrament. At the same time, he should protect the sacrament from being used in a trivial way. The Church does not refer to this sacrament any longer as the sacrament of the "last rites" or "extreme unction." Elderly people who are in a weak condition may be anointed. For example, an elderly person who has the flu may be anointed since that person could easily suffer a serious health problem. In a case where a serious illness is the reason for surgery, the person should be anointed. In the case of children, the anointing may take place if they have sufficient use of reason. The Sacrament of the Sick can be celebrated more than once by an individual.

b. Anointing may be conferred upon sick people who have lost consciousness or the use of reason.

If a person throughout life has freely chosen to receive the sacraments or has shown a desire to receive this Sacrament of Anointing in times of illness, this person may receive the sacrament even when unconscious or confused. Through an accident or aging, a person may lose the use of reason. Such a person may still receive this sacrament.

c. If a person has already died, the priest does not administer the Sacrament of Anointing.

At times, a priest is called to attend a person who is already dead. He should pray that God forgive the person's sins and that God receive this person into God's love and the priest prays for the family and consoles them. However, the priest is not to administer the Sacrament of Anointing at this time.

4. How is this Sacrament of the Anointing of the Sick celebrated?

a. Bishops and presbyters are the proper ministers of the Sacrament of the Anointing of the Sick.

Bishops and presbyters are the only proper ministers of this Sacrament of the Anointing of the Sick. With their pastoral responsibility of caring for the sick and preparing them for reception of all the sacraments, presbyters have the responsibility to share this sacrament with those capable of receiving the sacrament.

b. The minister celebrates this sacrament by laying hands on the head of the sick person, offering a prayer of faith, and anointing the sick person with oil especially blessed for this occasion.

As in other sacraments, the ordained minister lays hands on the sick person's head in silence, then anoints the sick person on the forehead and the hands with oil. The minister prays:

> *Through this holy anointing*
> *may the Lord in his love and mercy help you*
> *with the grace of the Holy Spirit.*
> *R. (Amen).*
> *May the Lord who frees you from sin*
> *save you and raise you up.*
> *R. (Amen).*

Although these actions confer the sacrament, the Church offers other prayers in preparation for the reception of the sacrament and prayers immediately after the reception of the sacrament. Through these prayers, the Church prepares the sick person and those who are assisting in this liturgy for the reception and significance of the sacrament. The prayers following upon this sacrament allow for the reception of the Eucharist if the person is physically capable of sharing in this sacrament.

5. What is holy viaticum?

a. When a person at the point of death receives the Sacrament of the Eucharist, this person is receiving a special grace of the sacrament which is called "holy viaticum."

The author of the Gospel of John links the importance of the reception of the Eucharist with our resurrection on the last day. The person who shares in the Body and Blood of Christ has a pledge of Christ's resurrection, "Anyone who does eat my flesh and drink my blood has eternal life, and I shall raise him up on the last day" (John 6:54). The Sacrament of the Eucharist most closely symbolizes the death and resurrection of Jesus Christ. For this reason, the Church has chosen to make this a most special sacrament at the moment of death.

In a sense, viaticum should be seen as the true "last rite," rather than the anointing of the sick. The Church says that viaticum is the true food for passage through death to eternal life. In some instances, when a person seems to be on the edge of death, a choice must be made, and, at such a time, the Church chooses viaticum over the anointing. If time permits, a person may then share in the anointing after celebrating viaticum. As anointing is the sacrament for the sick, viaticum is the sacrament for the dying.

b. All Catholics who can physically receive Communion must receive viaticum as they near death.

Because of the strength and blessings that flow from this sacrament, the Church reminds all Catholics of their obligation to receive the Eucharist at the point of death. During the celebration of viaticum, the Catholic should renew the vows of baptism by praying a profession of faith.

When persons near death, they are often conscious of their quickly fleeting life, and they wish to prepare themselves for their passover into eternal life. Some, trying to be compassionate, may tend to deny a person this time of preparation by not making this viaticum available to the dying person. This denial is contrary to the ideal of Christian life and preparation for death, and it deprives a person of a great gift for the passage into eternal life.

c. Where possible, viaticum should be received during the celebration of the Eucharistic Liturgy.

Since viaticum shows in a special way a union in the mystery of the death of the Lord and his passage to the Father, the most appropriate context for the sharing in this sacrament would be within the Eucharistic Liturgy. When possible the sick person should receive the Eucharist under both forms, that is, the form of bread and the form of wine. In some cases, where a person has difficulty swallowing, either a tiny piece of the consecrated bread, or the wine may be given to the dying person.

6. What is communal anointing of the sick?

a. Communal anointing consists in groups of people celebrating this sacrament within the Eucharistic Liturgy.

In certain cases, groups of people may celebrate this sacrament within a Eucharistic Celebration. Elderly people and people whose health is seriously impaired, should be urged to come and celebrate together in the Eucharistic Liturgy. The purpose of this action shows that even this Sacrament of Anointing of the Sick is an action of the community whereby all members are concerned for one another. As one member suffers, all suffer and as one member shares in the joy of a sacrament, all share in the joy of the sacrament. The group, coming together for communal anointing, manifests the great sign of a concerned community celebrating a joyful sacrament.

b. Others besides those who are to be anointed should share in the celebration of communal anointing.

Although those who are elderly or those who have certain illnesses are permitted to receive the Sacrament of the Anointing of the Sick, other members of the community should share in this Eucharistic Celebration. The reception of this sacrament is not only a special moment in the lives of those who receive this sacrament, but also in the lives of every member of the community. Others should come to share their concern, love, and support for those who show a need for this sacrament. Active participation of the faithful in a communal anointing is certainly preferred because of its great sign of a community concerned for its members.

Paul tells the Romans that they should have an attitude of concern for all the brothers and sisters in the faith, whom he refers to as the "saints." Paul writes, "Look on the needs of the saints as your own; be generous in offering hospitality." Hospitality in this sense not only involves welcoming a person into one's home, but also treating a person with the love one would have for a close member of one's family. The fears and joys of the members of the Christian community become the fears and joys of all members.

Conclusion

When Virginia visits her friends in the hospital, she tries to share with them her own experiences of love and healing. She had learned much from her own sickness, and she wanted to share what she had learned. As her sister lay dying some years later, Virginia came and sat quietly by her bed. The comfort of the Anointing of the Sick had helped her sister, but Virginia saw herself as an extension of that healing touch of Christ. She prayed with her sister, listened to her when she repeated those same stories over and over, and wiped her sister's forehead when her sister could no longer do these things for herself. Through her own sickness, Virginia had learned much about the healing touch of presence. The kind word, the thoughtful visit, the silent listening, the tender touch, and Sacrament of the Anointing of the Sick were all moments for the healing touch of Christ.

For Scripture reflection and discussion concerning this chapter, see Journeying in His Light, *"Anointing of the Sick."*

Death to Life

Introduction

When the doctor told Phil he was going to die, Phil scoffed at the doctor's appraisal of his health. He felt fine. A little more tired than usual, but still fine! As Phil lay in the hospital bed feeling more fatigued and frightened each new day, he became angry. Why should all those older people live when he had to die at such a young age? He had so much to give yet. Why not one of those people who spent their time begging food and drinking all day? He was not yet forty, and already he was dying. On another day, his anger turned to bargaining. He prayed, "God, if you give me a little more time, you won't believe how good I'll be. I'll go to church every day!" One day, Phil told his wife to leave him alone. He had fallen into a deep depression. His favorite television program, his new car, his daughter visiting from over two hundred miles away, and his wife who sat patiently day by day at his bedside—none of these seemed important to him. Finally, one day, Phil woke up and told his wife without emotion, "I'm ready." She tried to tell him that he would soon be up and around, but he shook his head and repeated, "I'm ready." Phil died peacefully a few weeks later.

A woman psychiatrist by the name of Dr. Elisabeth Kübler-Ross has studied the process of dying and has discovered stages that resembled Phil's process very closely. The dying patient goes through five steps. The first step is denial, where the patient objects, "No. Not me! Not yet!" The second step is rage and anger: "Why me?" The third step is bargaining: "A little longer, and I will really be good." The fourth step is depression, "Don't bother me!" The fifth step is acceptance: "It's all right. I'm ready."

For many people, especially those who have no belief in life hereafter, death is the frightening moment that should be avoided as long as possible. This chapter looks to the hope that Christ's message shares with us concerning death and beyond. For a Christian, death does not end life, but brings life to a fuller awareness of love and eternal fulfillment.

1. What is the Christian belief about death?

a. A Christian believes that there is eternal life after death.

Christians do not see death as the end, but rather as the beginning of a new life. The new life will be a different type of life which will last forever. Paul expresses it this way: "For we know that when the tent we live in on earth is folded up, there is a house built by God for us, an everlasting home, not made by human hands, in the heavens" (2 Corinthians 5:1). At the point of our passing from this life into eternal life, we will face God and receive the reward or punishment flowing from the way we have lived our life. The Letter to the Corinthians continues, "For all the truth about us will be brought out in the law court of Christ, and each of us will get what he deserves for the things he did in the body, good or bad" (2 Corinthians 5:10).

b. Christ shares with all Christians a hope for a new life.

In the discourses in the Gospel of John, Jesus tells his disciples that he is going to prepare a place for them. All Christians should see in these words of Christ a message that extends beyond the apostles to every person:

Do not be worried and upset, Jesus told them. Believe in God and believe also in me. There are many rooms in my Father's house, and I am going to prepare a place for you. I would not tell you this if it were not so. And after I go and prepare a place for you, I will come back and take you to myself, so that you will be where I am (John 14:1–3).

Throughout his life, Jesus told parables or stories concerning a continual life hereafter. He tells of a rich man who would not share his food with a poor man. The poor man enters eternal happiness along with Abraham, Isaac, and all the prophets. The rich man lives a life of eternal pain. The Scriptures tell us that in the resurrection of Jesus Christ, we receive a new dawn, a new hope in his resurrection. Until the coming of Christ, people wondered about the idea of life hereafter. Through his death and resurrection, Christ showed us a glory that he will share with all of us.

c. Faith in the resurrection does not take away our need to grieve.

Although we accept in faith the idea that the deceased are now living in Christ and are born into eternal life, we still experience human grief.

220

We should accept our human condition and realize that we feel lonely, lost, and deeply saddened when someone close to us dies. Grieving is a necessary and healthy aspect of our human condition. Through grieving, we too pass through the stages of accepting death, in this case the death of someone close to us. In time, we learn to turn our grief into fond memories. A tinge of sadness will return now and then, but God has given us an ability to get on with life. Grief, accepted maturely, will gradually give way to a life continually open to new joys and new tragedies. Instead of a "piece of ourselves" dying with someone, a "piece of that person" will live on through us. The faith that leads to a hope for resurrection for all of us should serve as a source of strength through moments of grief in life.

In the Gospel of John, we read the story about Jesus' raising Lazarus from the dead. Jesus had already proclaimed to Martha that anyone who believed in him would never die spiritually, although the person would die in the view of the world. Despite this belief, the sadness of the loss of Lazarus overcomes Jesus, and the Gospel tells us, "Jesus saw her (Mary) weeping, and he saw how the people with her were weeping also; his heart was touched, and he was deeply moved. . . . Jesus wept. See how much he loved him! the people said" (John 11:33,35–36). Some interpreters would claim that the weeping of Jesus showed how closely he followed the Father's will. They see the event as one which portrays Jesus as not yet certain that the Father would allow him to raise Lazarus from the dead. Like the rest of us who lose close relatives and friends in life, Jesus grieved for the loss of his friend Lazarus.

d. At the moment of passage from this life to the next, our time for gaining or losing merit has ended.

At the moment of our death, we stand before God as we truly are. We can no longer gain merit nor can we lose the merit we have. At this moment, our whole attitude of mind suddenly brings us into a direct confrontation with God. We experience the great loving presence of God and judge our own worthiness or unworthiness of entering God's presence. God need not judge us, because we judge ourselves. At this moment, we see ourselves as we truly are and realize most fully the goodness and love of God. We proclaim ourselves worthy or unworthy of this love as we look into our own attitude toward God. In the Gospel of John, we read the words the author attributes to Jesus, "If anyone hears my message and does not obey it, I will not judge him. I came not to judge the world, but to save it. Whoever rejects me and does not accept my message has one who will judge him. The words I have spoken will be his judge on the last day" (John 12:47–48).

2. What is heaven?

a. Heaven is a full and perfect sharing in God's loving presence for all eternity.

When we attain heaven, we experience the great joy and happiness of being in God's presence and sharing fully and perfectly in God's love. The love we feel for any other person here on earth is only a shadow of the love that we will feel for God at the moment of our death. The happiness of heaven can never be expressed in words. Speaking of the glory of heaven, Paul writes, "What no one ever saw or heard, what no one ever thought could happen, is the very thing God prepared for those who love him" (1 Corinthians 2:9).

b. In heaven, the struggles and pains of life will cease.

Throughout life, we live through moments of sorrow, as for example when we lose those close to us. We experience pain, frustration, discouragement, and we continually struggle against temptations that will seek to allure us from the main goal of our life. Once we reach heaven, all these sorrows and struggles cease to exist. We experience God's love, and that love so overwhelms us that all sorrow, suffering, and temptation can no longer touch us. In the Book of Revelation in the New Testament, we read about the new, heavenly Jerusalem. The author tells us that a voice from the heavens cries out:

Now God's home is with mankind! He will live with them, and they shall be his people. God himself will be with them, and he will be their God. He will wipe away all tears from their eyes. There will be no more death, no more grief or crying or pain. The old things have disappeared (Revelation 21:3–4).

c. Heaven is not a place but rather a state of existence.

We build homes on a certain parcel of land. We look and live and walk in time and space. Our whole universe is in place. When we speak of heaven, however, we speak of eternal happiness in God's presence. It is a deep experience of the overwhelming presence of God, yet a presence which does not exist in a place, but really outside of place. What this state of existence really encompasses cannot be understood with the human mind. In this state of existence, we are somehow capable of loving God deeply and experiencing God's love for us. We are capable of knowing one another completely and of sharing together the great joy of eternal happiness.

3. What is hell?

a. Hell is a state of eternal rejection of God.

At the moment of our death, we experience a deep yearning to be with God. At that same moment, we face the truth of our lives and see ourselves as accepting or rejecting God by the way we have lived. The fundamental attitude of mind with which we meet death directs us to accept or reject God. When we choose hell, our attitude of mind tells us that we are not worthy of spending an eternity with God who is all loving. We see ourselves as unloving, turned selfishly in on ourselves and having rejected God during life. At the moment of our death, we continue that rejection and cast ourselves out of God's presence for all eternity. We actually cannot choose God. Our attitude of mind at that moment could never allow the humility and love needed for that choice.

b. Hell consists in a state of deep, burning loneliness or alienation from God.

In the Scriptures, we often read of hell as consisting of fire. In Matthew's Gospel, we read Jesus' parable about the sheep and the goats: "Then he will say to those on his left hand, "Go away from me, with your curse upon you, to the eternal fire prepared for the devil and his angels!" (Matthew 25:41) When Jesus spoke of fire, he spoke of an imagery that was most accepted in his own day. Today, we can imagine many different images arising from the idea of fire. One common image all of us share is the experience of a deep loneliness when someone close to us passes out of this world. Within our own hearts, we feel a burning sensation, a sensation brought about by loneliness or an experience of lost love. When we die, we will experience a deep yearning to be with God. The pain of hell consists in the burning sensation of loneliness and alienation from God and our own inability to accept this love.

c. In hell, a person experiences a deep self-hatred.

In hell, a person accepts self over God, and this choice of self fills a person with deep self-hatred. When a person turns in upon oneself, that person finds only frustration and lack of love. In hell, people even hate others who are damned along with them. For all eternity, a person experiences loneliness, frustration, disappointment, deep hatred, and suffers continually in this alienation from God.

4. Has Jesus ever spoken of anyone going to hell?

a. Christ spoke about the experience of hell, but the Scriptures never tell us whether any person has ever been condemned to hell.

Jesus warns about the punishment of hell that awaits those who reject God throughout their lives. Neither Jesus nor the Scriptures speak of any specific person being condemned to hell. Even Judas, for his betrayal, is never explicitly mentioned as going to hell. The existence of hell is a fact that we believe as Christians. Whether anyone is in hell and who specifically is in hell can only be known by God.

b. The Scriptures tell us of Jesus' promising paradise to a thief on the cross.

In the Gospel of Luke, we read about two thieves who were crucified on either side of Jesus. One of the thieves berated Jesus and challenged Jesus to save them. The other, however, rebuked his fellow thief and turned to Jesus and said, "Jesus, remember me when you come into your kingdom." "Indeed, I promise you;" he replied, "today you will be with me in Paradise" (Luke 23:42–43). In this text, Jesus promises the thief that he will share in the glory of eternal happiness. While the Scriptures do not tell us of a specific person going to hell, they do tell us of a specific person gaining heaven.

c. We are incapable of judging whether or not another individual enters eternal hell.

Jesus, during his life, warned us about judging others. He told us, "Do not judge, and you will not be judged; because the judgments you give out are the judgments you will get" (Matthew 7:1–2). We have no way of judging another person. We cannot enter into that person's conscience and understand why that person acts in any particular fashion. We can say that certain actions in themselves are sinful actions. Whether or not that person is guilty of sin is beyond our ability to judge. Whenever we dare to judge the sinfulness of another particular person, God warns us that we must pass that same test.

5. What is purgatory?

a. Purgatory consists in the painful passage from this life into God's loving presence.

At our passage into new life, we yearn for an eternal presence in possession of God's love. We suddenly experience God and all God's love, and we painfully and shamefully face ourselves in our weakness. At this passover from death to life, we must pass through the purifying fires of God's love, and experience a deeper love of God than of our own selfish desires.

b. In the passage we call purgatory, we turn our love fully toward God.

Because of our selfish love and the continual turning away from God in many minor ways, we must suddenly confront God in our weakness. We know that we have not cut ourselves off so completely from God that we condemn ourselves to eternal hell, yet we also see the painful attachments that we have chosen over God. At this very painful, purifying moment, we turn ourselves fully toward God and reject all our own selfish desires. The word "purgatory" has within it the idea of purging or cleansing. We simply purge ourselves of all selfish opinions that have drawn us away from a full love of God so that we may fully enter into an eternal happiness and a purified love for all eternity.

c. Purgatory is not a place.

Purgatory does not consist of a place in which we spend a specific number of years. As with heaven and hell, purgatory is a state of existence. It is an experience of people who are saved and invited into God's presence for all eternity. Persons experience joy in this state because of a realization that they have gained an eternal happiness with God, yet joined to that state of joy is also a state of suffering. God wants us for all eternity in heaven, but God does not want us with our weakness and our self-centered attitudes. In the state of purgatory, this moment of passage, the self-centered attitude must painfully be purified for our entrance into an eternal happiness. Purgatory, although painful, is nothing like the eternal pain of loss in hell.

d. The Catholic Church teaches that our prayers can help others through this state of purgatory.

The Catholic Church teaches that the dead may profit from our prayers as they pass through the state of purgatory. In the Book of Maccabees, we read that Judas, a leader of the people, went to gather the bodies of the slain. The Scriptures tell us:

An altogether fine and noble action, in which he took full account of the resurrection. For if he had not expected the fallen to rise again, it would have been superfluous and foolish to pray for the dead, whereas if he had in view the splendid recompense reserved for those who make a pious end, the thought was holy and devout. This was why he had this atonement sacrifice offered so that they might be released from their sin (2 Maccabees 12:43–46).

According to this Scripture reading, Judas would have been foolish to pray for the dead if there were no chance of a resurrection and no chance of those prayers benefitting the dead. When we see purgatory as a passage from the selfishness of this life to the full love of heaven, we must ask how our prayers can benefit an event that apparently has taken place in a flash of light. By the time we pray for someone already deceased, that person is enjoying the reward of heaven. All we can say is that somehow our prayers affect the passage that took place in the past, even when we pray for that person today. The Church, in its reading of the Scriptures, believes that it is a "very excellent and noble" thing to pray for the dead. Our prayers benefit those who experience purgatory. We cannot explain how this happens, so we trustingly place our prayers in the hands of God and believe that it does happen.

e. On November second every year, the Church celebrates All Soul's Day.

On All Souls' Day, the Church remembers all those who have made the passage from this life to eternity. On this day, we pray for our relatives, our friends, and others throughout the world that their passage to God was less painful. We pray in faith, realizing that somehow in God's goodness and in the mystery of eternity, our prayers are able to affect a moment of passage from this life to an eternal reward.

6. What is the liturgy
of Christian burial?

*a. The liturgy of Christian burial consists in the celebration
of the Eucharistic Liturgy for a Christian who dies.*

When a Christian dies, the body is brought to the church where the Eucharistic Liturgy is celebrated. At this liturgy, we celebrate the fact that someone who was baptized in Christ has now risen in Christ. The signs, songs, and prayers of this liturgy point toward spiritual joy although the minds of those celebrating recognize the human sadness at the loss of someone close to them.

*b. The signs and symbols used in Christian burial refer to
baptism and resurrection.*

As was mentioned under the Sacrament of Baptism, a white robe is placed upon the person being baptized signifying a clothing in Christ. At a Christian burial liturgy, the presider meets the casket at the door of the church and drapes a white cloth over it. This white cloth symbolizes the link between baptism and Christian burial. A person who has been baptized in Christ is now risen in Christ. At the time of baptism, the Easter candle stood near the baptismal font reminding us of the day of Christ's resurrection. The Easter candle is also placed in a prominent place during the liturgy of Christian burial to again remind us of Christ's resurrection and our resurrection. The vestments worn at the liturgy are white vestments to symbolize the spiritual joy and hope of resurrection. In this way, the Church reminds us that we are celebrating a *Christian* burial.

7. What is a saint?

*a. The Catholic Church, after investigating the life of a good
person and demanding other signs of holiness, declares a
person as worthy of the title "saint."*

When the Catholic Church declares that a person who has lived and died well is worthy of the title "saint," the Church is actually using its authority, under the guidance of the Holy Spirit, to declare that the person is now sharing in the eternal presence of God. In other words, that person is now in heaven. Before a person is declared a saint, that person's life undergoes intense scrutiny while some sign, usually in the form of miracles in that person's name, is sought of God. By this sign from God, the

Church feels secure in naming a person a saint and declaring that person's life worthy of imitation. By honoring the saints, Catholics are really praising God for God's goodness in sharing holiness with our human condition. Without a good and loving God, no one would be able to become a saint. A saint points to this goodness and love of God.

b. All who have entered the eternal glory of God's presence, that is heaven, are considered saints in the Catholic Church.

There are many people sharing in God's eternal glory whose names we do not know. Many of these people are relatives and friends we have known in life and who have passed on to God. Because the Church is not able to know by name all the people who have lived and served God well, the Church celebrates a feast in honor of all these saints. On November first, the Church celebrates "All Saints' Day." On this day, we celebrate the fact that many Christians have lived and died in God's love and are now sharing in God's eternal happiness. Someday, the Feast of All Saints, hopefully, will be our feast day. This is a special "holy day" for Catholics. On this day, we are reminded of our calling to eternal happiness. We are a pilgrim people who strive to live well that we may come to share in All Saints' Day.

c. We should strive to enter heaven out of love for God rather than a fear of hell.

Many Christians carry out the law of God because they feel that if they die in sin they will be condemned to eternal pain. The real meaning of heaven, however, consists in a deep experience of love. Through baptism, we begin the reign of heaven within our own person and we grow in that reign as we grow in love through life. Our passage to eternal happiness will not depend on how well we kept the law, but rather how well we loved God in keeping God's law.

8. What do we know about the end of the world?

a. The end of the world comes with the fulfillment or completion of God's creation.

The world in which we live will eventually come to its day of fulfillment. This does not necessarily mean that the world will be destroyed at the end of time, but that there will be ". . . new heavens and a new earth" as we read in the Book of Revelation (21:1). We do not know exactly what this means, since the Scriptures speak about the end of the world in highly symbolic terms. Many interpret the words of Jesus who speaks of catastrophies as signs of the end of the world. Even Jesus, as did many of the people of his own day, used highly symbolic language when speaking of the end of the world. We know that the world will end and that it will consist in the completion or final fulfillment of the reign of God in creation. As we read the Scriptures, we are reminded to look forward with hope to this day.

b. At the end of the world, all will share in the general judgment.

The word judgment has many meanings. At the end of time, there will be many who have already shared in the "particular judgment," i.e., the moment when they will have chosen or rejected God for all eternity. The general judgment consists in the final gathering when all of creatioin comes before God, not to be condemned or rewarded, but to experience as one the fullness of God's creation. For those who have chosen a sinful attitude during life, the moment will be one of loneliness and rejection, while, for those who have chosen a loving attitude during life, it will be a time of fulfillment in joy and love.

During the early days of Paul's writings, the people expected the world to end soon, and they looked hopefully and expectantly toward this day. When it did not occur, they began to fear for those who had already died, wondering whether they had missed the second coming of Christ and thus missed eternal reward. Paul, in a letter to the Thessalonians, tells them that those who have died will indeed share in the final, general judgement. Paul writes:

> . . . We want to know the truth about those who have died, so that you will not be sad as are those who have no hope. . . . What we are teaching you now is the Lord's teaching: we who are alive, on the day the Lord comes will not go ahead of those who have died. There will be the shout of command, the archangel's voice, the sound of God's trumpet, and the Lord himself will come down from heaven. Those who have died believing in Christ will rise to life first. Then we who are living at that time, will be gathered up along with them in the clouds to meet the Lord in the air. And so we will always be with the Lord. So then, encourage one another with these words" (I Thessalonians 4:13,15–18).

c. At the end of time, Christ will turn over to God, the Father, the total gift of the reign which will have reached its fulfillment.

In the Gospel of John, we read that the Son of God, called the "Word" by the author of the Gospel, was with God, the Father, at the time of creation, and that all was created through the Word. The Word became flesh and was known to us in his human and divine nature as Jesus Christ, the one who brought salvation through his death, resurrection, and ascension. At the end of time, all creation will reach its perfection in Christ, and he will then offer the perfect and complete gift to God. In this way, we learn that the Son of God is central to creation from beginning to end, and that the total fulfillment of the gift is finally directed to the Father.

In his first letter to the Corinthians, Paul explains to his readers this wonderful mystery of creation. He tells them that everything, with the exception of the Father, became subject to Christ. At the time of perfect fulfillment, Christ will subject himself and the perfect gift to the Father. We read, "After that will come the end, when, after having destroyed every sovereignty, authority, and power, he will hand over the kingdom to God, the Father. Christ must reign until God has put all enemies under his feet, and the last enemy to be destroyed is death. Scripture reads that God, 'has placed all things under his feet.' But when it says that everything has been made subject, it is clear that he who has made everything subject to Christ is excluded. When, finally, all has been subjected to the Son, he will then subject himself to the One who made all things subject to him, so that God may be all in all" (I Corinthians 15:24–28).

The final mystery of creation will unfold at the end of time, when the Son joyfully offers to the Father the perfect fulfillment of the reign of God. Our hope is that we will share in that loving and joyful fulfillment.

Conclusion

Given enough time, we too will pass through the five steps of dying. Many Christians, in a loving way, have already begun this process in their lives, not knowing whether they have five or fifty years ahead and not waiting for any specific illness. The reality of their eternal destiny is always before them. The apostle Paul shares with us the image of a man who has already accepted the fact of his death and who even looks forward to that moment with some longing:

For what is life? To me, it is Christ. Death then will bring more. But if by continuing to live I can do more worthwhile work, then I am not sure which I should choose. I am pulled in two directions. I want very much to leave this life and be with Christ, which is a far better thing; but for your sake it is much more important that I remain alive (Philippians 1:21–24).

Paul's love draws him to the eternal joy of God's presence and his duty and love for the people draw him to living out his earthly life. He has reached the point of acceptance and now awaits the fulfillment of his desire for God's presence. Death holds no fear for Paul.

For Scripture reflection and discussion concerning this chapter, see Journeying in His Light, *"Death to Light."*

Epilogue

At the beginning of this book, we read about a young boy going out at night for the first time to feed the horses. He slowly followed a circle of light that led him down the path and out to the barn. Now the years have passed. The boy has grown up, married, and is presently rearing his own children. One night, he decided that it was time for his oldest son to go out to the barn on his own to feed the horses. The young boy showed no fear. He simply stepped out onto the porch, pulled a lever on the side of an electric box, and watched the yard and barn leap into light. He easily accepted the chore of going out at night to feed the horses.

As the months passed, the father had grown accustomed to the boy's routine. But one week, he noted that the boy was coming in from the barn a little later than usual. He questioned the boy, and the boy admitted that he slipped out behind the barn after feeding the horses to sit in the dark and enjoy the stars. The son envied the simplicity of the father's young life, where electric lights never dimmed the beauty of the stars. The father smiled as he remembered his own fear of the darkness.

In our early pages, we expressed a hope of lighting up a path to understanding Catholic belief. Just as the boy moved toward the barn with his lantern, lighting up only small areas of the path, so we moved slowly toward an understanding of our faith, lighting up only small areas of the faith. Now, as we look back, we see the path we have traveled a little more clearly. As we make new discoveries in our faith and light up the path of understanding a little more, we must continually test these new discoveries against the background of the early Church and the Bible. Like the boy who slipped out of the barn into the darkness, we must never lose sight of the stars.

Appendix

Throughout this book, we have shared some prayers and practices of the Catholic faith. This section will draw these prayers and practices together for quick reference as well as adding others that the reader may wish to know in living the Catholic faith.

Blessing with holy water on entering the church

In the Sacrament of Baptism, the minister of the sacrament baptizes "In the name of the Father and of the Son and of the Holy Spirit." As we enter the church, we bless ourselves with specially blessed holy water. The blessing with the water reminds us that we enter the church as baptized Christians ready to share our baptismal gifts in worship of God:

As we enter the church, we dip the tip of our right hand in the holy water and bless ourselves with our right hand in the image of a cross by touching our forehead first, then our chest, then our left shoulder, and finally our right shoulder. While we make this sign of the cross, we recite the words: "In the name of the Father and of the Son, and of the Holy Spirit. Amen."

Genuflection on one knee

If the Blessed Sacrament is present, Catholics show a special sign of reverence to this presence of Jesus. We genuflect (1) before entering our bench on first entering the Church, (2) whenever we pass in front of the Blessed Sacrament in church, and (3) as we leave our seat to leave the church.

We genuflect by touching the floor with the right knee. Even if the Blessed Sacrament is exposed for benediction of special occasions such as Holy Thursday, we still genuflect on only one knee.

The Lord's Prayer

When the followers of Jesus asked him to teach them how to pray, Jesus taught them the prayer commonly referred to today as "The Lord's Prayer." Through our baptism, we enter into a close, intimate relationship with God. We no longer approach God in a most formal way, but rather with the intimate manner of a child approaching a concerned, loving parent. Because of this relationship, we can now call God the Father "Dad" or "Daddy" which is the real meaning behind the very formal translation of "Father" in the Lord's Prayer. In reality, we are simply saying, "Our Dad, who art. . . ." Through the gift of the resurrection and our own baptism, we dare to say:

Our Father, Who art in heaven,
Hallowed be thy name,
Thy kingdom come,
Thy will be done on earth as it is in heaven,
Give us this day our daily bread,
And forgive us our trespasses
As we forgive those who trespass against us:
And lead us not into temptation,
But deliver us from evil. Amen.

The Hail Mary

The Scriptures continually need to be translated into a more modern language so that we may more clearly understand the message of the Scriptures. The first part of the prayer, "The Hail Mary," came from a previous translation of the Scriptures. In the infancy narratives, an angel appeared to Mary, called her "Full of Grace" and told her that the Lord was with her. When Mary visited Elizabeth, her cousin, Elizabeth proclaimed the blessedness of the "fruit of your womb." The Church added the name of "Jesus" to Elizabeth's greeting and added the second part of the prayer which is simply a request for Mary's prayers in the lives of its people.

Hail Mary, full of Grace!
The Lord is with you.
Blessed are you among women,
And blessed is the fruit of your womb, Jesus.
Holy Mary, Mother of God,
Pray for us sinners,
Now and at the hour of our death. Amen.

The Trinity Prayer

Besides making the sign of the cross in the name of the Trinity, the Church also makes use of a prayer of praise and glory to the Trinity. It professes a belief through prayer of God's glory, God's unity in three persons, and God's eternal existence.

Glory to the Father, and to the Son, and to the Holy Spirit. As it was in the beginning, is now, and will be forever. Amen.

The Apostles' Creed

The Apostles' Creed has its birth in the early Church, and is a basic profession of faith in God and God's plan of salvation. Legend has it that there are twelve articles of faith mentioned in the Apostles' Creed and that each apostle added one of the articles of faith. This does not seem likely, although the Creed does go back to the early apostolic age of the Church. Longer professions of faith, such as the Nicene Creed used in the Eucharistic Liturgy, are developments from the Apostles' Creed. Councils added more explanation to certain articles of faith and put them into the Creed. The Nicene Creed is actually the Apostles' Creed with further explanation of certain points that the Council of Nicea felt were necessary.

I believe in God, the Father Almighty, creator of heaven and earth; and in Jesus Christ, His only Son, our Lord; who was conceived by the Holy Spirit, born of the Virgin Mary, suffered under Pontius Pilate, was crucified, died, and was buried. He descended into hell; the third day he arose again from the dead; he ascended into heaven, sits at the right hand of God, the Father almighty; from thence he shall come to judge the living and the dead. I believe in the Holy Spirit, the holy Catholic Church, the communion of saints, the forgiveness of sins, the resurrection of the body, and life everlasting. Amen.

Act of Sorrow (Contrition)

In the Sacrament of Reconciliation, we pray an Act of Sorrow to express in words the sorrow we have already shown in the confession of sins. In this sacrament, we may choose to express our sorrow in our own words, or choose one of several different suggested acts of sorrow offered in the book of the *Rite for Reconciliation* itself. An example of an Act of Sorrow as found in the *Rite of Reconciliation* is the following:

My God,
I am sorry for my sins with all my heart,
In choosing to do wrong,
And failing to do good,
I have sinned against you
Whom I should love above all things.
I firmly intend, with your help,
To do penance,
To sin no more,
And to avoid whatever leads me to sin.
Our saviour Jesus Christ
Suffered and died for us.
In his name, my God, have mercy.

The Rosary

The rosary stands out as one of the major devotions of personal piety for many Catholics. Although St. Dominic gave great impetus to the recitation of the rosary as far back as 800 years ago, the practice of the recitation of the rosary seems to predate even St. Dominic. Its origin lies in the shadows of the past, but its use among Catholics has made the rosary one of the best known forms of Catholic devotion. The rosary beads could easily go back to some of the ancient religious customs of counting prayers on beads. The Church, however, has placed certain blessings upon the use of beads which are blessed by the priest. The rosary beads consist of a set of fifty beads, clustered together in groups of ten, called decades. A short chain with a single bead set in the middle separates the decades from each other. The chain is joined together to form a circle, and a small chain holding a crucifix, a single bead, and three beads grouped together extend from the circle. The praying of the rosary takes place as follows:

We bless ourselves "In the name of the Father, and of the Son, and of the Holy Spirit. Amen." We then pray the Apostles' Creed, holding the crucifix in our fingers. We pray one "Our Father" on the single bead, and three "Hail Mary" prayers on the cluster of three beads. These prayers are recited for "an increase of the virtues of faith, hope, and charity." At the end of each cluster of beads, we pray the "Glory to the Father. . . ." Each decade consists of one "Our Father," ten recitations of the "Hail Mary," and a single recitation of "Glory to the

The Rosary Beads

1. The Apostles' Creed
2. Our Father
3. Three Hail Marys
4. Glory to the Father
5. Our Father (Reflect on the mystery)
6. Ten Hail Marys
7. Glory to the Father

Father. . . ." At the beginning of each decade, we meditate on some event in the life of Jesus and Mary. When we finish praying the five decades, we again make the Sign of the Cross as an end to the prayer. The mysteries of the rosary are the following:

The Joyful Mysteries (Mondays and Thursdays)

1. *The Annunciation that Mary is to be the Mother of Jesus.*
2. *Mary visits her cousin Elizabeth.*
3. *Mary gives birth to Jesus.*
4. *Mary presents Jesus in the temple according to Jewish tradition.*
5. *Mary and Joseph find Jesus in the temple after three days.*

The Sorrowful Mysteries (Tuesdays and Fridays)

1. *The agony of Jesus in the garden on the night before his death.*
2. *Jesus is whipped by the Roman soldiers.*
3. *Jesus is crowned with thorns.*
4. *Jesus carries his cross.*
5. *Jesus dies on the cross.*

The Glorious Mysteries (Sundays, Wednesdays, and Saturdays)

1. *Jesus is raised from the dead.*
2. *Jesus ascends into heaven.*
3. *The Holy Spirit is sent upon the Apostles.*
4. *Mary is taken into heaven.*
5. *Mary is crowned Queen of heaven.*

Stations of the Cross

A station is a place to stop or linger for some set purpose. In some cases, these places signify or recall some great event in history. In most churches, plaques that show pictures of Jesus on his journey to death are spaced along the walls. Each of these pictures or plaques is a station where the person praying will stop to meditate on that particular event portrayed in the picture. During the season of Lent, the Church meditates through its liturgy on the passion and death of Jesus, but always with an eye to his resurrection. The stations of the cross enable the Catholic to pray in a personal way, especially during the season of Lent, by meditating on Jesus' journey to his death and resurrection. There are traditionally fourteen stations, and they are as follows:

First Station: Jesus is condemned to death by Pilate.
Second Station: Jesus is made to carry his cross.
Third Station: Jesus falls the first time.
Fourth Station: Jesus meets Mary his mother.
Fifth Station: Simon, the Cyrenian, helps Jesus carry his cross.
Sixth Station: Veronica wipes the fact of Jesus.
Seventh Station: Jesus falls the second time.
Eighth Station: Jesus speaks to the daughters of Jerusalem.
Ninth Station: Jesus falls the third time.
Tenth Station: Jesus is stripped of his garments.
Eleventh Station: Jesus is nailed to the cross.
Twelfth Station: Jesus dies on the cross.
Thirteenth Station: Jesus is taken down from the cross.
Fourteenth Station: Jesus is laid in the tomb.

Some books on the stations of the cross have added a fifteenth station to honor the resurrection of Jesus from the dead.

Fifteenth Station: Jesus is raised from the dead.

Acts of Faith, Hope, and Love

The virtues that lie at the foundation of the Christian life are the virtues of Faith, Hope, and Love. All other virtues flow from this foundation. When we pray these Acts of Faith, Hope and Love, we are actually putting into words what we are already living. The following prayers are simply examples of ways of expressing our living Faith, Hope and Love.

Through an Act of Faith, we profess a belief in the Trinity and the work of the Trinity in our lives. We may express an Act of Faith in the following fashion. . . .

Lord God, I believe that you are one God in three persons. I believe that you are Father, Son, and Holy Spirit. I believe that a new life opened for me through the death and resurrection of your Son and that your love and guidance continue through your Holy Spirit. I believe in the truths taught by your holy, Catholic, and Apostolic church. By responding in love to your gifts, I believe that I shall share in eternal joy with you. This is my belief, Lord God, and my belief is my joy. Amen.

Through an Act of Hope, we profess a confidence in God's promises as found in the Scriptures. We may express our Act of Hope as follows. . . .

Lord God, trusting in your deep love and goodness, I hope to receive continued forgiveness for my faults and your guidance and help in avoiding sin. My hope for eternal life and joy with you fills me with joy and love each day I live. Amen.

Through an Act of Love, we express our love for God and for our neighbor. This is the greatest of the virtues because it gives life to all the virtues. Paul writes of love, "There are in the end three things that last: faith, hope, and love, and the greatest of these is love" (I Corinthians 13:13). We may express our Act of Love as follows. . . .

Lord God, you continually share your great love with me through the gifts in my life. In an attempt to imitate your great goodness and show my love in return, I will strive to love you with all my heart, all my mind, and all my strength, and I will seek to love my neighbor as myself. Lord, teach me to love even more. Amen.

Special Holy Days

Besides Sundays, Catholics assemble together for special occasions or feast days at six other times during the year. These feasts may differ from country to country, although most countries retain the number of six holy days. The same obligation a Catholic feels in regards to the Sunday Eucharistic Celebration applies to these days also. The special holy days are:

1. *Christmas Day—celebrated on December 25*
2. *Feast of Mary, the Mother of God—Octave of Christmas, January 1*
3. *Ascension Thursday—celebrated on the fortieth day after Easter*
4. *The Assumption of Mary—celebrated August 15*
5. *All Saints' Day—celebrated November 1*
6. *Immaculate Conception of Mary—celebrated December 8*

Offerings for Intentions
of Eucharistic Liturgy

The Eucharistic Liturgy is always celebrated in union with the Church throughout the world. It is also celebrated for the intention of the universal Church. In the early Church, the assembly would offer at the Eucharistic Liturgy the necessary items for the celebration of the Eucharist, namely bread and wine. They would also make other offerings to be given for the poor or the support of the priest. The custom of making offerings for the support of the priest continued for some time. In this way, the priest would be free to carry out the service of the Church to the community.

As time passed, people would make certain requests for prayers in making their offering. An offering for certain sacramental functions performed by the priests came to be called "a stipend." In some places, priests depended solely upon this stipend for livelihood. Gradually, the prayer-request for which a stipend would be offered was announced, especially during the celebration of the Eucharistic Liturgy. The custom most Catholics are familiar with today is the custom of making an offering to the priest or parish "with the request that a special remembrance be given to the one "for whom the Mass is offered."

Actually, the Eucharistic Liturgy is still celebrated primarily for the universal Church. No amount of offerings can change this. But another intention can also be remembered for a specific person or intention. Besides making an offering for a specific intention, a person should not overlook the more important action of assisting at the Eucharistic Liturgy for that intention. An offering for a Eucharistic Celebration does not pay for someone else to pray in our place. It is an offering with the idea that the priest and the assembly will pray along with us. In many Churches, the priest has stopped announcing the intention because the primary intention is the universal Church. This is done to avoid the impression that the Eucharistic Liturgy is primarily for the intention requested, which it is not.

If a Catholic wishes to have the priest remember someone in a special way at the Eucharistic Liturgy, he or she simply calls the priest and makes the request. An offering is ordinarily given. The priest will often note the intention in the weekly bulletin.

Donations are given at the time of other sacramental celebrations, such as weddings, funerals, and baptisms. Where an offering cannot be made, the priest may never refuse a sacrament. No one "buys" a sacrament and no one "buys a Mass."

The practice of fasting from food and abstaining from meat

The Church, as a community reflecting Christ, has often called upon its members to put themselves in union with the suffering of Christ by sharing in certain types of personal sacrifice. Because Friday was considered the day of Jesus' suffering and death, the Church asked that Catholics abstain from eating meat on all Fridays of the year. Recently, the Church has urged all Catholics to continue to sacrifice in some way on Fridays in honor of the passion and death of Jesus, but the Church does not oblige Catholics to do this, except during the season of Lent. In some cases, abstaining from meat is not considered a sacrifice since seafood is enjoyed by so many. What was meant to be a day of sacrifice became for many a day of switching to another type of enjoyable food. The Church also recognized that in certain parts of the world, people had to eat whatever they could get within their financial means. In some cases, this meant buying certain types of meat where dairy products and fish were too expensive.

The Church, however, has not completely abandoned this obligation to abstain from meat and fast on certain days. **The obligation to abstain from meat binds Catholics on Ash Wednesday, and on each of the Fridays during Lent. Those fourteen years and older are bound by this law.**

The law of fasting allows for one full meal a day. It does not forbid the taking of food at the other two meals, but it ordinarily offers as a norm that the other two meals may not equal the main meal in quantity. Also, eating solid foods between meals is not permitted. The main meal of the day may be taken at whatever meal a person chooses. **The obligation to fast binds Catholics only on Ash Wednesday and Good Friday. This law binds everyone from eighteen to the beginning of their sixtieth year.**

The Church urges Christians to place themselves in union with the passion and death of Jesus by performing some type of voluntary sacrifice during the season of Lent.

Symbolic offering of oneself at Eucharist

In many churches, a tray or basket filled with the bread to be used for the Eucharist is placed near the entrance. When Catholics enter the church, they take the bread from the tray or basket and place it in another container. It is this bread which will be used during the Eucharistic Liturgy. In moving the bread from the tray or basket to the other container, Catholics are symbolically making an offering of their lives in this offering of bread. In the early Church, the people brought the bread and wine from home to be used during the Eucharistic Celebration. After the General Intercessions, these gifts of bread and wine are brought forward and are presented to the presider who prepares them for use in the liturgy of the Eucharist.

Manner of reception of the Eucharist

When Catholics share in the Eucharist, they celebrate the presence of Christ under the appearance of bread and wine. In the early Church toward the end of the Eucharistic Celebration, the people would pass around the one bread and the one cup for all to share in the Eucharistic presence of Christ.

In receiving the Eucharistic bread, Catholics have two options. They may receive communion on the tongue by extending the tongue after they have arrived at the Eucharistic table. The priest or minister of the Eucharist will place communion on the tongue of those who approach the table in this manner or Catholics may choose to receive communion in the hand. This is an ancient tradition by which those approaching the priest or minister of the Eucharist extend a hand resting on the other, palm up, forming a type of cradle in which the priest or minister places the bread. Once the bread has been placed in the hand, the communicant steps aside, takes the consecrated bread from the cradle of the one hand with the other hand, and places the consecrated bread in his or her mouth. Those who are right handed place their left hand on top of the right with palm up when taking the consecrated bread and those who are left handed place the right hand on top of the left one with palm up when taking the bread. In this manner, a person communicates himself or herself with the hand that person customarily uses for most activities in life.

At their meeting in November 1978, the Bishops of the United States extended the practice of sharing in the cup to the Sunday Eucharistic Liturgy. The custom of the laity sharing in the cup was an ancient custom in the Church, now revised by the Church. Many Churches use two ministers of the consecrated wine for every minister of the bread, thus avoiding lengthy lines for those sharing in the consecrated wine. The use of tiny, individual drinking cups should be avoided since it destroys the symbolism of the sharing in the common cup. The one bread and one wine are a symbolism of the one community in Christ.

When sharing the Eucharist, the priest or minister says "The Body of Christ" when offering the bread, and "The Blood of Christ" when offering the wine. The communicant responds "Amen" to each of these prayers.

In the Church, sacraments are meant to be presented through a minister. Jesus offered his disciples the bread and wine at the Last Supper (Luke 22:17–20). Except for the presider who takes, eats, and drinks, no one else, including the Eucharistic ministers, take the Eucharist themselves. It is presented to them, and they respond, "Amen."

Indulgences

To understand the meaning of indulgences, we must reach back to the roots of the Church and the understanding of the Church as the Mystical Body of Christ. All the merits of Christ and the saints are now shared through the Church. By its authority, the Church has the power to share these gifts with others.

To help overcome the consequences of our sinfulness, the Church offers us help by sharing with us the merits which flow from Christ and the saints. This help is called indulgences. It may be a "partial indulgence" if it does away with part of the consequences of sin, or it may be a "plenary indulgence" when it does away with all of the consequences of sin.

In the past, some have abused the idea of indulgences, and the Church is careful not to allow this to happen again. Pope Paul VI, in an Apostolic Constitution on the Revision of Indulgences (1967), spells out the types of indulgences used by the Church, and the occasions for these indulgences. Although we hear less about indulgences today than we did in the past, Pope Paul points out that the use of indulgences continues to be part of Church practice.

Index

Sermon on the Mount, 79
Sexuality, 178ff, 186ff
Signs, 103ff
Sin, 51, 69ff
   against self, 71
   forgiveness of, 76ff
   God and, 51, 69, 76, 168
   grace and, 88–89, 136, 167
   Jesus confronted, 51, 77–78
   less serious, 75
   original, 59, 73
   penance and, 165ff
   presence of, 15, 34–35, 73
   serious, 75
   social, 71
Sirach, 33
Social justice, 137ff
Social sin, 71
Solomon, 33
Son of God, 53
Song of Songs, 33
Sorrow, for sin, 174–75
Southern kingdom, 30
Stations of the Cross, 238–39
Stipends, 241

Suffering, 15–16, 235
Synod of bishops, 96

T

Temptation, 167
Ten Commandments, 29, 73
Testament, 22, 31
Tradition, 22
Trinity, 62ff
   prayer to, 67, 235
Twelve tribes of Israel, 28

U

Unbaptized, fate of, 123
Uriah, 168

V

Virgin Birth, 43–44
Vows, 206

W

War, 194
Wisdom literature, 33
Worship, 143ff

Other Books by the Author

Journeying in His Light

This formation guide presents thirty-five topics and session outlines. Using chapters from *In His Light* as background, sessions begin with a series of Scripture references and include questions for discussion and reflection. Space is provided for composing personal thoughts and prayers. Each session concludes with a simple prayer. ($4.95 Order #1858)

Journeying through the RCIA

This book is the first in the series entitled **Journeying with Christ**, a series of books concerned with living the Christian life. Through information, Scripture texts, personal reflections, and discussion options, this book offers a reflective approach to understanding and experiencing the RCIA. ($5.75 Order #1941)

Journeying toward Baptism

Because each birth is a unique and personal experience, this book gives parents the opportunity to reflect upon those special circumstances and special gifts.

In the journey of preparing for the Sacrament of Baptism, the book helps parents reflect on the family, the child, the religious community, and the sacrament itself.

The book covers each step of the ceremony and also includes a special section for recording important family memories. ($5.75 Order #2002)

Journeying toward Marriage

This book will help couples reflect on their relationship and to see the Sacrament of Marriage as a lifetime commitment rather than a solitary expression of love.

Special sections of this book include a selection of readings and prayers for the ceremony and worksheets for planning the wedding. ($6.75 Order #2059)

To order, send your name and address with the titles and order numbers of the books you wish to order. Please include $1.50 for postage and handling. Payment must accompany the order. Send to:

Wm. C. Brown Company Publishers
Religious Education Division
P.O. Box 539
2460 Kerper Blvd.
Dubuque, Iowa 52001